*With the Compliments of Captain Arata Oka,*

Japanese Naval Attaché.

Broadway Court,
Broadway,
Westminster, S.W.1.

# MANCHOUKUO: CHILD OF CONFLICT

THE MACMILLAN COMPANY
NEW YORK · BOSTON · CHICAGO · DALLAS
ATLANTA · SAN FRANCISCO

MACMILLAN & CO., Limited
LONDON · BOMBAY · CALCUTTA
MELBOURNE

THE MACMILLAN COMPANY
OF CANADA, Limited
TORONTO

# MANCHOUKUO
## CHILD OF CONFLICT

BY

### K. K. KAWAKAMI

Washington Correspondent of "The Tokyo Hochi Shimbun"

*Author of*

"Japan in World Politics," "The Real Japanese Question,"
"Japan's Pacific Policy," "Japan Speaks," etc.

NEW YORK

## THE MACMILLAN COMPANY

1933

SET UP BY BROWN BROTHERS LINOTYPERS
PRINTED IN THE UNITED STATES OF AMERICA
BY THE FERRIS PRINTING COMPANY

# PREFACE

THIS modest volume is a sequel to my *Japan Speaks on the Sino-Japanese Crisis* (Macmillan), published in March, 1932. In that book I tried to paint a picture of the Manchurian imbroglio against the historical background of Japan's relations with China, and to explain the causes of the trouble in the light of her treaty rights in Manchuria. The present volume approaches the same problem from a somewhat different angle, emphasizing what may be termed human factors rather than treaties and agreements.

While the world is discussing whether or not Manchoukuo should be recognized, Manchoukuo herself is making steady and signal progress as a new state. For some years to come, this youngest of nations will be much in the limelight. To some of her neighbors she may be an *enfant terrible,* even a nightmare. Geneva will continue to discuss her. America will reassert the non-recognition doctrine. For good or ill, the advent of Manchoukuo has registered a radical change in the Far Eastern situation. Certainly it is one of the most significant developments in the present century—a great experiment in the reorganization, regeneration and rejuvenation of an ancient nation long wallowing in chaos and maladministration so serious as to have become a menace to her neighbors. If it succeeds, the whole world will gain. If it fails, the failure will be due, not entirely to Japan's own

v

incapacity, but largely to the interference of third parties.
For the first time in history, a non-white race has undertaken to carry the white man's burden, and the white
man, long accustomed to think the burden exclusively his
own, is reluctant to commit it to the young shoulders of
Japan, yellow and an upstart at that. Stripped of all diplomatic verbiage, that is the long and short of the whole
story.

Whether recognized or not, Manchoukuo is a world
factor. Its population numbering more than 30,000,000,
its territory measuring 460,000 square miles and extending
from the Amur River to the Great Wall, its budget nearly
balanced, its exports exceeding its imports almost by 100,-
000,000 *yuan* a year even in these times of depression,
Manchoukuo challenges the attention of the whole world.
Such a nation must be watched and studied by friend
and foe alike. If the Powers have not recognized her, they
certainly do not and cannot ignore her. Their consuls are
in Manchoukuo looking after their trade and the interests
of their respective nationals there. Moreover, the Powers,
America not excepted, are taking, even indirectly demanding, a share in Manchoukuo's revenue. Soviet Russia has
welcomed the establishment of Manchoukuo's consulates
in several cities under its jurisdiction. A few European
capitalists have visited Manchoukuo with a view to finding a new field of investment.

Internally, Manchoukuo's pacification program is being
carried out with as great a success as has been anticipated
even by a sanguine observer. Her internal reforms, such
as the unification of the currency, reduction of the army,
readjustment of taxation, and opium control, are also

being carried out, not on paper, but actually and effectively—reforms which, all agree, China herself should long since have undertaken, but which she is incapable of undertaking.

The question of recognition or non-recognition is comparatively unimportant. It would be as useless for Manchoukuo to press for recognition at this moment as it is futile for Geneva to waste its valuable time in discussing the question.

Meanwhile, the important thing to be remembered is that Manchoukuo is here to stay, and that she already has enough achievements to her credit to justify the prediction that she is going to be a better-administered and happier country than China, and is bound to carve out for herself a significant place in the society of nations. It is, therefore, essential that the world at large should know what Manchoukuo is—its organization, its foreign relations, its finances, its problems and difficulties. That is the *raison d'être* of this book.

I am indebted to the authors and publishers of the following books for permission to quote: Mr. Owen Lattimore's *Manchuria: Cradle of Conflict* (Macmillan Company, New York); Senator Harry B. Hawes' *Philippine Uncertainty* (Century Company, New York); and Mr. J. O. P. Bland's *China, Japan and Korea* (Charles Scribner's Sons, New York), and *China, the Pity of It* (William Heinemann, London); Dr. Richard Wilhelm's *The Soul of China* (Harcourt, Brace & Co.); Liang Chi-chao's *History of Chinese Political Thought* (Harcourt, Brace & Co.); Woodrow Wilson's *A History of the American People* (Harper & Brothers); Arthur H. Smith's *Chinese*

*Characteristics* (Fleming H. Revell Co.); and Ellen N. La Motte's *The Ethics of Opium* (The Century Company).

Chapter I of this book, entitled "The Storm Gathers," has been published in French in *L'Esprit International,* of Paris, under the title of "The Real Causes of the Manchurian Trouble." Considerable parts of the chapters on Jehol and on "volunteers" and bandits have appeared in the *National Review,* of London. I wish to thank the editors of these reviews for their courtesy in allowing me to reproduce them in this book.

K. K. KAWAKAMI.

Washington, D. C.

# CONTENTS

# ILLUSTRATIONS

# MANCHOUKUO: CHILD OF CONFLICT

# INTRODUCTION

## I

On February 24, 1933, the League of Nations Assembly adopted the report of the Committee of Nineteen, which caused the immediate withdrawal of the Japanese delegation. For this deplorable pass both Japan and the League are equally to blame.

On Japan's side the chief fault lies in the fact that she did not present her case clearly enough before the League in the early stage of the Manchurian conflict, when Geneva, unsympathetic as it was, was still in a mood to listen to her. Japan's failure or negligence in this respect was so obvious that on January 30, 1932 (four months after the Mukden incident of September 18, 1931) the *New York Times* editorially observed that "Japan has lacked what is called good publicity," though "she had, in many respects, a good case," and that "for a time, the Chinese there [at Geneva] had all the better of the controversy, and indeed let the League of Nations too hastily take a position favorable to the Chinese contention."

When the Japanese Government at last realized this mistake and sent Mr. Yosuke Matsuoka, unquestionably one of Japan's ablest spokesmen, to Geneva in November, 1932, it was too late, for Geneva had already been swayed by the preconceived opinion formed in the months when Japan was singularly reticent. In fact, Mr. Matsuoka arrived in Geneva when Geneva was no longer in a mood to listen to Japan. In such a hostile atmosphere, what was needed more than anything else was tact, patience, and soft-speaking—*suaviter in modo, fortiter in re*. Few men have ever been asked to undertake so difficult and delicate a task in Geneva as has been thrust upon Mr. Matsuoka. If the result has been disappointing to him, it certainly is not his fault, but the fault of the Government, which was too slow in awakening to the necessity of arguing its case clearly and convincingly before the League.

It must also be observed that neither the Japanese Government nor the Japanese delegation made the best use of the Lytton Commission's report. To be sure, that report contains statements which, from our point of view, are not entirely pleasing; but, taken as a whole, it is a commendable document, with observations and suggestions which Japan could have used to her advantage. Does not the report plainly say that until China has established a reliable central government, nothing worth while can be accomplished in the way of readjusting her relations with Japan or her position in Manchuria? Instead of taking the report by and large in a friendly spirit, Japan seemed to be bent upon ferretting out misstatements and erroneous judgments, some of which are of minor importance. She missed the wood for the trees.

On the other hand neither the League Council, nor the Assembly, nor the Committee of Nineteen, between November, 1932, and February, 1933, was disposed to give Japan a fair hearing. It was a "packed" jury which faced Japan. This I shall explain in the following few paragraphs.

The Committee of Nineteen, in preparing its report to the Assembly, claims to have taken the Lytton Commission's report on the Sino-Japanese situation as the basis of deliberation and to have been guided by it. Indeed, the Committee adopted *in toto* the recommendations of the Lytton report by saying that "the settlement of the [Sino-Japanese] dispute must conform to the principles and conditions laid down by the [Lytton] Commission of Inquiry." As a matter of fact, however, the Committee of Nineteen wandered very far afield from those "principles and conditions," and was guided, not by the facts presented by the Lytton report but by their own prejudices and preconceived notions. This is obvious in the conclusions of the Committee, which ignore the Lytton Commission's recommendations. And the Assembly, governed by mob psychology rather than by calm and independent thinking, has swallowed those conclusions, without, perhaps, understanding what they really meant. This is an all-important fact which no true friend of the League, no true lover of peace, should overlook.

First, then, let us carefully note the more essential of the "principles and conditions" (which we shall call recommendations) laid down by the Lytton Commission for the guidance of the settlement of the Sino-Japanese controversy. These are:

(1) "Recognition of Japan's interests in Manchuria."

(2) "A restatement of the respective rights, interests, and responsibilities of China and Japan in Manchuria in new treaties."

(3) "A large measure of autonomy [of Manchuria] designed to meet its local conditions and special characteristics."

(4) Organization of "an effective local gendarmerie force" for the maintenance of internal order in Manchuria,

and "withdrawal of all armed forces," Chinese or Japanese, after such a gendarmerie force shall have been organized.

At first glance, the above four conditions may appear sensible and reasonable. Close examination, however, reveals their essential defects. For one thing, how is the suggested gendarmerie force to be organized and maintained? Past experiences clearly show that such a force, even when officered by foreigners, will prove utterly inadequate to maintain order in so disturbed and so vast a country as Manchuria. At any rate, it will take many years to whip native material into an efficient police force.

But we shall overlook such defects and pass on to the next recommendation, which is couched in these words:

(5) *"Since the conditions enumerated above cannot be fulfilled without a strong central government in China, the final requisite for a satisfactory solution is temporary international cooperation in the internal reconstruction in China."*

To all practical purposes, the above thirty-two words constitute the essence and the only important part of the Lytton report. Until the condition expressed in these thirty-two words is fulfilled, the rest of the hundreds of thousands of words contained in that document are of no practical value. As is evident in the wording of the above-quoted final recommendation, the Lytton Commission itself thinks it of little use to discuss the recognition of Japanese rights, the conclusion of Sino-Japanese treaties, the organization of gendarmerie, the establishment of autonomous Manchuria, the withdrawal of troops, etc., until and unless China shall have succeeded in establishing a united, stable, effectual central government which is capable of observing laws and treaties and with which foreign governments may deal with confidence. To find out this simple truth, it should not have taken such a painstaking, arduous, and thoroughgoing investigation as was undertaken, at such a great cost, by so distinguished a body of diplomats, soldiers, statesmen and scholars as the Lytton Commission. Japan, for one, has known it for more than twenty years, and it is at least consoling to her that this simple truth has at last been presented as a revelation to Geneva, that hub of the universe, through the Lytton report.

But the Committee of Nineteen, which was supposed to have acted upon that revelation, completely ignored it, and jumped blindfolded into the topsy-turvy conclusion that the withdrawal of Japanese troops from Manchuria is the prerequisite of everything else. It even ignores the Lytton Commission's suggestion for the establishment of an efficient gendarmerie force as the prerequisite of withdrawal of Japanese troops. It is eloquently silent on the chaos and anarchy which is certain to follow troop withdrawal. Evidently the nineteen wise gentlemen thought that evacuation of troops would work miracles, producing automatically in its wake a powerful gendarmerie which would chase hordes of bandits in to the hills and make them stay there, and an efficient autonomous government capable of administering the vast territory of Manchuria. In short, troop withdrawal would at once usher peace, order, and happiness into distracted Manchuria. Once the Japanese soldiers turn their backs to bandits and Chang Hsueh-liang's "volunteers," everything good and desirable would just grow like Topsy. Beautiful vision this, but is it practical? Lord Lytton and his four associates and their learned expert advisers did not think so.

Let us, then, go back to the Lytton recommendations. Suppose that the League really acted upon those recommendations, and proceeded to overhaul and regenerate China herself, as the first step toward the readjustment of the Manchurian situation, what would happen? China, of course, would never permit Geneva to undertake this humanitarian task in her behalf, which would, of course, reduce the whole scheme evolved by the Lytton Commission to a castle in the air, alluring but unreal.

But let us suppose that China would be acquiescent. If this grand scheme of overhauling China should prove a success, and if the China thus regenerated should prove a better-governed and happier country than Japanese-tutored Manchoukuo, there is little doubt that Manchoukuo would of its own volition go out of existence as an independent state and would rejoin China. But the overhauling of so vast a country as China could not be accomplished in a jiffy—it would require many years and even decades. In the meantime, Manchuria, or Manchoukuo, should not be left adrift or to shift for itself—a prey of organized banditry, militarist exploitation, and whatnot. It might be just as well to leave it under Japanese tutelage, as it is at present, and let it progress on the road to modernization, while China, under the international tutelage envisaged by the Lytton recommendations, might also similarly progress. It would be interesting to watch which would make the greater progress. The competition thus kept alive might prove an incentive and encouragement for greater endeavor on the part of either nation. Should

China win this race for self-improvement, Manchoukuo would, I am sure, desert its Japanese tutor and return to China's arms. If, on the contrary, China should continue to wallow in the mire of chaos, while Manchoukuo made steady progress, then the four hundred million Chinese of China might wish to become the subjects of Mr. Henry Pu-yi. Who knows?

## II

The Lytton Commission's report on the Sino-Japanese dispute brings out the following points:

First: That the Sino-Japanese treaties which existed in September, 1931, are binding on both signatories, and that the Japanese rights defined by those instruments must be respected.

Second: That anti-foreign, and in this particular case anti-Japanese, boycott employed by China "involves a measure of [Chinese] Government responsibility."

Third: Nowhere in the report does the Commission suggest that the Japanese troops be withdrawn as a pre-requisite of negotiations between China and Japan on the basis of the above two general principles. On the contrary, it suggests organization of an effective gendarmerie force as a preliminary to troop withdrawal.

These points cannot be too strongly emphasized. Had the League Council taken the above stand in September or October, or even November, 1931, there is not the slight-est doubt that Japan would have been more than willing to negotiate with China (whatever "China" might have meant) and liquidate the Manchurian situation with dis-patch, because all that Japan wanted was a guaranty of her treaty rights in China, including her right to trade, free from officially encouraged boycotts. This Japan repeatedly made plain before the League and the world. Had this course been followed, the dispute would have been settled at once, and China and Japan would have been at peace, at least for some years.

But the League Council, instead of taking the above stand, concentrated its futile efforts upon compelling Japan to withdraw troops before Sino-Japanese negotiations could be opened for the guaranty of Japanese treaty rights. This produced two unfortunate effects. On one hand, it made China think that she had the League in her pocket. On the other, it stiffened the Japanese army, who knew, as did all Japanese, that the troops could not be withdrawn.

If the Lytton Commission, after a painstaking and exhaustive study of the actual situation, explicitly recognized (as it actually has) the legality of Japan's treaty rights in China, and implicitly recognized the necessity of maintaining Japanese troops in Manchuria, then the League Council (which, when Japan was anxious to negotiate with China on these very terms, refused to let her so negotiate, but merely insisted upon troop withdrawal) must, in the light of the Lytton report confess that it was shortsighted and committed an irretrievable error. The Council's dilly-dallying in the early stages of the Manchurian trouble brought about a situation which it could not foresee and which cannot now be altered—namely, the appearance of an independent Manchuria.

The logical conclusion is that the Council has its own lack of vision to thank for the independence of Manchuria. This it should have confessed before the world in sackcloth and ashes. Instead it whitewashed or rather completely ignored its own error, and made Japan the scapegoat.

In fairness, however, it must be admitted that this was not the fault of the Council alone; perhaps the fault lies in the nature of the League itself. This Manchurian controversy shows that no grave international problem can ever be settled at an international forum where all nations, most of which have not the slightest interest in and know nothing about the problem in question, are permitted to air their prejudices and views, each, as often as not, with an eye upon some third party or parties, or with an axe to grind.

### III

I have said that direct negotiations between China and Japan, if opened in the last months of 1931, on the basis of the then existing treaties (since recognized by the Lytton Commission), would have effected a peace which would have been maintained at least for some years. I say "for some years" advisedly, because it is doubtful that lasting peace could be secured through any agreement signed in any way between China and Japan. This difficulty is fundamental and inherent; it comes from the fact that China is a house divided against itself, not only between North and South, but also between East and West, northeast and northwest, southeast and southwest. China is a chaotic void. Dr. Wellington Koo, Mr. W. W. Yen, or Mr. Alfred Sze, do not represent China; they represent only a fragment of it and they know it. Any treaty signed with such a governmental void is a make-believe which can do no more than patch up peace of a sort only for the time being. This fundamental difficulty has always been, and still is, an insuperable barrier against any satisfactory arrangement calculated to ensure peace between China and such of her neighbors as have vital interests in her territory. In the light of this difficulty, it is perfectly understandable that Japan embraced the first opportunity to deal with an independent Manchuria which placed itself under her tutelage and which she thinks furnishes, in the long run, a better guaranty of peace than is afforded by a chaotic China.

This difficulty, as we have already seen in earlier paragraphs, was fully recognized by the Lytton Commission when it unequivocally stated that the establishment of an effectual, strong, responsible central government in China was the prerequisite of a satisfactory readjustment of the Manchurian situation with reference to its relations with Japan. And yet this fundamental fact was completely ignored in the Report of the Committee of Nineteen which was adopted by the Assembly on February 24, 1933, and which caused the immediate withdrawal of the Japanese delegation. The Report assumes that whoever pleads for China before the League represents a normal, ordered, effectual government. That is the fundamental error.

At this time of writing (March 10, 1933), it is reported from the Far East that Marshal Chang Hsueh-liang, the ousted war lord of Manchuria, has definitely resigned his post as commander of the northern army, and has agreed to place his soldiers, 150,000 strong, under the authority of Chiang Kaishek, the Nanking generalissimo. As far as the so-called Central Government at Nanking is concerned, this sudden development is entirely fortuitous; it is due, not to any increase in Nanking's ability to unify China, but to the crushing defeat which has been inflicted upon Chang Hsueh-liang by the Japanese-Manchoukuo campaign in Jehol province. This is exactly what Chiang Kaishek has for years been praying would happen. He himself has been powerless to eliminate Chang Hsueh-liang and his army, and has hoped that the Japanese would do the job for him. There is not the slightest doubt that the Nanking generalissimo is sincerely grateful to Japan and Manchoukuo for their Jehol campaign, which has led to Marshal Chang's resignation and possibly his definite elimination as a military factor in North China. That explains why Nanking had never sent a single soldier to the north to help Chang Hsueh-liang in Jehol. A shrewd politician, Chiang Kaishek, for reasons of domestic politics, will, in all probability, continue to proclaim to the world, as he has so often done, that he is a sworn enemy of Japan. But at heart he is thankful that Japan has fought his battle against the former Manchurian war lord, and has thus made it possible for him to send to Peiping his faithful aide, General Ho Ying-chin, as new commander of the northern forces. I should not at all be surprised if Chiang Kaishek, after making a feint of fighting the Manchoukuo-Japanese forces along the Great Wall for a while, should call a halt to his generals and then issue some such statement:

"I am as bitter an enemy of Japan as I have ever been, and I dedicate myself to the task of restoring Manchuria to China. But at this moment, and for some time to come, we must bend all our energies to the suppression of the Communist armies in Central China and to the unification of China proper. When this is accomplished, I shall go to the north and fight the Japanese to a finish."

Whether or not Chiang will take this course depends upon the attitude and strength of the semi-independent regional anti-Nanking governments, such as those of Canton, Shantung, and Shansi, as well as the Communist Government in Kiangsi. If these factional governments should prove too vociferous in denouncing Chiang Kai-shek's "lukewarm" policy toward Manchoukuo, the Nanking generalissimo may, in spite of himself, be forced to keep on fighting Japan and Manchoukuo. Thus we are forced to come back to the conclusion of the Lytton Commission to the effect that the establishment of a strong central government in China is the prerequisite of a satisfactory solution of her international problems.

Now let us go back to Geneva and see what would have happened had Japan accepted the recommendation of the Committee of Nineteen in January or February of this year when Chang Hsueh-liang's power was still intact and his troops were overrunning Jehol province. The Manchoukuo-Japanese campaign of pacification against Jehol would have been nipped in the bud, and all Japanese troops withdrawn from all points outside the South Manchuria Railway zone, thus casting the vast territory of Manchuria, except the said zone, a narrow ribbon of land, to the mercy of Marshal Chang. With the Japanese soldiers under the League's rigid order not to advance a step out of the railway zone, Marshal Chang would have been free to reënter Manchuria, set up his government at Chinchow or Shinminfu, and let loose forces of mischief all over the country.

In such circumstances, how could the League have expected to put the recommendation of the Committee of Nineteen into execution? To what Chinese authority

could it have restored Manchuria had Manchoukuo, under the said recommendation, gone out of existence?
Nanking, *faute de mieux?* Suppose, then, that the
League and Japan had agreed to hand Manchuria over
to Nanking, what would Chang Hsueh-liang (then still
entrenched in North China with 150,000 soldiers) have
done? He would have balked and blocked any such
agreement. At that time he still cherished the idea that
he, not the Nanking faction, should be the one to get
back Manchuria, if Manchuria was to be restored to any
Chinese authority; and he was then powerful enough to
make good this intention, for, under the League recommendation, the Japanese troops could not stop Chang's
reëntrance into Manchuria.

The Lytton Commission's report plainly says that "a
mere restoration of the *status quo ante* would be no solution" of the Sino-Japanese dispute, and that such "would
be to treat the whole question theoretically and to leave
out of account the realities of the situation." The Commission, however sympathetic to China, was forced to
recognize the state of flux prevailing in China and the
precariousness, or rather absence, of her central authority,
always militating against the satisfactory adjustment of
her foreign relations. This view, so unmistakably expressed by the Lytton Commission, has been ignored by
the Committee of Nineteen and the Assembly.

If Chiang Kaishek were powerful enough to defy all
the factions aligned against him, he would probably come
to terms with Japan on the Manchurian question, but he
is not. At this moment no one can tell what will be the
effects of his temporary advance to North China through
the entirely fortuitous event of Chang Hsueh-liang's de-

feat at the hands of the Manchoukuo-Japanese forces. If the past is a clue to the future any agreement signed between Nanking and Japan, no matter how reasonable, is certain to be assailed and even made a cause of fresh civil war by Canton and other anti-foreign regional governments, as well as the "Communist" forces, all firmly entrenched in their respective spheres of control. These factions, like the traditional Irishman, are always and unalterably "agin" any institution which claims to be the central government of China. They will exploit any agreement designed to settle the Manchurian dispute between Nanking and Tokyo, as humiliating to China, regardless of the merits of the agreement. They will incite anti-Japanese boycotts and violent agitation against the Japanese, just as the Cantonese did before the outbreak of the Shanghai incident of January 28, 1932, all for purposes of domestic politics—namely, to embarrass the Nanking régime. It makes no difference whether the agreement is just or not; it is enough that they pretend to believe that it is unjust. This is not a hypothesis or an assumption; it has happened again and again. Indeed, China's history since 1911 has been largely a repetition of the same process. Denmark, Switzerland, or Spain, may be indifferent to all this, but Japan, for obvious reasons, cannot be. Any academic and idealistic plan for Manchuria which does not take into account the realities of the situation is more mischievous than useless.

The League is asking Japan to do what no other Power, if similarly situated, would do. It proposes to make Japan the first object of its uncertain, grandiose experiment. Japan might have accommodated the League had her interests at stake been not so great as to affect her very existence. Things being as they are, Japan cannot afford to take the risk inherent in such an experiment.

It is not fair to compare Japan's vital rights in Manchuria with the comparatively small British oil concession in Persia. Japan would have gladly submitted to the arbitrament of the League any dispute developing from any oil concession in a country thousands of miles away. Comparison is odious, and, moreover, no case exactly analogous to the Japanese case in Manchuria can be found.

## IV

If the League thinks that its refusal to recognize Manchoukuo would force Japan to recede from her present stand, it is likely to be disappointed. It may be shocking to the protagonists of the non-recognition doctrine to learn that Japan, and for that matter Manchoukuo, too, are not seriously concerned with the decision made by the League in this respect, but it is a fact nevertheless. True, Manchoukuo has been clamoring for recognition as a matter of principle. As a practical matter, however, I doubt that recognition is desired by Manchoukuo in the immediate or even near future. I have a sneaky feeling of suspicion that neither Japan nor Manchoukuo really wants recognition, at least for some years to come. If Manchoukuo were recognized now, the Powers, by no means friendlily disposed toward it, will station at Hsinking their representatives, whose critical eyes will no doubt detect, even ferret out, flaws and faults in which the new State will not be lacking in its formative stage. For a while, it would rather be free from such critical eyes, so that it could carry out its program in its own way.

Morally, non-recognition, I fear, makes little impression

upon Japan, because she is convinced of the justice of her cause. Non-recognition may hurt a guilty conscience, but it is devoid of force when applied to a nation which believes itself in the right.

Japan believes that she has delivered the 30,000,000 inhabitants of Manchuria from the yoke of the worst tyranny known to the modern world, and that she is assisting in the establishment of a new government which promises to keep out Chinese anarchy and to give a benevolent and beneficial rule to the people who have long endured official extortion and militarist plunder with mute resignation.

Japan is confident that organized banditry, which has cursed Manchuria for centuries, will cease within a few years, and that peace and order will soon prevail throughout the region. Beginnings in that direction are perceptible. Manchoukuo, with Japanese aid, has already unified and stabilized its currency, has abolished a few taxes, and has reduced the rate of some of the taxes which are still levied. It has even taken a step toward the solution of the opium evil, the age-long curse of China.

The above statement finds unqualified support in the following passage from Mr. Hallett Abend's article in the *New York Times* dated Mukden, December 21, 1932:

After even a short trip through Manchuria has served to reveal strikingly the real progress which Japan has made toward stabilizing the country, any sojourner in Mukden must agree, at least to some extent, with the arguments of Japan's delegates at Geneva to the effect that China will almost certainly continue in a condition of turmoil and disunity for the next ten or twenty years.

Anyone who has visited Manchuria for from four to six different times every year during the last seven years, as has this correspondent, cannot fail to admit that Manchuria today, as it was six years ago and four years ago and two years ago, still is the most progressive and best administered portion of what maps and atlases label "China."

Conditions in Manchuria today, with all the drawbacks and serious problems, are better than conditions prevailing in the Yangtse Valley or in North or South China.

Yosuke Matsuoka, Japan's chief delegate to Geneva, expressed this general Japanese conviction when he said in a press interview:

We do not take. We are in a position to give. Japan has taken all she needs from the West, assimilated and naturalized Western mechanism and materialism. That much richer by a code and modernization which supplement our own traditional civilization, we hold a unique position among Far Eastern countries. Our occupation of Manchuria is not a question of "taking" Manchuria in a military sense or of taking anything away from Manchuria in a moral sense. It is Japan who is giving Manchuria precious principles of self-development, progress and spirituality. This melting-pot of Asia, where meet and mingle Japanese, Chinese, Manchus, Mongols, Koreans, Siberians, and Russians, Red and White, one day may be able to save the whole of China.

Mr. Matsuoka further said that if, in time to come, a renascent and vitalized Manchuria of Japan's molding and inspiration should desire to throw in her lot again with China, there would be none to hinder. "That would be but one of Japan's many contributions to humanity."

Japan, to take such an attitude, may be a modern Don Quixote. Perhaps she is fanatical. Perhaps she is mad. But whatever she is, she faces the world with a clear conscience; and the world, unable to fathom her mind, looks at her with mingled wonderment, perplexity, fear, and suspicion. It is a case of utter lack of understanding, comparable to the usual misunderstanding between a Victorian parent and a modern youth. That is the tragedy of it.

Meanwhile, the Powers cannot, and will not, ignore Manchoukuo, even though they are too prudish to recognize her. Her territory is too vast and potentially too rich to be ignored. As a matter of fact, some of the Powers are casting furtive glances toward her. They are accepting, even demanding, handsome sums from her. Who take the eleven million *yuan* or so which Manchoukuo is called upon to remit every year to the Inspector-General of the Maritime Customs at China out of her customs receipts? The Powers, America included. Again, who take the two and one-half million *yuan* which Manchoukuo sends to the Inspector-General of the Salt Gabelle annually? Again the Powers who have claims against China. And yet the Powers pretend that they have nothing to do with Manchoukuo. That is neither good sense nor good taste.

Furthermore, the Powers have been pressing upon the Manchoukuo Government the demand that it settle the claims of their respective nationals who had sold to the old Chang régime goods which had not been paid for when the new Government replaced it. Certainly the Powers have not ignored Manchoukuo. Their nationals will continue to live and trade in Manchoukuo. Their consuls are there to look after the interests of their respective countries. How can they perform their duties if they have nothing to do with Manchoukuo?

I agree with President Lowell, of Harvard University, when he says that the principle of non-recognition cannot be maintained for any length of time. "There are," he says, "profits to be made by outsiders in Manchoukuo, and, when the strength of feeling has subsided, will not some nation seek to obtain them—not at first by direct recognition, but in substance? Will not others follow suit, until practically the whole system has broken down?"

v

I have long felt that Japan will somehow, some time, retire from the League. If possible, she would leave it in the same friendly spirit in which she agreed to dissolve her alliance with Great Britain in 1922. For that reason she would, if she could have her way, withdraw under happier circumstances than are at present possible. But if she does not quit the League now, she will quit it eventually.

The League, in its conception and inception, is primarily and essentially a European institution. It was meant to solve, if possible, Europe's own problems which had so often converted the Continent into a battlefield. Japan stumbled into it by accident, or to be more accurate, by reason of the minor rôle she had played in the World War. Japan has contributed little, if anything, toward the solution of any of the multitudinous problems of Europe, as indeed she could not, but has imposed upon the League obnoxious problems of which the League would gladly have steered clear. Japan's withdrawal, then, may be considered a good riddance for Geneva.

Japan, on her part, realizes that she does not really belong to the League. Once out, Japan is more than unlikely to return to the League's fold, but will in all probability follow the American example, coöperating with the League in disarmament and in such humanitarian enterprises as may appeal to her. She feels that she could contribute nothing toward the unraveling of the tangled skein of Europe, and that Europe could do even less toward the solution of the problems of the Far East.

For a time, the League dazzled Japan. She was proud of the high place accorded to her in the League. The prestige thus given her was pleasing to her. Her diplomats presided over various commissions entrusted with the solution of European disputes, which satisfied their and her vanity. But nations have more vital matters to consider than national vanity or even prestige. Japan now realizes that for a Japanese diplomat to preside over a commission to solve any political problem of Europe which he does not really understand is as unnatural as for a European diplomat to preside over a commission to solve a Far Eastern problem which he does not comprehend. Japan now sees the League and herself without glamour and with no illusion.

The Manchurian decision of the League will serve to strengthen Japanese skepticism as to the capability of any European tribunal of rendering unbiased decision on any question involving the interests of an Oriental nation. Ever since the Hague Court of Arbitration, in 1905, decided against Japan on the question of foreigners' immunity from taxation, this skepticism has prevailed in large circles in Japan. Let me briefly describe this case.

When Japan opened her doors to foreign intercourse in the middle of the last century, she agreed to set apart certain sections in the open ports for the residence and trade of Europeans and Americans. In these "settlements" the foreigners secured from the Japanese Government perpetual lease of lands, tax-free and paying rents which were less than nominal. Of course the Japanese Government had no intention of extending this tax immunity to the buildings to be built upon those lands. But the foreigners refused to pay tax on these buildings worth tens of millions of *yen,* and this refusal was supported by their respective home governments. So the dispute was submitted to the Permanent Court of Arbitration at The Hague in 1904. The tribunal which considered this case consisted of two arbitrators and an umpire. The arbitrators were M. Louis Renault, professor of law in the University of Paris, representing the three European governments concerned, and Mr. Ichiro Motono, the Japanese Minister at Paris, representing the Government at Tokyo. The umpire was Mr. Gregers Gram, formerly Norwegian Minister of State. The decision rendered under date of May 22, 1905, sustains the contention of the European Powers that the treaties exempt not only the land but "buildings of every description constructed or which may hereafter be constructed on such land, from all imposts, taxes, charges, contribution, or conditions whatsoever."

The significance of this decision lies not so much in its material effects as in its moral influence. The point at issue was the principle involved. The Japanese were, and are, firmly convinced of the justice of their contention on the above tax question, and were grieved that their first experience with an international tribunal proved disappointing. What unbiased critic shall deny that the Japanese contention was just and incontrovertible? The Japanese disappointment experienced at The Hague and the consequent Japanese skepticism have been made infinitely more poignant by the sneaky manner in which the League Council whitewashed the grave and grievous error it had committed at the beginning of the Manchurian trouble and by the brusque and overbearing manner in which the

Committee of Nineteen and the Assembly have brushed aside Japan's arguments and even the recommendations of the Lytton Commission.

## VI

Finally, Japan now fully realizes that, however accommodating she may endeavor to be in dealing with China, she will always be exposed to the menace of Chinese boycotts, which, except in rare instances, are not motivated by patriotism but are a downright scheme of blackmail, as I have shown in my previous book, *Japan Speaks*. Japan has suffered from this Chinese "racket," which is employed as an instrument of national policy, at various intervals during the past twenty-seven years. Of course Japan denies emphatically the legality and justifiability of such boycotts, but insists that they are a clear violation of treaty stipulations. But whether legal or illegal, whether justifiable or unjustifiable, boycotts are a factor which Japan must take into account in formulating her future commercial policy abroad. More and more will she strive to deflect her trade from China to other parts of the world, and thus offset the effects of Chinese boycotts by trade gains elsewhere. Without in the least abandoning the contention that the boycott is a treaty violation, Japan will, at the same time, follow this course of readjustment.

And this process of readjustment has already begun to bear fruit. Japan's trade returns from January 1 to August 30, 1932, show that, while her exports to China, Hongkong, the Straits Settlements, and a few places where the Chinese population is preponderant, have decreased by 50,219,000 *yen* as compared with figures for the corresponding period in 1931, her exports to other countries such as India, the Kwantung Leased Territory, Java, Persia, Asia Minor, Africa, Oceania, and Europe, have increased by 58,892,000 *yen*—a net gain of 8,687,000 *yen*.

I have no later figures at hand, but I know that our export trade since August, 1932, has been even more favorable. Thus Japan is making up her losses in China by extending her export trade into new markets. The Powers at Geneva, by taking a suicidal attitude of encouraging Chinese boycotts, have virtually invited Japan to make incursions into their own markets. Moreover, I am convinced that the time will come when China will employ boycotts against other Powers than Japan. Some day the League's chickens will come home to roost.

# CHAPTER I

## THE STORM GATHERS

### I

THE Manchurian imbroglio has given birth to a plethora of books and articles on the subject. Students of international affairs have sought explanation for it in old treaties and musty documents. Professors of history have called to light past records of international rivalry to find the cause of the conflict. The League of Nations Commission, who were sent to the Far East to study the matter on the spot, have interviewed war lords and statesmen and politicians, hoping thus to unravel the tangled skein of a triangular wrangle involving Japan, China and Manchoukuo. Last but not least, foreign ministers and ambassadors, speaking in the usual language of diplomacy, have added much to the discussion.

And yet the composite picture thus produced is not a truthful portrayal. It ignores or does not give due importance to the human factors which were at the bottom of the trouble.

Nations, like individuals, are human. They have their moods and temperaments, their virtues and frailties. Naturally, relations between nations are often fashioned by human sentiments no less than by treaties and protocols. It would be difficult to name any international trouble which was not rooted in human factors.

Since the chief actor in the Manchurian drama was the Japanese soldier, it is essential to know something of his moods and feelings prior to the September incident. How did he feel about the way things had been going on in Japan? What was his reaction to the vital problems of his nation, which had been crying for solution? What did he think about statesmen, diplomats, politicians, and industrialists about him? Above all, what did he think about Manchuria? All these had conspired to make him restive, discontented, even defiant.

For well-nigh ten years preceding the Manchurian incident, the Japanese soldier had believed himself virtually standing at bay. It is not my intention to determine whether this belief was justifiable or unjustifiable; it is enough to say that the belief was generally prevalent. The soldier cherished the memory of the sacrifices he had offered upon the altar of the New Japan through its infant and formative stages, and compared it with the slight which he thought was now meted out to him by an ungrateful public. But for those sacrifices, what would have been the status of Japan today? Perhaps a second India, China, Persia, or Turkey. Through the years when the militaristic imperialism of the Occident was surging forth against the Orient, when the great Powers vied with one another in staking out for themselves vast areas in "backward" countries, Japan alone stood her ground. Had it not been for her hard-won victories at Port Arthur, at Mukden, in the Japan Sea, where would she have been? As the soldier looks at it, it was largely his achievements in the arts of war which inspired in the Western mind due respect for Japan's innate capacity for administration and other arts of peace and thus caused the Powers, willy-nilly, to restore to her the judicial and tariff autonomy of which they had deprived her when she was infant and helpless.

Then came the World War, ushering in, in its wake, a period of idealism in all the war-worn and war-weary countries. With apparent sincerity, the statesmen who had so lately advocated death and destruction now joined in a chorus of peace, friendliness and disarmament. It was an inevitable, though unfortunately ephemeral, recoil from the appalling holocaust which had almost spelled the destruction of civilization and humanity.

Japan, although she had participated in that war only in a minor capacity, proved no exception to this general post-bellum reaction. The wave of liberalism swept through the country. Public sentiment was in favor of armament retrenchment. The press supported liberal diplomacy and denounced whatever savored of militarism vis-à-vis Japan's continental policy. Domestically, too, Japan adopted a universal manhood suffrage, calculated to strengthen the hands of liberals. For the time being liberalism was the vogue and its advocates occupied the center of the stage. The famous Shidehara policy was a product of this period.

Along with this surging tide of liberalism came a sort of industrialism, also a by-product of the World War. Like the United States, though on a much smaller scale, Japan benefited by the war industrially and commercially. Her factories and mills expanded as never before. Her ships carried her manufactures over the seven seas. Her banks and commercial corporations reaped handsome profits. Her captains of industry and her merchant princes waxed wealthy and correspondingly influential, while men

MR. PU-YI
CHIEF EXECUTIVE

employed by them were paid higher salaries than were received by government officials. In former years the pick and flower of Japan's young men were attracted to the governmental service for the honor attached to it; now they preferred commercial positions for the material comfort they offered.

In this world of industrialism coupled with liberalism, the soldier receded, or rather was forced, farther and farther into the background, and his profession had come to be looked upon as a sort of necessary evil, of which the public was no longer proud. The soldier began to be regarded as the burden rather than the glory of the nation. There was really a time when crowds on the trams and in the streets started at men in uniform as if they were an anachronism and even objects of pity.

## II

Under these circumstances, the military program which had been formulated in the wake of the war with Russia, and which called for the inauguration of twenty-five divisions, went by the board. By the time of the Washington Conference of 1921-22, the four divisions which had still remained on paper had been entirely eliminated. About the curtailment of these paper divisions the soldier was not seriously concerned, for he recognized its reasonableness in the light of the collapse of the Czarist empire, the greatest military colossus of the world. But the ball of armament reduction, once set rolling, could not be stopped. It gathered momentum as it moved on and broke through all resistance offered by those directly concerned with Japan's national defense.

At the beginning of 1922, while the Washington Conference was discussing naval reduction, the Diet at Tokyo passed a resolution demanding that army expenditure be cut by at least 40,000,000 *yen* a year and that the term of service of conscripts be reduced from two years to one year and four months. So general was popular backing for this resolution that the army was obliged to take immediate steps in compliance with it. Thus, between 1922 and 1924, no less than 1,800 officers and 56,000 men, as well as 13,000 horses, were curtailed. The readjustment program thus adopted also shortened the term of service, abolished independent garrisons, and eliminated the higher officers' complement in Korea. The total reduction thus carried out amounted, in effect, to five divisions on peace footing. In terms of money the retrenchment between 1922 and 1924 amounted to 354,000,000 *yen*. Thus, at the end of 1924, though Japan's land force, on paper, still consisted of twenty-one divisions, the actual strength of these divisions, as compared with their former strength, was cut by five divisions.

Nor was this all. Even the twenty-one divisions thus weakened were not to be permitted to remain intact, for in May, 1925, another drastic reduction was put into effect, resulting in the abolition of four divisions which included sixteen infantry regiments, four cavalry regiments, four field artillery regiments, four engineer battalions, four commissariat battalions and a motor-car battalion. The number of officers and men thus eliminated totaled 37,000. The term of service of infantry was reduced from two years to eighteen months.

All this while the soldier remained quiescent, but with mingled apprehension, alarm, and resentment. As a strategist, he could not help observing the Red army, imbued with ideals diametrically opposed to those of the rest of the world, looming larger and larger upon the Siberian horizon. Today the Soviet forces, as the Japanese soldier looks at it, are much larger than the army over which the Czar had held sway. Nor could he ignore China's 2,000,000 soldiers, ill-equipped and inefficient, it is true, but none the less capable of converting Manchuria into a scene of civil strife and, what was more significant, believing themselves far more powerful than their Japanese fellows.

The soldier believed that the Japanese army, though nominally consisting of seventeen divisions, was actually little larger than thirteen divisions—the size maintained thirty years ago—because the personnel of the infantry, cavalry, artillery, engineering corps, and commissariat had been greatly reduced in order to supply men for the air force and various other new branches of national defense, those unexpected, unwelcome, costly offsprings of the World War. He saw that such new branches, though organized on paper, were not provided with the funds necessary to make them effectual. And while such restrictions and restraints were put upon the army, he knew that his duty as the defender of his country had become much greater, for the area which he was now expected to defend increased in the past three decades from 420,000 square kilometers to 680,000 square kilometers, with the corresponding increase in population from 49,000,000 to 85,000,000. He knew that the Japanese army ranked fifth in size among the armies of the world; that its expenditure amounted to 235,000,000 *yen* a year as compared with Soviet Russia's 1,040,000,000 *yen*, America's 880,000,000 *yen*, France's 635,000,000 *yen*, England's 486,-

000,000 *yen*, Italy's 307,000,000 *yen*, and Germany's 242,-000,000 *yen;* that Japan's per capita burden of land armament was 3.44 *yen* as compared with France's 15.58 *yen*, England's 10.80 *yen*, America's 7.99 *yen*, Italy's 7.67 *yen*, Russia's 7.01 *yen*, and Germany's 3.78 *yen*. He saw that the army's appropriation had been so drastically reduced that only 300 yen per annum was allowed each soldier for ration, clothing, and even maneuvers. As he looked at it, only the loyalty and patriotism which had won the wars with China and then with Russian remained to keep up the morale of the army, but he knew very well that in modern warfare loyalty and patriotism alone could not cope with the tremendous devices of destruction which had been developed by the Powers since the World War.

### III

On the other hand, the liberals of Japan advocated further reduction in the army. They thought that such reduction was in harmony with, and indeed a natural corollary to, the Washington Treaty of 1922 which had caused the Japanese navy to abolish 24 capital ships, built, building and projected, to delete 38 auxiliary ships, and to retire 12,200 officers and sailors. They reasoned that if Japan, an island nation, could dispense with so much of her navy, she could afford to reduce her army even to a greater extent. They ignored the army's view that Japan had long since ceased to be an island nation but had, for better or for worse, become a continental power with vast land frontiers to protect on the Asian continent. Some of them went so far as to urge upon the army a reduction of seven more divisions, which, if effected, would have reduced Japan's entire land force to ten divisions for the protection of Korea, Manchuria, Formosa, and Sagalien, as well as her home islands.

Such liberal ideas were favorably received, if not positively supported, by the press. They seemed to strike a responsive chord in the popular mind. It had indeed become unpopular to take up the cudgels in defense of the army and its point of view.

## IV

Then came the London Conference of 1930, which, as far as Japan was concerned, marked the climax of the liberal movement. That Conference dealt exclusively with the question of naval limitation, but the momentous decision which it obliged Japan to make produced a most far-reaching effect upon the army, as upon the navy. That decision, outcome of the now famous Reed-Matsudaira compromise, was made by Premier Hamaguchi and Foreign Minister Baron Shidehara without consulting, or at least without the consent of, those to whom had been entrusted by law and tradition the duty—and right—of formulating the nation's defense policy. The decision itself, accepting as it did a smaller ratio than had been asked by the navy, was objectionable enough to those high in the councils of Japan's national defense, but it was the above method of adopting it, deviating from the long-established precedent, which, more than anything else, stirred the ire of the soldier as well as of the sailor.

The question of the naval ratio, of course, was not the soldier's immediate concern, but if the Prime Minister and Foreign Minister were permitted to deprive the sailor of the authority he had long enjoyed, would they not mete out much the same treatment to the soldier? To the soldier, such a treatment was not a slight to him personally, but a challenge to the system of defense which, he believed, afforded the best guarantee of Japan's security. It, as he saw it, struck at the very foundation of Japan's national existence. That, to him, was the last straw.

Unfortunately, the condition of party government in Japan had been far from inspiring confidence and respect in the mind of the soldier. On the contrary, the soldier had for years watched party politicians and their performances with distrust and disgust. He had seen corruption in high political circles. He had seen national problems of great importance converted into pawns in the game of politics. He had seen political parties concocting questionable schemes in collusion with financial cliques for selfish gain. Of course party government, with all its foibles, follies, and futilities, had its bright side, but this the soldier could not recognize, for his eyes were fixed upon its dark side. Would not national defense, if entrusted to politicians, become one more pawn in their game? Could it, when subjected to the whims of party government, preserve the integrity and efficiency which it had managed to maintain? Above all, could it long remain free from the corruption which had besmirched many of the projects in which politicians were interested? So asked the soldier. To him the answer was obvious.

v

And so the soldier was in a defiant mood against the growing vogue of liberalism, democracy, industrialism, or what you will. His resentment became all the greater as he viewed this national trend in the light of the grave situation developing in Manchuria. To him Japan was a na-

tion asleep on a volcano about to erupt. He believed that
conditions in Manchuria, due largely to what he termed
the "weak-kneed" diplomacy of the Foreign Office, had
already become so intolerable that nothing but his firm
stand could save Japan's vital rights and interests there
from utter destruction. He was convinced that unless the
nation awakened, and awakened soon, it might some day
find itself at Armegeddon, where he would be called
upon to sacrifice his life as his sires had sacrificed theirs
twice upon the plains of Manchuria.

And indeed, in spite, or rather, as the soldier saw it,
because, of the "new diplomacy" of the Foreign Office,
the Manchurian situation had been going from bad to
worse. This new diplomacy, confronted by the "revolutionary diplomacy" of Nationalist China and the military
pressure of the Manchurian war lords, had met with nothing but reverses. The practice, followed both by Nationalist China and militarist Manchuria, of abrogating or disregarding whatever treaties were not to their liking, had
resulted in serious impairment of rights and interests
essential to Japan's existence.

In Manchuria the Japanese, instead of going forward,
had begun to beat a retreat. Everywhere his position had
become precarious. Even the South Manchuria Railway,
that gigantic economic organization owning property
worth more than a billion dollars, had been alarmed.
What more natural than that the Japanese in Manchuria
should unite and agitate for a firmer policy at the hands
of their home government? All along the railway they
held mass meetings to warn the Foreign Office against the
ruin which would stare them in the face unless the Chinese practice of treaty violations was stopped. They sent

a delegation to Tokyo to wait upon Foreign Minister Baron Shidehara, whose name will go down in history as Japan's great liberal diplomat. To their remonstrances Baron Shidehara replied, "It is not wise to think of the diplomatic problems of the twentieth century in terms of the nineteenth century."

Baron Shidehara's new diplomacy in China enjoyed public support; it was not seriously challenged even by the army as long as China's obstructionist policy confined itself within "reasonable" bounds. It broke down when China resorted to a policy of wholesale violation of treaties and struck at the vitals of the Japanese position in Manchuria. One may be permitted to wonder if President Hoover's and Secretary Stimson's new diplomacy *vis-à-vis* Central America and the Caribbean Islands, if subjected to a similar test, would not likewise break down. Suppose that Nicaragua repudiated the Bryan-Chamorro Treaty of 1916, which conceded to the United States the right to dig a canal through its territory and a 99-year lease of the Great Corn and Little Corn Islands and of a naval base on the Gulf of Fonseca, what would happen? Would America then appeal to Geneva? If a great Power, with unlimited resources within its own territory, refuses to appeal to the arbitrament of the League on a question which by no means affects its national existence, can we reasonably expect a nation existing in a hand-to-mouth fashion to refrain from direct action to safeguard the interests which are to it a matter of life or death? Such are the questions often asked by critics of Baron Shidehara's new diplomacy. And who shall deny that such questions, though unpleasant and perhaps impolite to ask, are of vital importance and will have to be answered some day? I have taken America and Nicaragua merely as an illustration. Many another analogy can be found in other quarters of the globe.

### VI

For some years since the war boom spent itself, Japan had been grappling with economic difficulties. The acute depression which followed in the wake of that boom had been accentuated by the great earthquake disaster of 1923. A pall of gloom had been cast over the people and they did not know how or when it could be lifted. Strikes became more and more frequent. Communistic ideas spread among college graduates who could find no employment. The agrarian problem grew increasingly acute. Farmers and peasants were harassed by mounting debts; nor could they raise enough to feed themselves, so small were their plots. To Japan such agricultural difficulties are of the foremost importance, for half her population are engaged in farming.

In such circumstances, it was inevitable that the eyes of the Japanese should turn to Manchuria. They, or at least many of them, felt that Manchuria was their salvation. They were not articulate, but they felt, in a vague and indefinable sort of way, that unless they were provided with a new outlet, a new field of activity, they had no hope of freeing themselves from their straits. Intellectuals there were many who would enumerate factors militating against Japanese settlement in Manchuria, such as banditry, official extortion, climatic conditions, and, above all, the war lords' deliberate breach of treaties. But the average Japanese, the man in the street, felt that somehow such obstacles could be overcome if only his

Government would take a firm stand in defense of the rights which he was entitled to enjoy. If the war lords or the Chinese Nationalists did not honor the treaties they had signed, his own Government had only to thank the vascillating policy it had itself followed in dealing with them. Why, he asked, does not the Government bestir itself and fulfill its bounden duty by settling the Manchurian question?

Perhaps I might illustrate this popular feeling by presenting a picture of the Ai-Kyo-Juku, literally "Love Neighbors House," a mutual-aid organization of farmers at Mito, a hundred miles from Tokyo. It is an institution both fraternal and patriotic in spirit. It has become notorious through the arrest of its founder and president, Tachibana, the "Gandhi of Japan," as a possible instigator of the assassination of Premier Inukai, which shocked the civilized world in May, 1932.

Tachibana, now forty years of age, had a high-school education and spent three years in college. While at school he was studious and was known to have a philosophical turn of mind. He read much of Tolstoi and Bergson. He was so deeply interested in the problems of small farmers and peasants that he quit college before graduation and resolved to devote his life to their cause. He had inherited a plot of land which, small though it was, he thought could be so utilized as to make him and his family entirely self-supporting. Having succeeded in this experiment for himself, he spread its gospel among his neighbors, whose hard lot he thus hoped to alleviate.

On the spiritual side he was a man of peace. He did not believe in Communism, and he deprecated the Marxian idea of class struggle. On the contrary, he urged

sympathetic understanding between the landlord and
the tenant as the first step to the solution of agrarian difficulties.

On the material side Tachibana's idea was simplicity
itself. Its essence was frugality plus good management.
He realized the meagerness of the farmer's resources and
believed that a most rigid economy was essential if he
was to balance his budget at all. He emphasized the
necessity of divorcing the farmer from the city with its
luxuries, its temptations, its system of gambling in farm
products at the expense of the son of the soil. Then he
introduced new elements into the traditional method of
farming. Besides growing enough rice for the use of his
family, he kept a milch cow, an ox for field work, a
breeding sow, and one hundred hens. To the Occidental
farmer there is nothing new in this, but to the Japanese
it is a novel thing to combine the culture of the main
staple, rice, with the raising of cows, pigs, and poultry.

When Tachibana organized this society four years ago
his own family was its sole member. Now it comprises
two thousand families. He was a man of a retiring disposition, and shunned the limelight of publicity. Yet his
fame spread so far and wide that even so distinguished a
personage as Lieutenant-General Prince Higashi Kuni, a
scion of the imperial house, a progressive who had studied
in Paris for ten years, went out of his way to call upon
this farmer-philosopher to inquire about his plan to save
the farmer.

Tachibana's idea of making the farmers self-supporting
by the practice of frugality, independence from the city,
and new management, would have been entirely practicable had there been enough land for them. The simple

fact was that most farmers did not have even the minimum of land necessary to produce barely enough for self-
support. Tachibana's own holdings amounted to only
four acres, and he managed to support his family of five
with what he wrested from this small plot. Yet a farmer
who owned "so much" land was far above the average;
indeed, he was considered one of the "upper class." In
his locality the average income of the farmer was 436
*yen* a year, and his outlay or cost of production, including taxes, fertilizer, seeds, and interest on debts, amounted
to 256 *yen*. This left only 180 *yen* for living cost for a
family of five. In Tachibana's estimate, the minimum
cost of living for a farming family of five was 325 *yen*
apportioned as follows: food, 200 *yen;* clothing, 25 *yen;*
education of children, 31 *yen;* repair of the dwelling, 15
*yen;* luxury, such as tobacco and wine, 15 *yen;* entertain-
ments, 12 *yen;* miscellaneous, 8 *yen*. Put this total living
cost of 325 *yen* against the net income of 180 *yen,* and
there is a clear deficit of 145 *yen*. Only by borrowing
could the farmer exist. Many of the farmers in Tachibana's locality borrowed money on the uncertain security
of prospective crops two or three years ahead. Many
ate up the rice they had produced in the previous season
long before the new crop was available.

The root of this dire plight was, as Tachibana saw it,
dearth of land. How could farming be diversified as he
had planned, when the average size of farms was only
a little over an acre, including the dwelling site and the
surrounding yards? To this question Tachibana could
give no answer except emigration.

Naturally, Manchuria, to him, seemed to offer one, if
not the only, solution. To Manchuria he went, hoping to

work out there a plan to emancipatae his fellow farmers at Mito. It was there that he was put under arrest on the suspicion that he had instigated, or at least was incriminated in, the assassination of Premier Inukai. Could it be that he considered Inukai's policy too weak to create a Manchuria which would serve to alleviate the agricultural problem of Japan?

Tachibana is under arrest. The Court may sentence him to a life term, but many another Tachibana may follow in his footsteps as long as the problem which produced him remains unsolved. That is why in some quarters the feeling prevails that Tachibana is as much a martyr as the Premier, a victim of a condition the radical alteration of which is the crying need of Japan.

## VII

The moral of the Tachibana incident is clear. It points out the difficulty of solving Japan's chronic and growing trouble of overpopulation without resort to emigration. What Caucasian nation, situated as Japan is, has not encouraged emigration or acquired colonies? They tell us that England solved her population question, not by emigration, but by industrialization. That is not true. When England's population-increase was at its height, her sons and daughters emigrated to the United States and her own overseas dominions by the hundred thousand. Before the American Immigration Act of 1924 restricted immigration by the quota system, most European countries, especially Italy, counted upon emigration to America as a means of allaying their economic ills.

Ever since the United States and the British overseas dominions raised a barrier against Japanese immigration,

our Government, to be polite and "gentlemanly," handled the knotty problem with kid gloves. It pretended
that Japan was interested, not in emigration, but in the
academic question of equality. As Viscount Ishii, one-
time Ambassador to Washington and Paris, puts it, "Our
primary concern in this respect is not whether or not a
few thousand or a few hundred Japanese immigrants shall
be admitted to America, but whether Japan shall be accorded the courteous treatment which is due to her as
one of the civilized Powers of the world. To us it is a
matter of ideals rather than a question of material interest." According to this view Japan would be satisfied
if the United States should apply the general quota system to Japanese emigration, although this would, in
effect, be the same as the exclusion now in force. That is
the official Japanese attitude.

But the average Japanese, the man who lives by the
sweat of his brow, is not concerned with the question of
national "face." To him, the emigration question means
his right to emigrate, not his nation's theoretical equality
with other states which confer no material benefit upon
him. He wants to go wherever he has the best opportunity to work and live. When this freedom is denied
him, when he sees himself cooped up in his narrow confines and his energy and enterprise thus throttled, he not
only blames the foreign nations which exclude him but
rails at his own Government, which pretends that emigration is of no serious concern to it. While the Government has been thus pretending, the noose of exclusion
laws adopted by foreign governments has been tighten-
ing around the nation with increasingly telling effect.
Why disguise the obvious fact that there are too many

Japanese living in Japan, and that the exclusion policy of the Caucasian nations is slowly but surely smothering the Japanese? As long as Japan was more or less benefited by the general prosperity of the world, the Government's pretension that it was interested only in theoretical equality was not seriously challenged by the people, but when the bubble of prosperity burst, with all its dire consequences, this tolerant popular attitude had to be changed.

### VIII

Much has already been written on the question of Japan's overpopulation. Yet now and then casual observers and even serious critics from the West deign to tell us that Japan is not overcrowded and that she still has much area which can be profitably developed. They are like a millionaire preaching thrift to the poor. Is there any civilized country in the world where cities, towns, villages and hamlets are so close together as they are in Japan?

Japan proper consists of four islands. Hondo, the largest island, has 732 inhabitants to the square mile, Shikoku 433, and Kiushiu 484. The average density of these three islands is about 550. But these figures do not tell the true story. Even school children know that these islands consist of volcanic ranges. They are virtually covered with mountains, affording but some 15,000,000 acres of tillable land, or only 16 per cent of the total area. In Great Britain 77 per cent of its land area is arable; in Italy 76 per cent; in France 70 per cent; and in Germany 65 per cent.

The fourth island, Hokkaido, is not so thickly populated. Yet its 78 per square mile is much more than three times the density of California. Moreover, Hokkaido, like the other three islands, is traversed by many mountain ranges which severely restrict the area of its tillable land. Because of its vigorous and protracted winters, farming on its northern slopes is not profitable

On the basis of the above figures, the average area of arable land for each of the population, urban and rural, is only one quarter of an acre. If we confine our consideration to the farming population, we find that 35 per cent of the total number of our farming families cultivate less than 1.22 acres each, 34 per cent between 1.22 and 2.45 acres each, and 31 per cent more than 2.45 acres. The arable area attached to each farming family in Japan is only one as compared to thirty-one in the United States, sixteen in Denmark, nine in England, six in Sweden, five in Germany, and three in Ireland. The result is that, in lean years, rice produced in Japan proper is not enough to feed the population. In 1930 the total yield was 10 per cent less than the home demand. True, Japan exports rice to a considerable extent, but this is possible only because most of our farmers, for reasons of economy, eat rice mixed with cheaper food stuffs such as millet, oats, Burma rice, or even vegetables.

Such is Japan's predicament. A nation less virile, less determined might have bowed to the inevitable. It might have adopted birth control as a national policy and have acquiesced in the fate which it thought could not be changed. Not so the Japanese. He preferred forward movement to defeatism, struggle to strangulation, when at last he was forced to make the choice. He has repudiated birth control, not only because it spells national decline, but because he has to consider his neighbors with vast territories and vast man power which may some day be turned against him.

IX

The scene now shifts to Manchuria. While the Japanese soldier watched with grave concern the Foreign Office's new diplomacy and its effect on China—while larger and larger circles in Japan began to realize the seriousness of the situation which confronted us in Manchuria—while the man in the street and the average farmer, unable to make ends meet, vaguely felt the need of a "place in the sun," conditions in Manchuria became more and more ominous. But for those conditions, the explosion of September, 1931, might have been averted.

So much has already been written on treaty violations by China and Manchuria that I think it unnecessary to discuss this matter here at length. Suffice it to enumerate the covenants which were broken. Here is the list:

1. The Treaty of Commerce and Navigation of 1896.
2. The Supplementary Treaty of Commerce and Navigation of 1903.
3. The Sino-Japanese Treaty of Peace, 1895.
4. The Treaty Relating to Manchuria, 1905.
5. The Agreements on the Establishment of the Maritime Customs Office at Dairen.
6. The Agreement on Inland Waters Steam Navigation.
7. The Agreement Concerning Chientao, 1909.
8. The Agreement Concerning Mines and Railways in Manchuria, 1909.
9. The Regulations Concerning the Fushun and Yentai Mines, 1911.
10. The Treaty Respecting Shantung Province, 1915.
11. The Treaty Respecting South Manchuria and Eastern Inner Mongolia, 1915.
12. The Notes Exchanged Respecting the Matter of Hanyehping, 1915.

13. The Treaty for the Settlement of Outstanding Questions Relative to Shantung, 1922.
14. The Agreement on Detailed Arrangements for the Execution of the Above Treaty, 1922.
15. The Notes Exchanged in Regard to the Construction of Certain Railways in Manchuria and Mongolia, 1913.
16. The Notes Exhanged Regarding Four Railways in Manchuria and Mongolia.
17. The Notes Exchanged Regarding the Recognition of China's New Import Customs Tariff, 1929.
18. The Agreement Regarding the Customs Tariff.
19. The Washington Nine-Power Treaty, 1922.
20. Resolutions Adopted at the Washington Conference, 1922, Regarding Extraterritoriality, the Abolition of Foreign Postal Agencies, the Withdrawal of Foreign Military Forces, and the Reduction of Chinese Military Forces.
21. The Reorganization Loan Agreement with Great Britain, France, Germany, Russia, and Japan, 1913.
22. Various Contracts between the Chinese Governments, Central and Local, and Japanese Banks, Corporations and Individuals.

This wholesale disregard of treaties was no doubt largely due to the encouragement which China derived from the new peace or pacifist system reared upon the ruins of the World War. She felt that the peace doctrine, which had become the vogue of the world, virtually made the weak nations powerful before great Powers and the great Powers helpless before weak nations. She thought that Japan's hands were tied by the League Covenant, the Peace Pact, and other similar treaties, and that, however irresponsibly she might act, Japan would not dare invoke punitive measures against her.

x

If the mood of the Japanese soldier did much to tip the balance of peace, so did the temper of the Chinese, especially the Manchurian, soldier. Remember that Manchuria had, to all intents and purposes, no civil government but was under the dictatorship of the soldier. There the soldier was law. His whims, his likes and dislikes, were of great significance even in international affairs.

When Chang Tso-lin, father of the "Young Marshal," ruled Manchuria, his policy was to get as much help from Japan, giving Japan in return as little, as possible. But for Japanese help, his régime would have been wiped out by the Kuo Sung-ling rebellion in December, 1925. When his son, Chang Hsueh-liang, succeeded him in 1928, the "Young Marshal" not only launched a vigorous anti-Japanese propaganda but also adopted a policy of personal slight in dealing with the Japanese. Indeed, he seemed to take delight in rebuffing and snubbing Japanese dignitaries, both military and civilian. Was he a victim of megalomania? Was he addicted to drugs, the use of which is so common among Chinese officials? Whatever the cause, the studied insults which he was in the habit of administering to Japanese diplomats, generals, nobles, and officials, were deplorable, and had, in my judgment, a far-reaching influence.

To make this point clear let me cite an extraordinary yet typical case, the story of which was told to me by a Japanese peer, a Baron, who was himself the unenviable hero of it.

The Baron had many friends among the high officials of Chang Hsueh-liang's Government at Mukden. When, in the summer of 1929, Soviet Russia, taking umbrage at Chang Hsueh-liang's high-handed measures *vis-à-vis* the management of the Chinese Eastern Railway, dispatched troops and war planes into North Manchuria, Mr. Tsai Yun-shen, Mukden's Foreign Commissioner, who had known the Baron for some years, asked his (the Baron's) opinion as to the course the Mukden Government should follow in dealing with the unfortunate situation. The Baron expressed the view that it would be the part of wisdom for Mukden to conclude "peace" with Russia as soon as possible. Whether or not Mr. Tsai acted upon this advice, he signed a provisional "peace treaty" with Soviet representatives at Khabarovsk in December of that year. Soon thereafter Mr. Tsai called upon the Baron, thanked him for the advice he had given, and asked him if he would accept an invitation to dine with Marshal Chang Hsueh-liang, who, Mr. Tsai said, was also grateful to him and would like to have a friendly talk with him.

The Baron, having accepted the invitation, went to the Marshal's mansion at 6:30 o'clock of an evening, the appointed hour for the dinner, only to find that the Marshal was not there. The clock struck seven and then eight, but the Marshal did not appear. The Baron, justly provoked, cared to wait no longer, but Mr. Tsang Shi-yi, then Civil Governor of Mukden, was in the room and begged him to stay, pleading that the Marshal was delayed by an unexpected matter. Another hour passed, and the Marshal did at last show up!

The dining-room was immediately opened, and the Baron was asked to sit beside the Marshal. But as soon as the Marshal sat down, he was so deeply interested in feeding himself that he seemed to have forgotten the presence of the guest of honor. The dinner over, the Marshal said a few words to the guest and retired! The Baron was flabbergasted.

From various reliable sources I heard many other stories

of a similar nature. The Japanese personages who were
thus victimized include a number of prominent officers of
the Japanese army. Such stories are not generally known,
for no man would care to advertise his own humiliation.
Certainly the Lytton Commission heard none of them.

If the young generalissimo himself took this attitude of
deliberate effrontery toward the Japanese, what would not
his officers and men do? Indeed, Marshal Chang's hatred
of Japan was reflected throughout his vast army. Of this
pernicious influence the notorious murder of Captain
Nakamura by Manchurian soldiers was only an indication.
The idea that the Japanese must be driven out from Manchuria, and that the Manchurian army was far superior to
the Japanese, was generally inculcated in the minds of
Marshal Chang's officers and men, as was revealed in the
documents and posters seized by the Japanese immediately
after the September incident of 1931. What wonder that
the "Young Marshal's" soldiers were itching for a fight.
They had virtually thrown down the gauntlet to the Japanese and said, "If you want to know who is boss here, start
something." Of this I shall have more to say in the next
chapter.

## XI

Thus did the storm gather over Japan and Manchuria
for a number of years. When at last it broke, its fury was
as great as the time in which it had accumulated was long.

The unthinking are wondering why the little explosion
on the track of the South Manchuria Railway on the night
of September 18, 1931, should have started the great conflagration that it did. In reality it was an explosion of the
whole of Manchuria and Japan—Manchuria because of its

deliberate policy of courting trouble with Japan, Japan because of general discontent, restlessness, resentment, and desperation born of the circumstances I have recounted.

The explosion was not physical—it was moral, political, and even spiritual. Unless it is viewed in this light, its true meaning will never be understood.

# CHAPTER II

## AGGRESSION OR SELF-DEFENSE?

### I

ONE day last autumn I motored through the Chinese city of Mukden with an English journalist. Presently we came upon a vast space enclosed by brick walls some eight feet high. Inside were many brick buildings with tall chimneys.

"This is the famous Arsenal," informed my English friend. "How many miles around do you think it is?"

"The way we are driving along it must be ten miles," I ventured.

The Englishman laughed. "Not four even," he said, "but it's big enough, the biggest in the world, as the Young Marshal was fond of calling it. No wonder he thought he could beat the Japanese to a frazzle. Poor fellow!"

No wonder! Marshal Chang Hsueh-liang had a great army variously estimated at between 250,000 and 300,000. And he had this great Arsenal capable of producing all the monstrous paraphernalia of modern warfare—rifles, guns, shells, poison gas, armored cars, bombing planes, tanks, and whatnot. The Arsenal was established by Chang Tso-lin, father of the Young Marshal, some ten years ago at a cost of 500,000,000 *yuan* (Chinese dollars). It was chiefly the work of Danish engineers, though, later, German, French, British, Japanese and other experts were also employed. Chang's ambition was to make the Arsenal larger and better equipped than any arsenal in Japan. In the palmy days of his régime between 1924 and 1927 no less than 20,000 men were working in the Arsenal. In later years this staff, for financial reasons, was reduced considerably. Yet, on the eve of the September, 1931, incident, it consisted of at least 8,000 men, of whom more than a thousand were foreign advisers and experts. For some years before that incident the Arsenal was known to have been producing 4,500 shells and 40,000 bullets a day, and 12 guns per month, but the output of rifles and machine guns had been most rigidly guarded. Annual outlay for the Arsenal alone was 50,000,000 *yuan,* while other military expenditures amounted to another 50,000,-000 *yuan,* all representing 86 to 92 per cent of the Government's total expenditure.

In the preceding chapter it has been made clear that Chang Hsueh-liang was a confirmed Japanophobe, taking personal delight in provoking the Japanese. His father, Chang Tso-lin, had, perhaps, no love to lose upon the Japanese, but being a shrewd man and conscious of what he owed to Japanese backing, he was careful not to try their patience too severely. But the Young Marshal had no such adroitness. Apparently, he was so sure of his military power that he thought he could provoke the Japanese with no fear.

Under Chang Tso-lin's régime anti-Japanese agitation occurred only occasionally in Manchuria; during his son's régime it was widespread and systematic. In Chang Tso-lin's days there were no established organizations to promote agitation against Japan; in his son's days such organizations were launched as the Foreign Affairs Association and the Northeastern Cultural Organization, whose real work was anti-Japanese movement by means of lectures, mass meetings, radio broadcasts, and pamphlets. Again, under the former régime there was no open demand for the rendition of the leased territory of Port Arthur and Dairen; under the latter it became quite open. It was also under the Young Marshal's rule that his officials, disregarding treaty obligations, began to levy taxes in the leased territory of Dairen and in the railway zone, and openly persecuted the Koreans as an official measure. He dismissed practically all Chinese officials who had been educated in Japan and surrounded himself with young Chinese imbued with anti-Japanese sentiment. Last autumn I was shown the room in the Young Marshal's former mansion in which he trapped and caused the murder of Yang Yu-ting, a favorite of his father and director of the Mukden Arsenal, and Chen Yin-hai, both of whom had studied in Japan, in the midst of a mahjong party to which they were invited by the Marshal.

II

Such was Chang Hsueh-liang's Japanophobia. And it spread, or rather was sedulously propagated, throughout his army. The barracks were placarded with anti-Japanese slogans. The officers were exhorted to prepare for *den Tag*. The men were taught to march to the cadence of anti-foreign songs obviously directed against Japan. One of these songs, when rendered into English, runs somewhat like this:

> We will knock you down and leave you powerless.
> We will cast your rifles away.
> We will hurl down your cannon.
> We will trample on your ferocious hegemony.
> We will brace our spirits in firm unity,

Fixing our mark and arousing our courage,
That we may overthrow Imperialism.
Overthrow! Overthrow!
Your political authority is already gone.

We will abolish your exorbitant taxes.
We will break your banks.
We will cancel your credits.
We will sweep away your gold, silver and jewelry.
We will brace our spirits in firm unity.
We will overthrow Imperialism.
Overthrow! Overthrow!
Your economic power is already useless."

The Young Marshal's soldiers were made to believe that while they had acquired much military experience, skill, and prowess through the perennial civil wars they had fought, the Japanese soldiers had been enervated by the long period of peace they had enjoyed. Obstructions on the tracks of the South Manchuria Railway became numerous. Some of them had been done by soldiers themselves or under their connivance. Bandits, too, were instigated to make raids upon railway towns.

In Mukden, the center of this agitation, it became unsafe for Japanese to venture into its Chinese section. Japanese women were abused in broad daylight, Japanese men were assaulted, and even Japanese police officers were not free from similar treatment.

General Wang I-che, one of the Young Marshal's favorites and commander of the Pei-Tai-Yeh, the famous North Barracks at Mukden, with 13,000 of the Marshal's best soldiers, whole-heartedly sympathized with his master's Japanophobia. Before the September incident these troops had held night maneuvers around Mukden more and more often, evidently for the purpose of parading their strength before the Japanese. General Wang placarded the walls of the North Barracks with posters bearing such incendiary words as, "See that railway [South Manchuria Railway] running so close to our barracks!", and, "Recover Formosa, Port Arthur and Dairen from Japan."

Of this general attitude, an incident of May 18, 1931, is highly illustrative. A Chinese soldier was found piling up stones on the track of the South Manchuria Railway near the North Barracks, and this in clear view of Japanese railway guards patrolling near by. When the Japanese guards caught this Chinese mischief-maker, many soldiers rushed out of the Barracks and threatened the Japanese. But the Japanese stood their ground until a Chinese officer bowed smilingly and offered them what he said was a letter of apology. The Japanese, unable to read Chinese, accepted the letter graciously. When the letter was brought to the Japanese headquarters in Mukden, it was found to read: "While our soldiers were marching along the railway, the Japanese soldiers, with no valid reason, obstructed the march." Imagine the chagrin of the Japanese! Such deliberate military insults were even more indicative of the tenseness of the situation than the murder of Captain Nakamura, of which the world has heard so much and to which the League Commission's report devotes much space.

### III

Thus was Manchuria converted into a powder magazine. Only a spark was needed to start a conflagration. In this ominous situation there were only 11,000 Japanese railway guards scattered along 600 miles of railway. Conscious of the danger confronting them, the commanding officers evolved a plan of precaution to meet any emergency which might be forced upon them. Colonel Ishihara, who played a very important rôle in the September incident, told the Lytton Commission that the "major part" of this precautionary plan "was to concentrate at Mukden in an instant all the forces" scattered over the neighboring territory. He stated that under this plan "we could concentrate all the railway guards in twenty minutes and the divisional troops in one hour's notice," and that "we established confidence in our ability to do this through intensive training and numerous maneuvers."

Then came the lurid night of September 18, 1931, which will go down in history as a turning point not merely in the Manchurian situation but in the situation of the whole world, drawing into the controversy which followed the League of Nations, the United States and Soviet Russia.

At midnight of that fateful night Lieutenant Kawamoto, with six of his men, was on patrol duty on the South Manchuria Railway line north of Mukden. As they were walking along the track about 500 meters southwest of the North Barracks, commanded by General Wang I-che, they heard a terrific sound just behind them. They hurried back and found that the railway track had been considerably damaged by an explosion, though they could not clearly see the extent of damage through the blackness of the dark night. At that instant they espied, or rather heard, a number of men running away from the scene. Instinctively they knew what those fleeing figures were, and they fired. In reply, volleys of shots came from among the tall kaoliang (millet) stalks growing on either side of the railway track. Again, intuitively, the Japanese knew that the shots came from Chinese soldiers in ambush. Judging from the number of shots, they thought that the enemy force consisted of four or five hundred.

Realizing the seriousness of the situation, Lieutenant Kawamoto let one of his six men apply the telephone apparatus (which every railway guard carries with him) on the jack-box on the railway telephone post near by and notify the Third Company of the explosion and what followed. This company, of some 130 men under the command of Lieutenant Kawashima, was engaged in night maneuvers a few miles away in the railway zone. So they rushed to the rescue of Lieutenant Kawamoto and his men. As they arrived upon the scene, they were greeted with a rain of shots from the Chinese force. After sharp fighting the Chinese began to retreat. The Japanese pursued them to the North Barracks, into which they fled. Then the main body of the Chinese troops within the Barracks opened fire upon the pursuing Japanese, using machine and field guns as well as rifles. There was no alternative for the Japanese but to accept the challenge. They broke through the northwest corner of the wall surrounding the Barracks and occupied one at the south end.

Meanwhile, a telephone message was sent to Colonel Shimamoto, the battalion commander at Mukden. How did he act upon receipt of the message? I shall let the Colonel himself answer in the following words which he spoke before the Lytton Commission:

I had already gone to bed when I received a telephone call from the officer of the day on duty. He informed me that the Third Company was attacked by the Chinese troops. I knew that the strength of the Chinese in the North Barracks exceeded 10,000, and I knew what steps my troops should take in case they should be attacked by the Chinese. I had under my command two companies in Mukden, one company in the north of the North Barracks and one company in Fushun. It takes one and one-half hours to bring troops from Fushun to Mukden by train, so I had only three companies under my command which could be brought together at that time. The strength of the three companies was about 500. The step that should be taken in case my troops were attacked, I knew, was to take the offensive. This was the only possible course, because there were only 500 men under my command and the strength of the Chinese was 10,000. So I sent an emergency call to those troops. My plan was to have them assemble at the Mukden station in order to proceed to the spot. This was the Japanese station in the railway zone. Our barracks are situated just across the road from the station, and the troops under my command were well trained to answer such emergency calls, because they had long been accustomed to fighting bandits.

At once, my troops proceeded to the small station of Liu-Tiao-Kou, where they got off the train, as I was afraid that the tracks might have been blown up north of that point. They rushed northward along the railway, and as they reached that point (indicating it on map) they were fired upon by the remaining forces of the Chinese from the east side of the tracks.

It was a little after 12 o'clock midnight. Then extending two companies on the first line there, an attack was made. That was 20 minutes after 12. As soon as they extended, the enemy poured on them terrific shots from behind the low banks outside the barracks (indicates map). We drove them back and proceeded close to the buildings (showing map) there. Six Japanese were wounded. The barracks were all lighted with glittering electric lights within, and the Chinese fired from within the buildings. We had advantage of it, as they could not see us well, while we could distinguish them clearly. They also fired rifles over their heads, and the shots flew high in the air. Because of that method of firing we suffered comparatively small casualties, only six being wounded, and as the result, we captured that section of the barracks soon. The Third Company then penetrated to the north end of the barracks.

Thus 600 Japanese soldiers defeated some 10,000 Chinese soldiers entrenched in the North Barracks. The barracks were taken by the Japanese at 5:30 o'clock on the morning of September 19, after a fight of six hours. At 8 o'clock of the same morning the Chinese city of Mukden was also cleared of Chinese troops, 3,000 strong.

Meanwhile, Lieutenant-General Honjo, commander of the Japanese forces in Manchuria, was in Port Arthur, the seat of his headquarters. What happened at the headquarters that night was explained by Colonel Ishihara, Honjo's staff officer, before the Lytton Commission:

In Port Arthur at about 11:40 of the night of the 18th we received information about the incident. A little after 12 o'clock midnight when I arrived at the Kwantung Army headquarters all the officers were in doubt as to whether that incident was a local one or whether it involved a large scale movement. At 12:30, however, we received the following information: the Chinese forces in North Barracks have blown up the track of the South Manchuria Railway and the strength of the Chinese forces is about three or four companies; a little after 11 o'clock the Third Company engaged the forces in the North Barracks and occupied a section of them after severe fighting; Lieutenant Noda was severely wounded.

This report indicated the importance and gravity of the situation. Our decision was reached after receiving this report. By that time Lieutenant General Honjo, our Commander, had arrived, and we expressed the opinion that all troops should be concentrated in Mukden. Quite difficult discussions continued among the officers, but the final decision was reached at 1:20, as a result of which a notice was sent out to the commanding officer of the second division, while orders were given at 2 o'clock to Yingkow and Fengcheng, near Antung [on the Yalu River]. These two orders were to carry out attacks against the Chinese for the purpose of protecting the railway transportation facilities. In order to ensure the safety of railway passage, it is always in our

minds to keep the Antung and Mukden line perfectly free from
any attacks from the outside. The same is true of the line between
Port Arthur and Mukden.

One major problem was what to do with Changchun. We felt
that the Chinese Changchun troops would not cooperate with the
Chinese Mukden troops, and therefore we even thought of bringing the Japanese troops from Changchun down to Mukden. There
were stationed in Changchun one infantry brigade and one artillery regiment of Chinese troops very close to the Japanese troops.
The order was given to attack the Chinese troops in case it was
necessary, but first to ensure the safety of the Japanese residents in
Changchun. The order was given to be prepared to attack the
Chinese army only in case of emergency; this order was sent out
at about half past two in the morning of September 19.

But of course the commanding officer at Changchun felt uneasy about his position because he was not sure that the Chinese
would not attack his forces. He received instructions from General
Honjo to be prepared for an emergency but he felt it necessary to
take the offensive and he did so on his own initiative.

### III

Now we have a complete picture of what happened
from 10 o'clock of the night of September 18 to about 3
o'clock of the afternoon of September 19. In the light of
the tense situation, which had, as I have already described,
long existed before September 18, it is easy to understand
why the Japanese acted so swiftly and decisively. It was
more than natural that they should take the explosion on
the railway track and the firing by the soldiers of the
North Barracks as the signal for a general assault against
the Japanese forces along the entire railway line. And if
they were justified in this belief, they should not be
blamed for the measures they took, and for not waiting
and exposing themselves to the danger of being over-
whelmed by the superior number of the Chinese army, of

which at least 100,000 remained in Manchuria, the other 100,000 or more having gone to Peiping with Marshal Chang.

One of the secret documents found by the Japanese army in the inner sanctuary of the General Staff Office of the Mukden army immediately after the September 18 incident was a book of 400 Chinese pages giving details of the plan for a general drive which was to have been launched. This plan included these items:

1. The Japanese army units at Liaoyang, Mukden, Changchun, etc., on the South Manchuria Railway lines shall be attacked simultaneously at a date to be decided upon.

2. The positions of the Northeastern (Manchurian) army shall be decided upon before the offensive.

3. The positions of the Japanese army and the strength of the Japanese troops immediately available in such an emergency are fully described.

4. At the outset of the offensive the Dairen wharves, the railway bridge across the Yahu River (between Korea and Manchuria), and as much of the South Manchuria Railway as possible shall be blown up.

5. Also a large number of leading Japanese residents shall be kidnapped as hostages to hamper the operations of the Japanese army.

6. To provide against the possible coöperation of the Red army with the Japanese, defense shall be strengthened at the strategic points on the Siberian border.

7. If possible, the Red army shall be won over by a pretended promise to hand over to Soviet Russia the control of the Chinese Eastern Railway in the event of the Manchurian army's victory.

8. As soon as our offensive begins we shall proclaim, both at home and abroad, that the conflict originated in Japanese aggression.

9. All inequitable treaties with Japan shall be abrogated, the lease of Port Arthur and Dairen repudiated, and the South Manchuria Railway taken over by us.

Evidently the plan miscarried through the untoward incident of September 18. When General Wang I-che's soldiers blew up a small part of the South Manchuria Railway track at the North Barracks, it was perhaps meant to be a mischief similar to those which had been played by them with increasing frequency. The Chinese, mistaking the long patience of the Japanese guards for cowardice, thought they could indulge with impunity in more provocative pranks. They did so once too often. The Japanese, fully conscious of the tense situation which had confronted them for some years, took the explosion as the signal for the long anticipated drive, all along the railway, of the Manchurian army against them.

That Marshal Chang had planned to launch a general drive against the Japanese at the first convenient opportunity there is no doubt. But September 18, 1931, was not the date of that coveted opportunity. He had gone to Peiping to mend, to use the parlance of American politics, his political fence there. He wanted nothing untoward to happen before he could return to Mukden to handle the Japanese situation himself. But fate played evil tricks upon him. His underlings, misunderstanding both their master and the Japanese, threw a lighted match into the powder magazine, thus causing the explosion which the Young Marshal did not want as yet to happen.

IV

The explosion on the railway track and the shooting that followed are two related incidents, but for our present purpose they must be considered separately. This is important because many are under the misconception that it was the explosion which caused the Japanese guards to attack the North Barracks. It was not. On the contrary, the firing by the Chinese soldiers near the scene of the explosion upon the Japanese railway guards was what caused the Japanese to attack them.

The explosion itself was not serious. As Mr. Horiye, the engineer who attended to the repair of the damaged track, told the Lytton Commission, "the sleeper on the north side was blown up from underneath the rail; also the sleeper from the south side. The inner side-plate was bent and warped, while some parts of the outer one were broken off. We put in two new sleepers and two new rails. The length of rails put in was 10.05 meters."

That was all. Evidently the explosion was the work of inexperienced men in the engineering corps of the North Barracks. It has been charged, in Chinese circles, that the incident was a premeditated Japanese plan. Had such been the case, the Japanese certainly would have notified the South Manchuria Railway, warning the trains not to pass the section where the track was to be blown up. Then the explosion would have been much more serious and the resultant damage to the railway so great as to furnish plausible justification to the military action which followed.

No, it was not the explosion which started the conflagration. It was the volleys from Chinese guns which kindled it.

V

Now we shall again take up our narrative of the military operations where we left off. Immediately after the September 18 incident, Marshal Chang Hsueh-liang, then at Peiping, made frantic efforts to retrieve his lost ground in Manchuria. By September 27 he had established a provisional government and headquarters of the "Frontiers Defense Army," in Chinchow, 150 miles west of Mukden, with his uncle General Chang Tso-hsiang as its commander. At the same time, Marshal Chang, through General Chang, issued orders to General Wang I-che and other regimental and battalion commanders who had remained in various parts of Manchuria west of the South Manchuria Railway, urging them to feign submission to the Japanese army for the time being but to attack it in unison as soon as the forces, which were being mustered at Chinchow, were ready for an offensive movement. By October 1, six regiments had been detailed between Kaupang-tsu and Taku-shan, on one side, and Chinchow on the other, while more troops were coming from inside the Great Wall. Moreover, General Chang had seized 800 cars belonging to the Peiping-Mukden Railway. Fearful of the apparently impending fight and the inevitable looting by Chinese soldiers, Chinese residents in towns and villages west of the Liao River poured into Mukden, then fairly quiet under Japanese military influence. It was significant that they preferred Mukden to Chinchow.

This menacing development could not be ignored by the Japanese army. Consequently, on October 8, between two and three o'clock in the afternoon, the Japanese sent out eleven planes from Mukden for scouting purposes in the Chinchow area. When they were fired upon by the Chinese army in Chinchow, they responded by dropping some forty bombs upon the headquarters of the Frontiers Defense Army, the Barracks, and the Communications College buildings which housed the provisional government. This was entirely justifiable in the light of the aerial warfare agreements adopted at The Hague, in February 1923, in compliance with a resolution passed at the Washington Conference in the preceding year. Yet the League of Nations Council, without knowing the actual developments of the situation, was so excited over this Chinchow affair that, on October 9, M. Lerroux, President of the Council, addressed a note of warning to both Japan and China, which was, however, obviously meant for Japan only.

## VI

The scene now shifts to the Nonni River region. On October 1, General Chang Hai-peng, division commander at Tao-nan-fu, declared independence against the Young Marshal with a view to wresting Hei-Lung-Kiang province from the old régime. The governor of the province, Wan Fu-lin, was then in Peiping with the Young Marshal, but his subordinates agreed to transfer the provincial government to Chang Hai-peng. So Chang began to march his troops toward Tsitsihar, the provincial capital.

Meanwhile General Ma Chan-shan, an old-régime man commanding a division at Heiho on the Amur River, had also declared independence and declared himself prepared to oppose Chang Hai-peng. Whereupon the Young Mar-

shal at Peiping promised material help to General Ma
and encouraged him to fight General Chang.

General Ma, in order to impede the advancing troops
of General Chang, destroyed two of the five railway
bridges in the Nonni River area. That was on October 15,
just in the midst of the season when the railway was busy
transporting the bean crop for which this region is famous.
The repair of the bridge was imperative. So the railway
authorities, acting upon an understanding with General
Ma, sent, on October 28, a corp of engineers, not soldiers,
to the river, but as soon as they began repair work they
were fired upon by Ma's troops.

Here it is necessary to explain the international nature
of this line called the Taonan-Angangchi Railway, 146
miles in length. It was built in 1926 by the South Manchuria Railway under contract for the old Mukden Government, and on December of that year it was handed
over to that Government. According to the construction
agreement, the Mukden Government was to have paid the
South Manchuria Railway the cost of construction, 14,000,-
000 *yen* (including 1,000,000 *yen* for rolling stock), upon
the taking over of the railway by that Government. In
case the Government failed to make the above payment
within six months, the obligation was to have been converted into a loan agreement.

But the Mukden authorities neither paid nor signed a
loan agreement, notwithstanding repeated protests by the
South Manchuria Railway. By June, 1931, the indebted-
ness, with accrued interest, had amounted to 26,000,000
*yen,* and yet it was impossible for the South Manchuria
Railway to obtain any loan agreement signed by Mukden.

Naturally, Japan was vitally concerned with the destruction of the Nonni bridges. Therefore, when General Ma refused to let the railway authorities repair them, or to repair them himself, it became the right and duty of the Japanese army to do the necessary work, and Colonel Hamamoto, with a battalion of infantry and a battalion of artillery, was ordered to proceed to the scene for the purpose of protecting the engineers.

When Colonel Hamamoto and his detachment arrived, on November 4, at a point near the Nonni, General Ma's staff officer, Colonel Shieh, accompanied by the Japanese Consul and a Japanese army officer at Tsitsihar, came down to meet him and conveyed General Ma's message that he (Ma) had no earthly intention to obstruct repair work, much less to attack the Japanese forces. Colonel Hamamoto accepted the message with appreciation. But as soon as his soldiers came near the river, they were greeted with a terrific bombardment, resulting in fifteen dead and wounded. Later it transpired that while Ma's "friendly" message was being delivered to Colonel Hamamoto, he sent bombastic messages to Marshal Chang at Peiping declaring that "I have attacked the Japanese forces and am advancing along the railway," and that "I am going to destroy more bridges and I am determined to fill the Nonni River with corpses rather than retreat." Ma was a born actor!

General Ma's forces on the north banks of the Nonni were estimated at 2,500, while his main force of 17,000 was at Tsitsihar. Against this large army, the Japanese force consisted of only 600.

To make a long story short, Ma's forces were driven away and the bridges repaired. Among 200 killed left behind by them were found two Russians. Whether they were Red or White could not be ascertained. But they lent color to the boastful pronouncement repeatedly made by Ma that he had the backing of the Red army.

Again the League Council, utterly uninformed of the actual condition on the spot, became nervous and, on November 6, cabled Tokyo in the name of its president, warning it against "the extention of incidents toward northern Manchuria."

The Japanese contingent, content with the protection of the Nonni bridges, did not pursue the enemy. But General Ma, with his army now increased to 30,000 was determined to regain the lost ground. He had been receiving telegram after telegram from Chang Hsueh-liang exhorting him to "exterminate the Japanese army." The Young Marshal also ordered General Ying Shin, commander of the Chinese forces at Chinchow, to attack the Japanese from the south while Ma would launch the offensive from the north. On November 13, General Ma surrounded the Japanese Consulate in Tsitsihar with his troops as if to hold its entire staff as hostages. Moreover, some of his battalions had moved toward the Nonni with the obvious intention of engaging the Japanese. In fact, his cavalry had already attacked the Japanese lines. Had the Japanese receded, Ma would have again destroyed the bridges.

As long as Ma's forces were concentrated at Tsitsihar and Angangchi (the northern terminal of the Japanese-financed railway described above), there was no safety for the railway nor for the Japanese forces. Angangchi was only 15 miles from the Nonni, and from Angangchi to Tsitsihar the distance was only 18 miles. On November 13, the Japanese army urged Ma to evacuate Tsitsihar and to withdraw to their original positions the large force he had mustered at Angangchi and other places further south. To this, Ma's reply was a general offensive launched on November 17. His army, 20,000 strong, had 30 field guns, more than ten trench mortars, two anti-aircraft guns, the last of which were said to have been obtained from Russian sources. Against this formidable array the Japanese infantry and cavalry, commanded by Lieutenant General Tamon, numbered 3,000 with 20 guns and a few planes. The Japanese commander issued this order to his troops:

> Avoid the Chinese Eastern Railway and all the buildings belonging to it. Do not enter the town of Angangchi [where a station of the above railway is located]. Do not harm non-combatants. Do not become involved in trouble with foreigners [mostly Russians].

Thus, on the early morning of November 18, the opposing armies came to a collision in full strength, and by the following morning General Ma, having been decisively defeated, had evacuated Angangchi and Tsitsihar. From that time to January 1, 1932, Ma thrice professed loyalty to the new régime and as often changed that attitude. But on January 2 he assured General Chang Chinghui, pro-Japanese governor of the Special District of Harbin, who had declared independence of Hei-Lung-Kiang province from Marshal Chang Hsueh-liang, that he had definitely made up his mind to coöperate with him. Upon this assurance, Chang Ching-hui entered Tsitsihar and organized a new government there.

How good this assurance of Ma's was we shall see in Chapter III.

VII

Now we shall retrace our steps southward from Tsitsihar, and return to the Chinchow area. We have noted the Chinchow incident of October 8. In the few weeks following that incident, Marshal Chang Hsueh-liang's forces in that area were increased to 50,000, and these were further augmented by reënforcements from Tientsin and Peiping. His object, of course, was to launch a general offensive against the Japanese. Pending this offensive, organized bandits, as well as regular soldiers were constantly employed to harrass the Japanese at this, that and other points. On November 23 the Japanese Consulate at Hsin-min-fu was attacked. On November 26, Marshal Chang ordered general mobilization of his forces in and near Chinchow, and Chinchow is only 150 miles from Mukden. The next day these forces began to advance along the Mukden-Shanghaikwan Railway, the Yinkow branch line, and the Takushan-Payantara line.

On the same day, Marshal Chang's forces attacked the five companies of Japanese infantry stationed in the Japanese Concession at Tientsin under treaty. Partly to send reënforcements to Tientsin, partly to counteract the offensive movement undertaken by the Marshal's forces in the Liao River and Chinchow areas, the Japanese contingents under Lieutenant-General Tamon and Lieutenant-General Suzuki crossed the Liao River on November 27 and were ready to advance. But on November 28 they received from the General Staff at Tokyo an unexpected order to halt. The reason given was that Marshal Chang Hsueh-liang had intimated a plan to withdraw the main body of his troops from the Chinchow area. All knew that this

was a make-believe reason, and that Marshal Chang had
no intention of withdrawing. The real reason, generally
conceded, was that Secretary Stimson had again remonstrated with Ambassador Debuchi, or directly with our
Foreign Office, and that, in consequence, our Foreign
Minister Baron Shidehara had prevailed upon the General
Staff to issue the above order.

It was then that a large number of the younger officers,
indignant at the "weak-kneed" attitude of the Foreign
Office, were said to have schemed to kidnap Baron Shidehara and several other statesmen who were of the same
mind as the Foreign Minister. The plot was nipped in
the bud, but the group involved in it was so formidable
that the ringleaders were merely nominally reprimanded
and none were really punished. The full story of this
incident is yet to be told, for the press has never been
allowed to report anything about it.

The halt of the Japanese advance had a deplorable
effect. It encouraged the Chinese army at Chinchow in
the belief that the Japanese, fearful of foreign interference,
dared not advance, and that the recapture of Mukden by
it was quite possible. Of course Marshal Chang never
withdrew any of his forces. As soon as the Japanese contingents under Tamon and Suzuki returned to their original positions, the Chinese regulars and organized bandits
began to advance and to menace the Japanese railway
zone. They occupied Fakumen, Shenshan and other
strategic points, evidently with a view to attacking Mukden. Such railway towns as Changtu, Ssupingkai, and
Chengchiatung were also menaced. By December 15, a
general offensive by all the forces of Marshal Chang,
40,000 strong, had become imminent.

The long and short of it all was that, on January 3, Marshal Chang's forces were driven out of Chinchow and forced back to the other side of the Great Wall. Then it was that Secretary Stimson notified Japan and China that the United States would not recognize any situation, treaty or agreement brought about by means contrary to the Peace Pact.

And as for the League, all this while it did naught but say to Japan, "Withdraw your troops. Quick! Quick!" That was not constructive. It asked Japan to do the impossible, and it made China think that she had the League in her pocket, which destroyed what chance there might have been of direct parley between the two nations. The League should have told Japan and China to get together and settle the matter between themselves. Had the League done this immediately after September 18, all that China would have had to do would have been to live up to the then existing treaties with Japan, and there would have been no independent Manchoukuo to worry about, as I shall show in the next chapter.

# CHAPTER III

## ENTER MANCHOUKUO

### I

WRITES Woodrow Wilson in his *A History of the American People*: *

There had been no thought, when this [Spanish-American] war came, of sweeping the Spanish islands of far-away seas within the sovereignty of the United States. But Spain's empire had proved a house of cards. When the American power touched it it fell to pieces. The Government of Spain's colonies had everywhere failed and gone to hopeless decay. It would have been impossible, it would have been intolerable, to set it up again where it had collapsed. A quick instinct apprised American statesmen that they had come to a turning point in the progress of the nation, which would have disclosed itself in some other way if not in this, had the war for Cuba not made it plain.

Something of this nature may be said of the developments which followed on the heels of the September, 1931, incident in Manchuria. When the Japanese railway guards, on the night of September 18, returned the fire of the Chinese soldiers of the North Barracks and drove them out of Mukden and other strategic points on the South Manchuria Railway, they had no idea of what was ahead. Even in the days immediately following, they thought they were fighting merely in self-defense. The Government at Tokyo and even the General Staff thought the incident only a minor military collision capable of localization and quick adjustment.

* Published by Harper & Brothers. Reprinted by permission.

But Marshal Chang Hsueh-liang's empire had proved even more fragile than that of Spain. Its deceptive grandeur was entirely due to the imposing war machinery which he had built up at the expense of the people. When that machinery crumbled to pieces from the impact of the shots fired by the Japanese railway guards, there was nothing left to prop up the tottering structure. For more than ten years the two Changs, father and son, had exploited Manchuria for their selfish ambitions and profit. Their military expenditure had amounted to one hundred million Chinese dollars per annum, representing 85 to 93 per cent of the total expenditure. It put a staggering burden upon the people. Not only had taxes been high, but the unlimited issuance of inconvertible paper currency had driven farmers and traders to the wall. Not less than 700,-000,000 of these bills, printed in Mukden and New York, had been foisted upon the people. The Changs, through the government banks which were, in reality, their private institutions, compelled the farmers to sell their crops for these worthless notes and then resold them at Newchwang or Dairen for silver or gold. It was a most profitable "racket" unequaled even in the gangdoms of Chicago or New York. Is it any wonder that the Changs earned the enmity of the people and alienated the loyalty of many of their adherents?

II

It must also be remembered that for many years there had existed among the leading men of Manchuria a sort of *esprit de corps* emphasizing the need for promoting local welfare and for keeping Manchuria from becoming involved in the politico-military wrangles of China proper.

This sentiment was pertinently expressed in four Chinese characters—*Pao-Ching An-Min,* signifying, "Peace within the Borders, Security for the People." It was the doctrine of "Manchuria for Manchurians," or "Manchurians for Manchuria." It encouraged Manchurians to devote their energies to the promotion of peace and welfare in Manchuria and decried any attempt to venture forth to the other side of the Great Wall. Quite naturally, local leaders who held this view watched with no small misgiving the two Changs' repeated incursions into North China where they squandered upon aimless and futile adventures hundreds of millions of *yuan* (Chinese dollars) which they had extorted from the innocent people of Manchuria. Thus did Chang Tso-lin and Chang Hsueh-liang deliberately flout, for more than a decade, the sentiment of the Manchurians expressed in the watchword of *Pao-Ching An-Min.* Only by force of arms was it possible to maintain that attitude.

When, therefore, the bubble of the vast armament built up by the Changs burst on the night of September 18, 1931, nothing was more natural than that independence movements should crop up in various sections of Manchuria. On September 27 there was organized in the city of Mukden a "Committee for the Preservation of Peace and Order" for Fengtien province. Its chairman was Yuan Chin-Kai, one-time governor of the province. It consisted of men who were in sympathy with the principle of *Pao-Ching An-Min.* At its inception, this Committee was not exactly separatist, but the logic of events soon forced it to change its attitude. On September 30, Lieutenant-General Hsi-Hsia, acting governor of Kirin province, declared himself independent from Marshal Chang and set up a new government for that province. This example was immediately followed by General Chang Ching-hui of Harbin, General Chang Hai-peng of Taonan, and General Tang Yu-ling of Jehol. Of course the Mongol princes and Banners were jubilant over the opportunity of shaking off the yoke which had been placed upon them by the Changs.

To make the picture of this movement clearer, I shall quote some of the statements made by Dr. Chao Hsin-po, one of the prime movers, before the Lytton Commission at Changchun (now Hsinking) on May 5, 1932. In reply to some of the questions asked by the Lytton Commission, Dr. Chao said:

In 1926 Chang Tso-lin attempted to capture Peking with the help of Wu Pei-fu. At that time the internal conditions were not very satisfactory. As a lawyer I contended that internal order should be the first to be in some way remedied. "Peace within the borders and security for the people" was my motto. I held that internal order should first be restored in Manchuria, and that only then other plans could be put into execution. Marshal Chang Tso-lin did not pay much attention to my proposals, and our opinions differed. Then, later on, Marshal Chang Tso-lin was killed in an unfortunate incident, and his son succeeded him.

I then hoped that the Young Marshal, with modern ideas and education, would be more liberal and adopt my proposals. I associated myself with the teaching staff of the Feng Yung University in Mukden, and I planned with my associates a movement of political reform in Manchuria, in opposition to the militarist policy of the Young Marshal. In this movement were included many students of the Northeastern University.

I then approached some of the leading Japanese military in Mukden and tried to reach some understanding with them on the subject of this movement, and I also got in touch with some of the Railway officials for the same purpose. I failed to obtain any result; but then came the September incident, and my associates and I felt that this was our opportunity to realize some of our plans. The Japanese leaders were then quite in agreement with my plans for a reform movement, but they were absolutely against the use of aggressive measures in this connection. I was then also President of the Association of Lawyers and Scholars. This Association formed a committee and despatched representatives to various Provinces to find out the sentiments of the leaders in different parts in regard to the establishment of a new Government. But the means of communication were very poor at the time, and we could not reach all the leaders we wished to or obtain the desired results.

We then organized in Mukden the "Committee for the Maintenance of Peace and Order." I was not a member of that Committee. The members were those who were highly respected in the community, and I was a sort of midwife to it. I then supervised the fixing of the prices of commodities. One of the first activities of the Committee was the reorganization of the currency of the Bank of the Three Eastern Provinces and the Frontier Bank. We contemplated the formation in Mukden of a new Administrative Organization, to be formed chiefly by the members of the "Committee for the Maintenance of Peace and Order." Then the Kuomintang Headquarters issued an order prohibiting all political activities in the city at that time. Conditions became such that the activities of the Municipal Authorities were turned over to the Committee of Peace and Order. On October 20, I was made Mayor of Mukden, succeeding Colonel Doihara, the Japanese officer who had, since the September 18 incident, been temporarily entrusted with the municipal administration of the city. I took over the duties of the Municipal Office. The Municipal Police Force was placed under my personal supervision. I worked hard to advance my plans to establish a new Administrative Organization.

### III

Meanwhile, what were the Japanese military in Manchuria doing? What was their attitude toward the secessionist movement? I shall let Lieutenant-Colonel

Takeshita, one of the spokesmen before the Lytton Commission, answer these questions.

First we shall see what happened in the city of Mukden, the center of the upheaval. Immediately after the September 18 incident, the administration of the city was completely disorganized. In such circumstances, it was imperative that the Japanese military should "do something for the establishment of local peace and order." "We (the military) therefore consulted the leaders of the Japanese community here and, in coöperation with them, formulated a plan under which the Japanese assisted in municipal affairs." "The telephone and telegraph systems, gas, waterways, and railways," explained Lieutenant-Colonel Takeshita, "are of vital interest to the population of the city. Due to the disorganization of their administration, and the disappearance of both officials and employees, following the incident of September 18, the military authorities took protective measures until such time as the officials in the different establishments returned to their posts or until their office staffs could be reorganized. At such a chaotic stage, we felt that this was necessary for our own protection as well as for the maintenance of peace and order in the interest of the general public. But the supervision and protection by the military authorities were gradually withdrawn when the officials and civil authorities returned to their respective posts." Thus from September 19 to October 20, 1931, the municipal administration of Mukden was practically in the hands of the leading Japanese residents of the city, under the supervision of a Japanese military officer, Colonel Doihara. There was no military government, nor was martial law declared. There was no military occupation, as Lieutenant-Colonel

Takeshita took pains to make clear to the Lytton Commission.

Explaining the emergency measures taken by the military authorities in regard to financial institutions in Mukden, Lieutenant-Colonel Takeshita stated that, "generally speaking, there was no change in the banking business except in the case of the Bank of the Three Eastern Provinces and the Frontier Bank which closed their doors after the September incident. These two banks were the central banks of Manchuria. The Frontier Bank was practically organized by Marshal Chang Hsueh-liang, while the Bank of the Three Eastern Provinces was established by the Government of Manchuria. In order to see that the funds owned by Marshal Chang and other military leaders would not be removed from these banks, we placed guards at these two institutions. When the banks were reopened, the people were still restless, and it was feared that there might be a run on them. To forestall any embarrassment from such a possible run, the bank officials adopted an emergency measure which restricted the amounts to be withdrawn." In the case of the funds belonging to Marshal Chang and other military leaders hostile to us, "we made an examination of records, and stopped the funds from going out of the banks."

So much about Mukden. As to other centers, Lieutenant-Colonel Takeshita explained that both in Kirin City and in Kirin Province the old officials remained undisturbed. "In Changchun, the same municipal officials as before continued to function. In Tsitsihar the municipal police took charge of municipal affairs. So no cities or localities other than Mukden were disturbed."

## IV

Now we must turn our eyes toward Tokyo and Geneva, and see what the Japanese Government and the League of Nations were doing, or trying to do, in the month or so following the September incident.

At this stage, Tokyo was thinking of the Manchurian situation largely in terms of treaties and agreements which had been disregarded by the Chinese and Manchurian Governments. What the Tokyo Government wanted was nothing more than the respect and recognition by China and Manchuria of the rights and interests which Japan had enjoyed by virtue of various treaties. It was not interested in the secessionist movement one way or the other. It was more than ready to enter into negotiations with the Nanking Government or Marshal Chang Hsueh-liang or whoever would agree to observe the treaties and whoever was in a position to carry out such agreements with a view to safeguarding Japan's established rights in Manchuria.

Nor was this a mere assertion. Immediately after the September incident, the Japanese Government through its Minister to China, Mr. Mamoru Shigemitsu, opened conversations with Mr. T. V. Soong, Finance Minister of the Nanking Government, with a view to finding out whether amicable adjustment was possible. Had the League, instead of urging Japan to withdraw troops unconditionally, at that time told Nanking and Tokyo to enter into direct negotiations on the basis of the Japanese terms, that is, the recognition by China of the then existing treaties regarding Manchuria, the trouble would have been settled and the independence of Manchuria forestalled.

The Japanese military, too, no doubt, had in the back of their minds the idea and hope that once the Manchurian army was driven out of Mukden and a few other strategic points, Marshal Chang Hsueh-liang would admit his defeat and would wish to salvage the situation through direct negotiations with the Japanese authorities. No doubt he would have taken this course had he not been given to understand, by acts and utterances at Geneva, that the League of Nations would somehow or other pick his chestnuts out of the fire. Encouraged by those acts and utterances, the Young Marshal cherished the vain hope that the Japanese troops would be forced to evacuate without obtaining any assurance that Japanese treaty rights would be respected, and that he would, under the League's protection, be permitted to return "triumphantly" to Mukden, thus turning the tables once again against Japan, and adding humiliation to the injury he had already done to the Japanese. In such circumstances, of course, the Japanese military could not back out and meekly obey the mandate of the League, which was naught but unconditional evacuation in favor of the Young Marshal.

The inevitable result was the unnecessary prolongation of the deadlock, which gave the Chinese secessionists the desired opportunity to promote and develop a movement for an independent Manchuria. No one conversant with the general discontent and restlessness which had long prevailed among the people of Manchuria could have failed to foresee this secessionist movement, certain to develop from any prolonged stalemate of this nature. But the European statesmen at Geneva, many thousands of miles away from the scene of conflict and knowing little of the real causes and significance of the trouble, thought that the situation would right itself only if Japan would withdraw her troops at once and unconditionally. In reality, those statesmen, by taking this attitude, prolonged the deadlock and thus gave the Manchurian secessionists an opportunity to realize their cherished scheme. In effect, it was they, as much as the Japanese military, who assisted in the birth of Manchoukuo.

The Japanese Government, on October 26, communicated to the League of Nations Council a declaration in which it signified its willingness to enter into direct negotiations with China on the basis of these "basic principles":

1. Mutual repudiation of aggressive policy and conduct.
2. Respect for China's territorial integrity.
3. Complete suppression of all organized movements interfering with freedom of trade and stirring up international hatred.
4. Effective protection throughout Manchuria of all peaceful pursuits undertaken by Japanese subjects.
5. Respect for treaty rights of Japan in Manchuria.

That these terms or principles were reasonable no one could deny. But the League, instead of favoring direct negotiations on these terms, nagged Japan to withdraw troops regardless of the actual condition of the affected areas in Manchuria, which made the presence of the Japanese soldiers absolutely necessary. The League would not permit Japan to negotiate with China unless and until her troops were withdrawn into the railway zone. Thus the League, to use Sir Austen Chamberlain's language, "got between the two parties" and prevented them, in effect, not from making war, as Sir Austen had in mind, but from making peace by negotiations. It inspired false hopes and futile expectations in the Chinese mind and

thus prevented China from acting upon the Japanese overtures. In the end it cost China the whole of Manchuria.
Had she accepted the Japanese overtures, all that she
would have had to do would have been to recognize the
rights of the Japanese as defined in the treaties then in
effect.

In view of what I have said, the Report of the League
Commission is nothing short of a tragedy. It virtually
admits the validity of the treaties, the persistent violation
of which by China had been Japan's only complaint. Of
course, there was no rhyme or reason why the Commission should have taken any other stand, unless it was
desirous of throwing international relations into chaos by
encouraging all disgruntled nations to violate such treaties
as were distasteful to them. The validity of the Sino-Japanese treaties in question must have been obvious to the
League Council at the time when the question was
brought forth by Japan. Certainly it did not require a
protracted study by a special commission. A few hours'
examination of related and relevant documents, all available at Geneva, was all that was needed to determine the
justice of the Japanese contention. As I have said in the
introductory chapter, had the League Council taken this
course in October or even November, 1931, instead of pursuing the futile course of prolonging the controversy by
merely asking Japan to withdraw troops, the dispute
could have been settled by direct parley between China
and Japan. Now, at the eleventh hour, when Manchoukuo, already eight months old, has become a going concern, the League, upon the basis of the Lytton Commission's suggestions, recognizes the legality of the treaties
and suggests negotiations between the two nations con-

cerned. It is too late. Manchoukuo is independent. Neither China nor Japan can abolish it at her own sweet will.

The question has often been asked why Japan had not appealed to the League before the Manchurian situation became so hopeless as to cause the explosion of September 18, 1931. Mr. Yosuke Matsuoka, Japan's able new delegate to Geneva, perhaps the ablest Japanese spokesman who has ever appeared before the League, answered this question in his speech before the Council on November 21, 1932—as follows:

> The answer, in brief, is, first, that Japanese national sentiment would not permit outside interference on the Manchurian question. We have taken that attitude all along. Secondly, had we referred the matter to the League, the position of Japanese subjects, including Koreans, in Manchuria would have been seriously undermined, in view of the delay invariably incidental to League procedure, and there are over one million Japanese subjects in Manchuria, including those of Korean origin. Thirdly, there is a difference between Japanese and Western mentality. The Westerner would begin to argue before the situation became acute, while the Japanese persists, perhaps too long, in the hope of a solution. Fourthly, when the breaking point came unexpectedly, events took their own natural course.

All this may be true, but I believe that there was another reason more important than the four given by Mr. Matsuoka, namely, that Baron Shidehara, as Japan's Foreign Minister, had, when the September 18 incident happened, been striving to adjust the situation by conciliatory policy and friendly negotiations without the intervention of the League. He did not see that his endeavors had not been nor ever would be requited by China, and that the two nations had been headed for a crash. And

CHAO HSIN-PO
PRESIDENT OF THE LEGISLATIVE COUNCIL

when the crash did come, "matters," as Mr. Matsuoka pertinently stated, "pursued their natural course."

### V

Now we must return to Manchuria to observe the further developments of the independence movement. In the first stage of that movement, the Manchurian leaders interested in it had no clear conception of how far they would go. Quite possibly independence, to them, or at least to some of them, meant simply revolt against Chang Hsueh-liang and not necessarily severance of all ties or relations with China proper. A few of them were, no doubt, actuated by selfish motives. But the independence movements, at first without coördination and inspired by various, even conflicting motives among different leaders, soon developed in such a way as to convince them of the wisdom of joining hands with one another in a united effort to establish a new State, whose jurisdiction would extend over the whole of Manchuria. This, they thought, was the best and only way to realize the traditional local ideal of "Peace within the Borders, Security for the People," thus barring out the chaos of Chinese nationalism and forestalling the perils of communism. Furthermore, great movements of this nature, when once launched, develop their consequences with a logic of their own, overriding the volition of those identified with them.

Up to the end of December, 1931, there had been no definite and organized movement to unite, under a common flag, all the privinces which had severed their allegiance to the Chang Hsueh-liang régime since the fateful eighteenth day of September of that year. But on January 4, 1932, Marshal Chang's army, which with its base of operation in the Chinchow area, had been creating disturbances in large sections of Fengtien province, was decisively defeated by the Japanese and was soon entirely driven to the other side of the Great Wall. Up to this point the Manchurian separatists had still been uneasy lest the old régime should "come back." The elimination of this obvious menace heartened them and made them feel entirely safe in pressing the independence movement to its logical conclusion. That was the beginning of the real movement for a united Manchuria under a new government.

In the furtherance of this movement the activities of the Tzuchi-chihtao-pu, litrally Self-Government Guidance Board, must be noted. The Board, with Yu Ching-han as president, had come into existence late in November or early in December. It had its headquarters in Mukden, and its activities were confined to Fengtien province. At its inception, its object was to inform the officials and people in the interior towns and villages that the province had been freed from the tyrannical old régime, and that thenceforth it would be governed in accordance with the principles of justice and equity. It also purposed to guide self-government in the right direction by enjoining district magistrates and other local functionaries to abolish the old practice of peculation and corruption. As there were not enough Chinese qualified for field work to carry out the ideals of the Board, a number of Japanese were drafted. At one time the organization employed some two hundred workers. How many of these were Chinese I was unable to ascertain.

When, after the fall of Chinchow on January 4, 1932, the separatist movement took a new turn for a united as well as an independent Manchuria, as we have already noted, the Board also widened its outlook and adopted as its ultimate goal the establishment of a new Manchurian State. Its slogans were "Maintenance of Peace and Order"; "Nurture the Economic Strength of the People"; "Destroy Pernicious Traditions"; "Promote Education"; "Readjust the Agricultural and Iudustrial System," etc.

On February 16 and 17 there was held at Mukden a meeting of six leaders interested in the independence project. They were Tsang Shih-yi, governor of Fengtien province; Hsi Hsa, governor of Kirin province; Chang Ching-hui, governor of the Special District of Harbin; Chi Wang Kuei Foo, representing the Mongol Banners of the Cherimu League; Ling Sheng, representing Hulun-pei-erh or the Barga district of Inner Mongolia; and last but not least, the notorious Ma Chan-Shan, of Nonni and Tsitsihar fame. General Ma had been sulking in his lair at Hailun since his defeat at Tsitsihar, but on February 7 he had been coaxed to come to Harbin for a conference with General Chang Ching-hui, governor of the Special District. He was promised the governorship of Hei-Lung-Kiang province and was, moreover, to be made War Minister in the Manchurian Government then in the making. As a result, Ma attended the Mukden Conference of February 16-17. He had already tricked the Japanese more than once. Was he sincere this time?

The immediate outcome of the Mukden Conference was the Declaration of Independence of February 18, signed by the above-named six representatives and Tang Yu-lin, governor of Jehol, who then constituted themselves into the Northeastern Administrative Committee.

Tang Yu-lin did not attend the Conference in person, as railway communication had been interrupted, but had agreed by telegram to put his name to the Declaration.

On February 25 the Northeastern Administrative Committee, in pursuance of the Declaration of Independence of February 18, issued an outline of the draft organic law of the projected new State, which was to be called Manchoukuo and whose head was to be known as Chih-Cheng, or Chief Executive. The Committee also adopted a new national flag of five colors, representing Fengtien, Kirin, Jehol, Barga and Hei-Lung-Kiang provinces. Changchun, renamed Hsinking (New Capital), was chosen as the seat of the new Government. Tatung was to be the name of the new era.

On February 25 a meeting of representatives of Kirin province was held at the City of Kirin, and a resolution was passed urging the immediate establishment of a new State.

Meanwhile, in Hei-Lung-Kiang province, similar meetings had been held at Harbin and Tsitsihar between February 22 and 25, and had resulted in much the same resolutions as were adopted in Kirin.

On February 28 the representatives of all the fifty-seven *hsiens* or districts of Fengtien Province met at Mukden and adopted a resolution in favor of independence.

On February 29 seven hundred delegates representing the various provinces and *hsiens,* as well as Mongol Banners, met at Mukden and passed a resolution recommending the inauguration of the new State without delay. The resolution also urged that Mr. Pu-yi, the last of the Manchu emperors, be asked to become the Chief Executive.

Prior to these meetings, on February 10, representatives

of various Banners in Eastern Inner Mongolia had met at Taonan-fu, in Fengtien province, and had memorialized the above-mentioned Northeastern Administrative Committee, expressing the desire of the Banners to swear allegiance to the new State when established. There are more than a million Mongols in that part of East Inner Mongolia which had traditionally been included in Manchuria. According to the Lytton Commission's Report, "the Mongols in Feng-tien and Jehol have formed Leagues [Meng], the most influential of which is the Cherim [Cherimu] League." The fact is that there is no Cherimu League in Jehol; it exists in Fengtien, Kirin, and Hei-Lung-Kiang provinces. The Mongol Leagues in Jehol province are called the Chosoto League and the Chaouda League.

On March 1 the Northeastern Administrative Committee, in the name of the new Manchoukuo Government, issued a proclamation apprising the world of the establishment of the new State of Manchoukuo. On the same day, the Committee telegraphically informed China that Manchoukuo had severed all ties with the Nationalist Government. Manchuria had crossed the Rubicon.

The culmination of all these concerted movements was the formal inauguration, at Changchun, of the new Government of Manchoukuo on March 9, 1932, with Pu-yi as Chief Executive. Simultaneously, the Organic Law of the Government and the Law for the Guaranty of Personal Rights were promulgated. On March 10, the Cabinet was organized, with Chang Hsiao-hsu as Prime Minister. On March 12, the Foreign Minister, Mr. Hsieh Chieh-shih, telegraphed the Foreign Offices of seventeen countries, which were represented in Manchuria by consular officials, advising them of the advent of Manchoukuo and asking them to open formal diplomatic relations.

VI

Perhaps I might write here a finis to the story of Ma Chan-shan. He attended the inauguration ceremonies of the Manchoukuo Government and was given the portfolio of War Minister. Yet he was not happy. He was utterly out of his element in the new surroundings. When, at Cabinet meetings, he was asked to sign documents, he had to confess before his colleagues his inability to write even his own name. What embarrassment! Having risen from the ranks of bandits, he had lived a rough but free life on the plains of North Manchuria, and he relished no thought of adjusting himself to the conventions of civilization. He simply could not play the part. True, his colleagues, Tang Yu-lin and Chang Ching-hui, had also been bandit leaders, but they had long since acclimatized themselves to the ways of civilization.

Furthermore, the policy of the new Government was to transfer the control of all military units from the provincial governors and generals to the central authorities. This meant that Ma would eventually be deprived of his troops. Nor was that all. He would no longer be permitted to levy taxes at his own sweet will, but he would be required to adhere to the rates fixed by the central government, and to forward to the central treasury all that he collected. All he could get would be his regular salary, which, however generous, would no longer permit him to lord it over his officers and men. To him the portfolio of War Minister and the governorship of Hei-Lung-Kiang province seemed but an empty glory.

Thinking thus, Ma Chan-shan returned to Tsitsihar, the capital of Hei-Lung-Kiang province, after a very short stay at Changchun (now Hsinking), the seat of the new Manchoukuo Government. The secret emissaries of Marshal Chang Hsueh-liang, the deposed war lord now in Peiping, had already been awaiting Ma in Tsitsihar. Chief among them were Han Shu-yeh and Yu Kwang-mo. They told Ma that the Manchoukuo Government, as the result of the Lytton Commission's investigation, was certain to collapse, and that wisdom and foresight demanded his immediate revolt against that Government. They assured him that large sums of money were forthcoming from Peiping, and that high honors would be conferred upon him even if the revolt should not be a complete success. Above all, they urged Ma to send radio messages to the Lytton Commission, and to his compatriots in Peiping and Shanghai, "exposing" the real nature of the Manchoukuo Government.

Ma could not resist the temptation. He made up his mind to revolt, and by April 7 he had set up his new headquarters at Heiho, just across the Amur River from the Siberian town of Blagoviestchensk. To Mr. Pu-yi, Chief Executive of Manchoukuo, he wired:

"Immediately after the Lytton Commission leaves Manchuria, your Government will be overthrown and Manchoukuo annexed by Japan. Therefore, it would be the part of wisdom for you to request that the Commission arrange for your safe departure from Manchuria."

He also addressed much the same message to Premier Cheng Hsiao-hsu. All such messages were, of course, written by Marshal Chang's emissaries.

The reason why Ma chose Heiho as his new base was

because of its proximity to Russian territory. He had counted upon Russian help. He thought that he could obtain arms, even men and money, from Russia. But Russia was shrewder and knew that Ma's case was hopeless and that his army, formerly estimated at 25,000, had dwindled to 2,000. She knew, too, that Ma had no conviction of his own and was entirely unreliable. What was more important, Russia had no desire to court trouble with Japan and Manchoukuo.

Nor did the money promised him by Marshal Chang reach him. His old colleagues and subordinates, who had flattered him and pandered to him when he was at the height of his power, deserted him now that he had little money and had lost his influence.

For almost four months from the beginning of April, 1932, Ma Chan-shan, constantly hounded by the Manchoukuo and Japanese forces, had no safe shelter. On July 29, he was killed at a small village near Hailun to the north of Harbin. When his body was found, the Japanese buried it with the honors due to a soldier.

Thus ended the colorful life of Ma Chan-shan. Was he a hero or a faker, a patriot or a knave?

VII

The Lytton Commission's Report, discussing the creation of Manchoukuo, has this to say:

The local self-governing administrations thus established in all the Provinces were subsequently combined into a separate and independent State. To understand the ease with which this was accomplished and the amount of evidence which it has been possible to bring forward of Chinese support for it when it was accomplished, it is necessary to consider a peculiar feature of

Chinese organised life which in some circumstances is a strength and in others a weakness. As has been already stated, the community obligations recognised by the Chinese are rather to the family, to a locality, or to persons, than to the State. Patriotism as it is understood in the West is only beginning to be felt. Guilds, associations, leagues, armies, are all accustomed to follow certain individual leaders. If, therefore, the support of a particular leader can be secured by persuasion or coercion, the support of his adherents over the whole area of his influence follows as a matter of course.

All this may be true, but the greater reason why the independence movement was so easily brought to fruition was that the people of Manchuria had no love to lose upon Chang Hsueh-liang, who had exploited them, as did his father, for selfish gain and self-aggrandizement. They had been powerless to put an end to that evil régime themselves, but they were glad enough to see it challenged and, if possible, ousted by any power which promised to give better administration. Another reason was the underlying spirit of independence which had for centuries been among the Manchurians, both Manchus, Mongols and Chinese. This "regionalism" will be more fully discussed in Chapter IV.

This, however, does not mean that Manchoukuo was the result of self-determination, that it represents the unanimous will of 30,000,000 Manchurians. No government in China, ancient or modern, has ever been founded by the will of the people. For many centuries China's history has been a periodic repetition of records of tyrannical governments overthrown by powerful militarists who, by benevolence and good government, gradually won the tacit approval of the people. Even American independence was not the work of a united people, nor did it represent a great popular uprising. According to Dr. Samuel Eliot Morrison, out of a total of 2,500,000 colonists then in America, less than one third may have actively supported independence; over one half remained neutral; while at least 250,000 were loyal to the British Crown.

Manchuria had no group of its own powerful enough to overthrow the Chang régime. Fortunately or unfortunately, Marshal Chang, by his ill-advised policy, forced the Japanese to take up the cudgels in defense of their own interests. And when this burst the bubble of Chang's apparently imposing empire, a comparatively small group of local leaders who had been dissatisfied with the Changs' policy of exploitation and extortion, took advantage of this fortuitous development and established a new Manchurian State upon the ruins of that shattered empire. That is the long and short of the whole story. If the new Manchoukuo Government proves benevolent and just, it will gradually win the trust of the people. If it fails to live up to the promise it has made, it will go the way of all the preceding governments which have destroyed themselves by reason of their own misgovernment.

The Lytton Commission makes a great deal of the 1,550 "unsolicited" letters which it received from Chinese in Manchuria and which were "bitterly hostile to the new Manchoukuo Government and to the Japanese." How did the Commission know that those letters were unsolicited? If it did not know that Chang Hsueh-liang had secret agents and emissaries manipulating the Manchurian situation in his interest, it was too saintly to investigate this mundane question. It is much easier to "buy" such letters in China than to "buy" votes at elections in Chicago or Philadelphia. One could just as easily obtain "unsolicited" letters highly favorable to the Manchoukuo Government. That the Lytton Commission was not deluged with letters in praise of the new régime seems to show that neither the Manchoukuo officials nor the Japanese concerned thought of emulating the manipulations of the Young Marshal.

# CHAPTER IV

## REGIONALISM IN MANCHURIA

### I

In the preceding chapter, reference has frequently been made to Manchuria's regional consciousness expressed in four Chinese words, *Pao-Ching An-Min,* "Peace within the Borders, Security for the People." Although this expression is comparatively new, this consciousness itself has its root planted deeply in the long history of Manchuria. For Manchuria—contrary to the popular Occidental conception that it is a new country like America's "wild west" of a century ago, and in spite of the contemptuous epithet of the "Land of Alien Barbarians" by which it was long known to China—has a history of more than two thousand years, in the course of which kingdoms and empires rose and fell within its borders. In this long history, periods of conservatism alternated with ages of forward movement, when the Manchurians surged over the Great Wall and attempted, often successfully, to impose an alien rule upon the Chinese. But when the surge spent itself with the consequent resurgence of the Chinese power, the Manchurians, forced back to their native land, were inclined, at least temporarily, to heed the counsels of "Peace within the Borders, Security for the People."

From the dawn of their history, the Manchurians always looked upon China as an extension—a colony, if you

94

will—of Manchuria. Never did they consider their homeland as part of China. Why should they? It was they
who repeatedly carried invasion into China, while China's
attitude was entirely defensive. And the surprising fact
was that the Chinese, who had settled in Manchuria, had
become so regional in sentiment that, in these recurrent
invasions, they usually joined not their compatriots at
home, but their Manchurian neighbors. Even when China
reasserted her power, drove out the invaders, and pursued
them beyond the Great Wall, her motive was not to conquer and occupy Manchuria but to keep the "barbarians"
out of her own territory. This fact has been known to
few Europeans or Americans, because few have studied
the history of Manchuria.

The known history of Manchuria dates back to about
400 B.C., when the Chinese called the country Su-shen and
Wei-ma, which were the names of the Tungusic tribes
who had settled and dominated it. These tribes had
plagued China so much that Emperor Shih-Huang Ti,
of the Chin Dynasty (246-210 B.C.), built the Great Wall
as a boundary and barrier between China and what was
later to be called Manchuria. Yet, in spite of the Great
Wall, the barbarian tribes continued to be a constant cause
of worry to China—so much so that Emperor Wu-ti (140-
88 B.C.) of the Han Dynasty, was forced to invade Manchuria, hoping thus to put an end to the pestiferous
inroads of the barbarians. He was doomed to disillusion-
ment, for he was able to conquer only a comparatively
small part in the south of Manchuria, leaving by far the
largest part of the I-lou and Fu-yu tribes, descendants,
respectively, of the Su-shen and Wei-ma tribes. Moreover, even this partial conquest proved short-lived, for by

30 B.C. the Han, or Chinese, invaders had been driven out by the Kao-kou-lie tribe (a branch of the Fu-yu tribe), who had established a kingdom covering the southern half of Manchuria. This lasted for seven centuries.

## II

In the early part of the seventh century, China, then under the Tang Dynasty, again invaded South Manchuria. As a consequence, the Kao-kou-lie Kingdom fell in about 668 A.D. But the power of the Tang Dynasty did not extend to North Manchuria, which was held by the Me-he tribe (descendant of the I-lou tribe), whose chieftain, King Kao, had established a kingdom there. The Tang Dynasty, instead of fighting King Kao, made him an ally so that it could remain in South Manchuria without molestation from the northern tribes. Under this alliance, the kingdom of the Me-he tribe was known as the Kingdom of Po-hai (sometimes spelled Puh-hai), which lasted from 713 A.D. to 926 A.D. At the height of its power, this Kingdom extended as far as the Amur River on the north and the Yalu River on the east. It also covered a large part of what is now Fengtien province in South Manchuria. Although the Po-hai Kingdom adopted much of the culture of the Tang Dynasty of China, it was a kingdom of and for the natives of Manchuria.

At the beginning of the tenth century, the Po-hai Kingdom succumbed before the onslaughts of another Manchurian tribe, which had established the Kingdom of Kitan by 916 A.D. In about 926, it, having overthrown the Po-hai Kingdom, assumed the name of the Kingdom of Liao. Not only did Liao rule the whole of Manchuria and Inner Mongolia, but it occupied a large part of North

China. This great Manchurian kingdom lasted some 200 years, till 1113 A.D.

After the Liao Kingdom came the Chin Kingdom, established by another Manchurian tribe known as Nuchen. The Chin rulers, like their predecessors of the Liao Kingdom, carried conquest inside the Great Wall and drove the Sung Dynasty, which then ruled China, to the south of the Yellow River. Thus the Chin Kingdom extended from the Amur River on the north to the Yellow River on the south, including within its confines Manchuria and a part of Mongolia, as well as North China. It lasted 120 years, till 1234 A.D.

Then came the great Mongol Empire, which, under the dynastic title of Yuan, embraced not only Mongolia and Manchuria but most of China as well. This lasted from 1279 to 1367.

After the Yuan (Mongol) Dynasty was driven out of China by the Ming (Chinese) Dynasty, South Manchuria was again invaded by the Chinese. But the Chinese influence thus established was, as before, limited to a comparatively small part of South Manchuria, mostly on the lower reaches of the Liao River. By far the largest part of Manchuria remained under the control of the Nuchen tribes. In order to avoid conflict with these tribes, the Ming Dynasty cajoled them into entering into an alliance with it, as had the Tang Dynasty in dealing with the Pohai Kingdom in the eighth century. Neither the Tang nor the Ming Dynasty ever established anything like absolute control over Manchuria. What semblance of control they did establish was in reality, a measure of self-defense conceived in a desire, not to conquer Manchuria, but to protect China from the assaults of the "barbarian" tribes. "Throughout history," writes Mr. Owen Lattimore in his scholarly *Manchuria, Cradle of Conflict,* "it can be seen that the fundamental aim of Chinese statecraft was to control the border territories, not to occupy them. Colonies were planted always as expedients to control strategic points. There was no general urge toward the complete occupation of outlying territory; for a general spread of population toward the north would have upset the balance of the State, which was identified with a very ancient drift toward the south and east. The north was, in general, the rear; only exceptionally the front."

III

From about 1360 to 1620 A.D., when China was ruled by the Ming Dynasty, Manchuria was divided among various tribes, none of which was powerful enough to unite them all under a common banner. Thus, it was comparatively easy for the Ming Dynasty of China to keep them outside the Great Wall under a nominal alliance with some of their chieftains.

Toward the end of the sixteenth century, however, the Nuchen tribe, which had, four hundred years before, established the great Kingdom of Chin, again came into its own. Under the able leadership of Nurhachi (the ancestor of Henry Pu-yi, now Chief Executive of Manchoukuo), the Nuchens united North and South Manchuria, as well as what is now Eastern Inner Mongolia. By 1616 A.D., he had driven out of South Manchuria what Chinese (Ming) power had remained there, and had established the foundation of the great Tsing Dynasty which ruled China, Manchuria, and Mongolia until

1911. In 1644, the Tsing Dynasty moved its capital to Peking.

To the Tsing Dynasty, China was the colony of Manchuria, not Manchuria the colony of China. It distributed Manchu warriors, known as "bannermen," among the provinces of China in order to forestall any uprisings among the Chinese. At the same time, it prohibited the immigration of the Chinese into Manchuria. The Chinese had already settled in the south of Manchuria in such large numbers that the Tsing Dynasty was anxious to check their further increase. The Manchu Dynasty, moreover, looked upon Manchuria, its homeland, as a place of refuge into which it could retreat in the event of resurgence of the Chinese power.

## IV

From these historical antecedents we can clearly understand why Manchuria has developed a strong regional sentiment. And it is a fact of the greatest significance that this Manchurian regionalism was not confined to the original population of Manchuria, but was fully shared by the Chinese who had settled there to such an extent that they outnumbered the natives. At the time of the Manchu conquest of China, the Manchu population was known to have been a little over a million. After the conquest, much of this population was sent into the various provinces of China as officers and soldiers to maintain peace. The Manchus who remained in Manchuria could not have numbered much more than eight hundred thousand. As against this small number of Manchus, there were a million and several hundred thousand Chinese in Manchuria itself. And yet this Chinese majority not only docilely accepted the dominance of the Manchu minority but was entirely willing to work with it. As Mr. Lattimore says, the Chinese in Manchuria "were willing to accept the authority and identify themselves with the drive, of the rising and aggressive Manchu group, which promised them a share of the power and wealth to be garnered in China." The Chinese "were willingly incorporated, from the very beginning, in the Manchu military system, and thoroughly identified themselves, politically, with the Manchus. No one who has visited both the old Manchurian and old Chinese regions of Manchuria and noticed the number, distribution, and known age of towns and villages, can doubt that, long before the [Manchu] conquest [of China], the largest numerical element in the Manchu armies must have been Chinese."

But this regional solidarity, this willingness of the Chinese majority in Manchuria to follow and work with the native minority goes back much farther than the Manchu period. The Chinese, who settled in the south of Manchuria before the Christian era, during the Han Dynasty of China, joined first with the Ma-he and then with the Kitan tribe, which resisted the Chinese invasion under the Tang Dynasty and finally drove the Tangs out of Manchuria. And the Chinese, who had followed the Tangs into Manchuria and remained there, soon became so regional that these, too, joined the Manchurian drive against China during the Sung Dynasty and also during the Ming Dynasty. After the Ming Dynasty entered into a sort of alliance with the Manchu tribe or tribes, the Chinese population in the south of Manchuria was augmented by many newcomers from China. These new settlers, too, soon acquired the regional sentiment to such an extent that they joined the Manchus and helped them in destroying the Ming Dynasty, under whose protection or sponsorship they had emigrated to Manchuria. "However triumphant the northward spread of Chinese power," to quote Mr. Lattimore again, "any Chinese population flowing into the 'reservoir' region [that part of South Manchuria contiguous to North China] inevitably becomes even more conscious of the fact that it can now exercise a control over the affairs of China behind it than that it can press forward to fresh conquests of barbarian territories."

This is a point which should be remembered, for history repeats itself. In this year of grace 1933, the Manchoukuo army, consisting mostly of regionally minded Chinese, is advancing into Jehol. And Jehol is the most important section of what Mr. Lattimore calls "the 'reservoir' area of the successive northern invaders of China," for it dominates the Great Wall, the most fundamental line of demarkation between China and Manchuria, by virtue of the plateau formation of Inner Mongolia. To the Chinese in Manchuria, this campaign is but a repetition of the same process followed periodically by them in the course of their long history. The only difference this time is that they are following Japanese instead of native leadership.

Another important point deduced from the history of Manchuria, as succinctly set forth in the foregoing passages, is that as long as Manchoukuo and Japan confine themselves within the Great Wall, with Jehol as its westernmost province, China's resistance will be half-hearted and ineffectual. In their heart of hearts the Chinese of China cling to the traditional belief that Manchuria is a land of barbarians which does not belong to them. The Chinese politicians and militarists may shout from the housetops against the independence of Manchuria, but the mass of the Chinese population remains indifferent.

On the other hand, should Manchoukuo and its Japanese ally go beyond the Great Wall and venture forth into North China, the imagination of the mass of the Chinese population would at once be stirred, calling forth a most resolute and united resistance on the part of all Chinese. As I have already shown, this happened again and again in the long history of Sino-Manchurian relations. Invariably such Chinese resistance resulted in the ultimate dislodgment of the Manchurian overlord from China proper, forcing him back into Jehol outside the Great Wall and into regions further east. This process of expulsion usually required decades, often centuries, but its final outcome was never doubted. In the light of this history, it would be extemely unwise for Manchoukuo, even with Japanese support, to extend its jurisdiction beyond Jehol province.

v

In view of the regional sentiment and solidarity, so old and so strong, it is not difficult to understand why Manchurian independence has been so readily accomplished. It is but another demonstration of *Pao-Ching An-Min,* an articulate modern expression of an inarticulate ancient idea peculiar to this region. In Manchuria, since the beginning of its history, independence has always been in the air. The Manchus, defeated by the Chinese in the revolution of 1911, have retired into Manchuria, their homeland and place of refuge, and there, aided by the highly regional Chinese majority, have inaugurated an independent State. That is nothing strange. What is strange is the fact that the world is making so much ado about it.

### Postscript

Since this chapter was written, the Chinese soldiers, 150,000 strong, who had vociferously proclaimed to the world that they were impregnably entrenched at all the strategic mountain passes in Jehol, have fled without offering any serious resistance to the Japanese and Manchoukuo forces. Both at Kailu and at Chihfeng the Chinese "defenders" welcomed the "invaders" and proffered to follow their leadership in their march against the Great Wall. In some of the cities, the inhabitants hoisted the old dragon flag of the Manchu Dynasty when the Manchoukuo and Japanese soldiers entered them. On March 4 Chengteh, capital of Jehol, which, the Chinese had claimed, was invincibly defended, was taken by 128 Japanese soldiers without firing a shot.

All this is but a repetition of the same spectacle as was seen again and again in Manchuria's long history. It entirely bears out my statements in this chapter that the Chinese in Manchuria usually abetted, rather than resisted, the Manchu advance against China, and that as long as Manchoukuo and Japan do not venture beyond the Great Wall they will encounter no determined resistance from China.

# CHAPTER V

## *WANGTAO*, OLDEST IDEAL OF THE NEWEST STATE

### I

In Manchuria nowadays one constantly hears the classic Chinese word *Wangtao* from the mouths of Chinese statesmen and officials, from the Chief Executive, Mr. Pu-yi himself, down to bureau chiefs. The new State of Manchoukuo is founded upon *Wangtao*. *Wangtao* is the antidote to the republicanism and the nationalism which have plunged China into chaos and have brought her to the verge of disintegration. The peace and happiness of the people are possible only when the ideals of *Wangtao* are applied to the practice of administration. *Wangtao* is the only effective preventive of the inroads of Communism. *Wangtao* will do this, that, and the other thing. What, indeed, is there that *Wangtao* cannot do?

What is this *Wangtao*, which seems to be the panacea of all ills of the body politic? If you call on Premier Cheng Hsiao-hsu, of the Manchoukuo Government, he will give you an essay on *Wangtao* written by himself in classic Chinese. If you are an American or a European, he will give you an English translation of the same essay. You pore over it, ponder it, meditate about it for hours, and yet you are at sea as to the real meaning of *Wangtao*. The more you think about it the deeper you get into mystery.

Etymologically, *Wangtao* consists of two Chinese characters—*Wang,* meaning "king," and *Tao,* signifying "way." *Wangtao,* then, is the *Way of the King.* But what is the *Way of the King?* Before I try to answer this question let me introduce the story of the two kings who stand out, in Chinese eyes, as the most ideal rulers of all ages.

## II

In the twilight of history, no less than four thousand two hundred years ago, there lived somewhere in China a king named Yao. He was an unselfish man, ready to sacrifice his own comfort for the happiness of his people. After years of assiduous toil in the interest of good administration he made a tour of inspection, disguised as a peasant, to see for himself whether the people were happy. Presently he came upon a farmhouse in which an aged yet robust farmer was found playing a guitar and singing a song which, in English, ran somewhat like this:

> I plough my ground and eat my own bread,
> I dig my well and drink my own water;
> What use have I for king or court?

King Yao danced with joy. He knew that the farmers were so contented that they had no need of thinking about the government or the King. Returning to his palace, Yao redoubled his endeavors for the welfare of his subjects.

Yao's reign lasted a hundred years. When he was ready to retire he asked his ministers to recommend a worthy successor. Shun was the man unanimously nominated, and the reason for his nomination was that he had been widely known for his filial piety and fraternal kindness. Shun's father, so the story runs, was a blind man of extraordinarily bad temper. His stepmother was notoriously wicked, and his younger brother, the darling of his parents, was even worse. All three seemed to derive doubtful satisfaction from tormenting and maltreating Shun. But Shun not only bore it all without complaint or resentment but, by self-sacrifice and filial conduct, completely changed the nature of his parents and brother, and won their affection.

King Yao was deeply touched by the story but was not entirely sure whether Shun, a filial son and a kind brother, would also be a faithful husband and a good father. So Yao adopted Shun and gave him his two daughters at once. Shun proved himself equal to the new test and became a shining example of virtue and good behavior. The aged King was highly satisfied and put Shun upon the throne which he had vacated.

### III

To the Chinese mind, the story of Yao and Shun is not a myth or a legend. It is a force made immortal through the politico-ethical philosophy of Confucius and Mencius. These two sage-philosophers, revered by the Chinese through the centuries, idealized Yao and Shun and looked upon their period as a golden age, an ideal state which should be the goal and objective of all rulers. In their writings, both Confucius and Mencius frequently referred to Yao and Shun and constructed about the deeds of these classic kings a sort of political philosophy for the guidance of all rulers.

Foreign-educated Chinese may make light of Yao and

Shun, of Confucius and Mencius, but they are, after all, a handful among the teeming millions of China. The masses of people still look back with a sense of reverence to the golden age of the ancient sage-kings. Confucianism and Mencianism are to them, perhaps, what Christianity is to the peoples of Europe and America. To them, the new-fangled political theories of the Occident are couched in jargon strange to their ears, as to their minds. Parliamentarism and party government, propounded by Chinese educated abroad, have made no impression upon the masses of China. On the other hand, any Chinese with even a slight education knows something of Yao and Shun, of Confucius and Mencius, and cherishes affection and veneration for them. In the midst of all the tumults and confusions brought about by the sudden impact of western modernism, the soul of China still harks to her own great past.

Such being the case, the leaders of Manchoukuo were perhaps wise in adopting *Wangtao,* the *Way of the King,* as the ideal and guiding principle of the new State. As they see it, the condition of China since the overthrow of the Manchu Government, which, whatever its failings in its last years, was founded upon the noble ideals of *Wangtao,* has gone from bad to worse. The republic, which replaced the rule of *Wangtao,* has proved an utter failure—so much so that even Dr. Frank Goodnow, American adviser to President Yuan Shihkai, was constrained, as early as 1914, to express the opinion that republicanism was unsuited to China; and that, if any western form of government was to be imported at all, constitutional monarchy would be best suited to the existing condition of the country. But the forces of disorganization, once set loose, could not be easily checked, and China sunk deeper and deeper in the mire of chaos.

Sun Yat-sen's nationalism, as the leaders of Manchoukuo look at it, is but an evil child of the chaos which followed upon the heels of republicanism. This new *ism,* emphasizing China's antagonism toward foreign powers, simply aggravated the situation which had been bad enough. It offered no constructive program for the internal rehabilitation of the nation; instead, it put all the blame upon foreigners for the difficulties and troubles which were inherent in the country itself. It inculcated enmity where friendliness was needed. It emphasized discord where harmony was essential. It threw China into the violent vortex of international conflict and made her position intolerable among the nations of the world. Such, as the Manchoukuo advocates of *Wangtao* see it, is the whirlwind reaped from the wind sowed by the Nationalists of the Sun Yat-sen school.

Nor is this the worst. China today is in imminent danger of being engulfed by the surging tide of communism. For this condition Soviet Russia and the Third International alone should not be held responsible; China herself must shoulder the large part of the blame, for she has, by her own waywardness and negligence, furnished Red agitation with the most fertile soil.

What is the remedy for all this? The Manchoukuo leaders answer in chorus, "Back to *Wangtao.*" And the chorus strikes a responsive chord in the Chinese mind, because it is couched in words familiar to the Chinese ear for many thousands of years. Republicanism has failed. Nationalism has failed. Sun Yat-sen's "Three People's Principles" have failed. They have all failed, and will

always fail, because they are foreign to China and will
never be understood by her millions. And as for Communism, it will spell the end of China. The salvation
lies in *Wangtao,* which, in China's history of forty-
three centuries, has given her long periods of peace,
prosperity, and enlightenment, interspersed, it is true,
with ages of chaos when *Wangtao* was temporarily
ignored.

Such is the reasoning of Manchoukuo statesmen and
officials. It is understandable. It rings true at least to
the native ear. It has a certain sympathetic appeal which
even the average Chinese knows how to appreciate. There
is, of course, no need of questioning the sincerity of those
who advocate *Wangtao,* but even from the standpoint of
mere statecraft, of mere expediency, this ancient and
familiar doctrine—as a symbol and slogan—will serve to
rally the people weary of the disorganization and disorder
which have denied them the peace they have desired for
the last twenty years.

## IV

Now we come to the essential question, "What is
*Wangtao?*" We have seen that Yao and Shun, who ruled
a certain section of what is now China from 2356 B.C. to
2255 B.C., still stand out in the Chinese mind as ideal
rulers. It was around their deeds and utterances that
Confucius, two hundred years before Christ, built up his
politico-ethical theories.

Let us ask, then, "What did Yao and Shun do to endear
themselves to the people?" The answer has already been
intimated in their story introduced at the outset. They
were ideal sons, ideal fathers, ideal husbands, and ideal

brothers. In other words, they made their homes shrines of peace, harmony, and happiness. In the Confucian theory the state is but an enlarged family. A man who is not a filial son, a loving father, a faithful husband, and a kind brother, can never be a good member of the state. Therefore, an ideal family is the foundation of an ideal state. Furthermore, if each family is harmonious and happy within itself its relations with other families will also be felicitous. This will ensure the peace of the state, for the state is not only an enlarged family but also a society of families.

That Premier Cheng, of the Manchoukuo Government, like the multitudes of his fellow countrymen, looks upon Shun as an ideal ruler is evident from the frequent reference he makes to that classic king in his essay on *Wangtao* which it is his wont to give to all who come to him for explanation of the *Way of the King*. "The great Shun," it says, "had a great delight in what was good. He regarded virtue as the common property of himself and others, giving up his own way to follow that of others, and taking delight in learning from others in order that he might practise what was good in all."

To quote the Manchoukuo Premier again, "Shun, an emperor from the ranks of common folk, having given up his own way to follow that of others, enabled all the people under Heaven to come to him and willingly to be his subjects. Willingness to learn from others and to practise what is good in all remove entirely the distinction between one's self and others."

To Premier Cheng, a ruler must "cultivate" himself before he is able to give peace and happiness to others. He writes:

Yen Yuan asked about perfect virtue. The Master [Confucius] said: "To subdue one's self and return to propriety, is perfect virtue. If a man can for one day subdue himself and return to propriety, all under heaven will ascribe perfect virtue to him."

Tsze-lu asked what constituted the superior man. The master [Confucius] said, "The cultivation of himself in reverential carefulness." "And is this all?" said Tsze-lu. "He cultivates himself so as to give peace to others," was the reply. "And is that all?" asked Tsze-lu again. The Master said, "He cultivates himself so as to give peace to all people. He cultivates himself so as to give peace to all people—even Yao and Shun were solicitous about this."

The sentence "He cultivates himself so as to give peace to others" means that in regard to the aged, to give them rest; in regard to friends, to show them sincerity; in regard to the young, to treat them tenderly. The sentence "He cultivates himself so as to give peace to all people" has the same meaning as "Yu [the king who succeeded Shun] thought that if any one in the empire were drowned, it was as if he drowned him." Tseih thought that if any one in the empire suffered hunger, it was as if he famished him. Yao and Shun took the responsibility of the empire as their own. Thus they four had the same principle.

According to the Confucian theory, the King is an embodiment of *jen,* or "love for fellow men" or "fellow-feeling." Therefore, the *Way of the King* is government by "fellow-feeling" or love for mankind. In the ancient Chinese *Book of Rites* is the following glorification of this doctrine:

When the Great Doctrine prevails all under heaven will work for the common good. The virtuous will be elected to office, and the able will be given responsibility. Faithfulness will be in constant practise and harmony will rule. Consequently, mankind will not only love their own parents and give care to their own children; all the aged will be provided for, and all the young employed in work. Infants will be fathered; widows and widowers, the fatherless and the unmarried, the disabled and the sick, will all be cared for. The men will have their rights and the women their home. No goods will go to waste, nor need they be stored for private possession. No energy should be retained in one's own body, nor should it be used for personal gain. Self-interest ceases, and theft and disorder are unknown. Therefore, the gates of the houses are never closed.

The significance of *jen,* "fellow-feeling," as the essence of the *Way of the King* or the perfect state is more fully explained by Liang Chi-chao, a brilliant Chinese writer and lecturer who died several years ago, in his *History of Chinese Political Thought:* *

What I like to hold now I must hold together with my fellow-beings; what I wish to attain in the future I must strive for in co-operation with my fellow-beings. This is true because the progression of human life involves relationship. Unless all men stand together, no man can stand; unless all men strive for the attainment, no man can accomplish it. The real meaning of "establishing others" and "elevating others" comprehends not individuals but the whole of mankind. Since the whole of mankind consists of others and self, to elevate others is to elevate the whole of mankind; and to elevate the whole of mankind is to elevate oneself. To try to understand this principle by inferring the wants of others from our own desires is the way to "Jen." To be lacking in "Jen" is to be like a benumbed hand or foot which is insensitive to pains in other bodily members. So the wholeness of personality which comes from the association of two or more persons lacks "Jen" when it is insensitive to the pains of another; it attains "Jen" when sensitiveness is keen. In short, the lack of "Jen" is insensitiveness to fellow-feeling; the fulfilment of "Jen" is the state of keen sensitiveness.

From the foregoing it is clear that Confucius built up his world upon a magnificent harmony with the natural conditions of his day. "He," as Dr. Richard Wilhelm fitly says in his *The Soul of China,* "conceived men rooted in

* Published by Harcourt, Brace & Company. Reprinted by permission.

the intuitive cohesion of the family. His order of the world is founded upon this cohesion: the attachment which is natural within the family, the love of the parents for their children: feelings which manifest themselves in natural men of their own accord without compulsion. These feelings were the material which K'ungtse [Confucius] used for his teaching. He strove to find the right form, the right expression for their emotion, because feelings are corrupted or wither if they do not find their true and natural expression. K'ungtse therefore strove to find the true expression for this central harmony of the emotions. He attempted to attain this end by the establishment of firm customs for external behaviour and by the influence of music upon man's inner attitude. With the family as the centre he extended the range of his action. What is nature within the family was to be culture in the cohesion of the state, which represents an enlargement of the family. He fixed, as the star above all natural states, the vision of humanity: 'within the four seas all are brothers,' and as the father of men he set up the Godhead which, full of eternal wisdom, wrought without sound or scent what is right for all living things, and it is also the only source for all that lives in man of the highest thoughts and the happiest destinies." *

Such is *Wangtao,* as it manifests itself in the ideal state of Confucius.

## v

Premier Cheng believes that *Wangtao* should be applied to international relations as well as to internal administration. The *Way of the King* is the only way to international peace. He writes:

* Reprinted by permission of the publishers, Harcourt, Brace & Company.

It is argued that, in this age of nationalism and militarism, no nation can exist without military power. Yet history tells us that men like Napoleon and William the Second failed to achieve their ambitions though their military forces were more than sufficient for their own protection. Today we find small countries existing as independent nations regardless of their military strength. Larger and stronger nations are prevented from annexing them by the principle of the "balance of power," which protects the small nations from the fear of the larger. The safety of the small nations likewise is the protection of the larger, and thus we find a new means of mutual control in the halls of Lausanne and Geneva. Both these places are located in Switzerland, whose lack of military power disarms the Powers of jealousy and mistrust. Offering no occasion for fear, Switzerland becomes a political centre of the world.

Hence a similarly developed nation, a *Wangtao* nation in the Far East, if brought into existence, should be of enormous advantage to the whole world, as it then would be under the protection of the great nations. Its weakness will be its strength, for unjustifiable force used against it by any one Power would excite the rest of the powers to come to its assistance and prevent invasion. As a result of a surfeit of war the world is sick of war. If *Wangtao* is adopted the outlook of the whole world will be changed. The development of such an attitude should contribute to the solution of naval and military armament reduction problems. But the most serious menace which confronts us is Communism, because its aim is to overthrow world morality. Communism is our chief enemy, as its very use of the principles of force is contrary to the teachings of *Wangtao*.

To Premier Cheng's way of thinking, nationalism and militarism are what have brought China to the verge of destruction. It was they which doomed Chang Hsueh-liang, and they will also doom Chiang Kai-shek, unless he realizes the futility of the course he is pursuing.

Liang Chi-chao, whom I have already quoted, maintains a similar view. "The starting point of the Con-

fucian is totally different from that of the political
theories current today in Europe and America," he writes.
"The latter, encouraging differences in sentimental feelings, brings hatred; the former, nourishing the fellow-
feeling in human nature, brings amity. What the West
calls nationalism is the sanction of a narrow conception
of patriotism. Its attitude towards aliens is merciless, so
that people are beguiled into thinking of war as glorious,
'extending,' as Mencius says, 'unloving deeds even to those
whom they love.' The capitalist class ignores all con-
siderations of reciprocity, giving to the laborers what they
themselves dislike. On the other hand, the protagonists
of labor, notably the followers of Marx, are also daily
advocating retaliation, again giving what they themselves
dislike. It is unthinkable that a social revolution, inspired
by such motives, will uplift mankind. In the eyes of those
who study Confucian teachings, the non-alienation of
mankind must be the minimum basis of the social ethic;
fellow-feeling among men must be constantly developed.
God forbid that a diminution of this feeling should be
either encouraged or considered as right or propitious!
What is known as national consciousness and class consciousness is quite foreign to the Chinese mind. Whether
or not this constitutes a weakness of the Chinese people
is yet a debatable question."

## VI

All this is very beautiful, but it is too ethereal to be
realized in this mundane world of ours. While I was
listening to the Premier's exposition of the *Wangtao* of
the dim past my mind wandered into the hard realities
of the present. In the Arcadian days of Yao and Shun,

whom Confucius apotheosizes and whom Premier Cheng
idolizes, there was no question of taxation, no complicated
and vast system of government, no standing army, no
police force, no schools, no public sanitation—none of the
paraphernalia of modern administration requiring large
funds which must be levied from the people. King Yao
found the farmers so contented that they were able to
forget him. The farmers of Manchuria will never be
able to forget Mr. Pu-yi, because the Chief Executive's
agents will make periodic visits to the farmers to collect
taxes. King Yao had no prime minister who was paid,
as is the Manchoukuo Prime Minister, an annual salary of
30,000 *yuan* (silver dollars). Besides the Premier, the
Central Government of Manchoukuo has nine cabinet
ministers, four heads of Councils, and seven Privy Councillors, drawing annual salaries of between 20,000 *yuan*
and 25,000 *yuan*. That means that Manchoukuo has a
complicated and costly system of administration. Then
there are provincial governments. The army, though
greatly reduced, still comprises 100,000 soldiers.

All these must be maintained by taxation in one form
or another. The burden will fall largely upon farmers,
laborers, traders, etc. How can they be made so contented as was the Arcadian farmer of the pastoral age of
King Yao?

The ancient doctrine of *Wangtao,* as the ideal of government, is perhaps sound enough even today. But
modern administration requires modern technique which
*Wangtao* does not supply. It requires a mastery of the
science and technique of finance, taxation, public health
and education, public works, national defense, public
peace, and all that is essential to the welfare of the great

multitudes which constitute a modern state. *Wangtao,* divorced from this modern knowledge and technique, is of little use. Indeed, China's "backwardness," if we may use the word, is due largely to the importance she has so long attached to the classics to the neglect of modern sciences, thus limiting the mental and moral vision to the narrow horizon which confined the mind of Confucius two thousand four hundred years ago.

It is here, perhaps, that Japan can be of service to Manchoukuo. Herself a worshiper of Confucius up to some sixty years ago, she has since made feverish efforts to catch up with Europe and America in the study of the sciences and the arts which are the causes of Occidental progress. For some years to come Japanese administrators, Japanese jurists, Japanese educators, and Japanese experts will have to work in the government of Manchoukuo. They enjoy a certain advantage in that they, too, have the background of the Chinese classics, as no Westerners have. Their modern knowledge and technique, combined with the classic *Wangtao* cherished by the leaders of Manchoukuo, may yet wring peace, order, and happiness out of the land of banditry and official "squeeze" that has been Manchuria for unnumbered ages.

# CHAPTER VI

## HENRY PU-YI, SYMBOL OF *WANGTAO*

### I

On October 1, 1932, I received a telephone message from the Wai-Chao-Pu, Foreign Office of Manchoukuo, saying that the Chih Cheng, or Chief Executive, Mr. Pu-yi, would receive me the next morning at eleven o'clock.

At the appointed hour I arrived at the Executive Mansion, which stood upon a knoll overlooking well-cultivated farms on all sides. The building, or rather group of buildings, surrounded by a brick wall, appeared more commodious and respectable than I had expected. I had not thought that the drab native city of Changchun, now called Hsinking, could supply the Chief Executive with any residence which would do justice to his exalted station. The building, I later found out, had housed the office of the Salt Monopoly Bureau of Kirin Province. It is about two miles from the Japanese railway city of Changchun, and sits back a considerable distance from the main street of the Chinese city.

The outer gate of the mansion was guarded by four sentries, all Chinese. Entering the reception office, I handed my card to one of the secretaries, again all Chinese. The official, looking at the card printed in Chinese characters, addressed me in Chinese, a language which, when spoken, I could not understand. I replied in English and said that I had an appointment with the Chief Executive. He did not seem to understand, nor did any of the other officials present. Presently, however, a young man, a Chinese, was called in who spoke English. "Ah!" he said, "you are to be received in audience by the Chief Executive; I shall take you in."

Guided by the young secretary, I passed through another gate which was not guarded, walked through the inner courtyard, and entered a small office where I was introduced to a Japanese gentleman, Mr. Nakajima, who was to interpret for the Chief Executive and me. The gentleman took me through another courtyard into a commodious room provided with comfortable chairs and sofas. There were here a few Chinese officers whose uniforms were adorned with brilliant epaulets. Evidently they were *aides de camp*.

Presently, I was ushered into the Chief Executive's drawing-room on the second floor of the same building. Mr. Pu-yi was standing and extended his hand to me. I had heard of his plebeian manners, but the woolen vest or pullover which he wore under his sackcoat rather surprised me. Was this unconventional attire an affectation or an expression of his genuine desire to be "democratic"? I had expected him to be a bit formal in receiving a foreigner, and I came in the regular habiliment of a motoring coat and striped trousers. He beckoned me to sit down across a small table before him, while Mr. Nakajima, the Japanese interpreter, sat at another end of it. Although Mr. Pu-yi had for some years been under the tutorship of a devoted Englishman, Sir Reginald Johnston, he was modest enough to say that his English was very limited and that he preferred to speak in Chinese. What we talked about was immaterial. To spare him embarrassment I steered clear of political topics and confined our conversation to social matters.

Our conversation lasted half an hour. When I was leaving, the Chief Executive came to the door of the room and cordially shook my hand. Surely a new era had dawned upon the Manchu House! The time was not so far back when Pu-yi's imperial sires demanded of all the foreigners—European, American, or Japanese—the humiliating curtsy of *kowtow,* which made an American Minister to Peking so indignant that he blurted out, "I *kowtow* only to God and woman"—a speech utterly incomprehensible to the Chinese. Now, Mr. Pu-yi, who had himself once graced the dragon throne in the innermost sanctum of the Forbidden City in Peking, receives all foreigners—scribes, journalists, even tourists, as well as ambassadors and generals—upon an equal footing.

## II

The choice of Mr. Pu-yi as the head of the new State is, perhaps, a wise one. He is a symbol of unity and harmony, around which various factions could rally as under no leadership supplied in any other way. Pu-yi leads without seeming to lead, because he represents an ideal and a tradition which are expressed by the classic word *Wangtao,* the *Way of the King.* He is neutral. He transcends factions. Toward politicians and militarists of diverse affiliations he can be and is impartial. Moreover, Pu-yi is the only man who can win the trust of the Manchurian Mongols, still numbering a million and a half. As Mr. Owen Lattimore, a profound scholar of the regions on the fringes of China, says in *Foreign Affairs* (New York) for January, 1933, "The difficulty among the princes of Inner Mongolia is to find one who can be accepted there as ruler by all the others. They are all so nearly equal in status and lineage that there is no obvious leader by right of birth. Allegiance to, or alliance under, a Manchu Emperor would solve the problem." From the Mongol standpoint, Mr. Lattimore thinks, an Emperor would have been more welcome than a ruler with the peculiar title of "Chief Executive."

If, on the contrary, the conferees at the independence meeting, held at Mukden on February 16 and 17, 1932, had elected one of their own number as president or head of the new Government there would have been no harmony but plenty of jealousies and insidious intrigues such as had time and again disrupted the Republican and the Nationalist governments of China. Immediately, those who failed to be chosen for the high honor would have concocted plots to pull down the man whom they had themselves elected. Ignominious wrangles would have developed among self-seeking politicians and ambitious generals. To be sure, General Ma would not have been the only rebel against the new régime. By placing Pu-yi—a symbol, an ideal, and a tradition, rather than a person—upon the dais of Chief Executive, this probable development has been forestalled.

Pu-yi's is a great heritage. The last of the Manchu Dynasty, he can name among his sires such great rulers as Kwang Hsi and Chin Lung. So great an authority as the late Dr. W. A. P. Martin goes so far as to say that the "Manchus gave to China a better government than any of her native dynasties." Emperor Kwang Hsi, a patron of literature, appointed a commission of scholars who compiled the immortal dictionary known as the *Kwang Hsi Dictionary*. Another commission, also appointed by the Emperor, compiled a great encyclopedia of 5,026 volumes. Himself a scholar of no mean order, Kwang Hsi wrote sixteen moral maxims which were afterwards published under the title of *Sacred Edict,* a book which, in the palmy days of the Manchu Dynasty, was read and expounded throughout the empire. His was perhaps the most brilliant and enlightened reign in the whole of Chinese history.

Almost as brilliant was the reign of Emperor Chin Lung, which lasted for sixty years from 1736. Under his rule the vast domains of the Manchu Empire, extending from Formosa to Nepaul, from Manchuria and Mongolia to what are now Burma and Siam, were unified, solidified, and tranquillized.

As far back as 1625 Nurhachu, founder of the Manchu Dynasty, established his court at Mukden and brought most of Manchuria under his flag. Twenty years afterwards the Manchu Regent, Durgan, conquered North China and removed his government to Peking, where the dynasty assumed the title of Ta Tsing, or Great Purity. From that time to 1911 the dynasty produced great rulers and great statesmen. Only when it had permitted itself to be enervated and corrupted by the wealth and power which it had itself accumulated did it collapse under its own weight, for then it had ceased to observe *Wangtao,* the *Way of the King,* and had exhausted the mandate of Heaven.

That is why Pu-yi and his ministers are anxious to restore *Wangtao* to its proper place, fitting it, not to a dynastic government, but to a new régime which will gradually develop into a constitutional government.

### III

Great though his heritage was, Pu-yi's life has been full of tragic vicissitudes. On November 14, 1908, Pu-yi, then an infant of three summers, was literally pushed onto the dragon throne upon the sudden demise on the same day of his uncle, Emperor Kwang Hsu. The power which was instrumental in enthroning the child was his great aunt, the aged Empress Dowager Tsu Hsi, that masterful woman who had, for almost fifty years, held the Manchu Court in the hollow of her hand, and who had twice resorted to a *coup d'état* to prove that she was the real ruler behind the throne. Though she was seventy-three years old when she proclaimed Pu-yi, her third puppet, emperor, she was still full of ambition and no doubt expected to rule for some years to come. But on the day after Pu-yi was enthroned the Empress Dowager suddenly died.

The infant Emperor, Pu-yi, whose dynastic title was Hsuan Tung, had been on the throne only two years when a serious revolution broke out in central China in the Yangtse valley. Unable to quell the uprising, the Manchu Government at Peking bowed to the inevitable, and on February 12, 1912, Pu-yi, or Emperor Hsuan Tung, still only five years old, "voluntarily" abdicated to make room for the Republic which had already been set up at Nanking with Dr. Sun Yat-sen as provisional President.

Before Hsuan Tung's abdication, there had been signed between his representatives and the new Republican Gov-

ernment at Nanking a set of three agreements, the terms
of which included the following:

1. The Emperor, after his abdication, shall continue to
use the dynastic title of Emperor Hsuan Tung, and the
Republican Government shall accord him all the respect
due to the sovereigns of foreign countries.

2. The Emperor shall receive from the Republican
Government an annual allowance of 4,000,000 *yuan* (silver
Chinese dollars).

3. The Emperor shall continue to occupy the imperial
palaces in Peking.

4. The Emperor shall enjoy all the private properties
which have belonged to the Imperial House. The Republican Government shall accord due protection to such
properties as well as to the imperial tombs.

The agreements were by no means one-sided. No less
an authority than Tang Shao-yi, a high official in the
Manchu Government, but later Prime Minister in the Republican Government, frankly admitted that "we [Repub-
licans] agreed to that treaty because, by abdicating, the
Manchus made it unnecessary for us to prolong the period
of the revolution, saved human life, and gave us an opportunity to settle down to reconstruction." Had the Manchus decided to prolong the struggle the revolutionists,
even if they were ultimately victorious, would have had to
make infinitely greater sacrifices in blood and treasure
than were actually offered by them in the above agreements. It so turned out that even the small sacrifices they
offered were only on paper, for the Republican Government never fully observed the abdication agreements.

The above compact was communicated to the foreign
legations at Peking. As Dr. L. R. O. Bevan, professor of

International Law at Peking University, fitly observed at
the time, the "final agreements are in the nature of a treaty
between two independent communities." Simultaneously
with the conclusion of the agreements the infant Emperor,
at the instance of his advisers, issued a decree which, in
part, said:

Since the revolutionary war was started, many provinces have
been drawn into it. The country is in turmoil and the people are
suffering indescribable hardships. Some time ago I ordered Yuan
Shih-kai to send our representatives to the South to confer with
the representatives of the revolutionary army. They agreed upon
general principles. Nevertheless, two months have passed with
no definite plan adopted between the two parties. The consequence is that the northern and the southern armies are still facing each other. The soldiers are suffering on the field. The
merchants are facing ruin. The longer the delay in deciding upon
the form of government the greater the suffering of the people.

Today national sentiment seems to be inclined toward republican government. We can understand the will of Heaven through
the feeling of the people. I have no solicitude for my personal
interest against the desire of the multitudes.

In another decree the Emperor said:

In ancient times our sage-emperors considered the protection
of the people their absorbing duty. They were solicitous for the
welfare of their subjects and never committed any act which
would do them harm. It is for the same solicitude that we have
agreed to the change of government. Our sole desire is to forestall civil war and to preserve peace in the interest of the people.

It is our desire that our subjects, far and near, shall appreciate
the motives which actuated us to make this decision for supreme
renunciation. They must avoid intemperate utterances and suppress extravagant emotions so that our state and people shall not
suffer. Our officials shall endeavor to make it widely known that
the Imperial Court, obeying the mandate of Heaven and the will
of the people, is acting in accordance with justice and rectitude.

Soon after these decrees were issued the Court withdrew to Chengteh, or Jehol City, the capital of Jehol province, as it did in 1860 when combined British and French troops entered Peking and sacked and burned the summer palace as a punishment for the murder of a company of men and officers under a flag of truce. The Manchu Dynasty had always regarded Jehol province as part of its ancestral domain, and had maintained a detached palace in Jehol City.

## IV

Although Emperor Hsuan Tung (Pu-yi) graciously said, or rather was made to say, in his abdication decrees, that he had decided to retire in deference to the will of the people, it was not at all clear that the people preferred a republic to an empire. The revolution of 1911 was, at its inception, the rebellion of the Chinese against the Manchus. It was the old story repeated many times in China's long history—the northern "barbarians" conquering and imposing an alien rule upon the Chinese, but, under the enervating influence of the highly developed civilization of the conquered, gradually losing their vigor and finally giving way to the Chinese power which was certain, sooner or later, to return to the north, usually as far as, but sometimes beyond, the Great Wall. As long as the Manchu Dynasty had sagacious and vigorous leaders, the Chinese were apparently satisfied or acquiescent; but when the scepter passed into feeble hands, with consequent misrule and corruption among the officials, the old feeling of racial antagonism cropped up among the Chinese.

Had the Manchu Government at that moment proposed that it would surrender China proper to the Chinese, retire to Mukden and establish an independent Manchurian state, the revolutionists would have accepted the proposal without hesitation. With the exception of a few leaders, the revolutionists had no definite idea as to what sort of government they were going to set up. They adopted republican government simply because that seemed to be the quickest way out. As for the multitudes, they cared nothing about republican principles, and thought, perhaps hoped, that another emperor would soon come to grace the dragon throne. As recently as 1921—ten years after the abdication of Emperor Hsuan Tung—Mr. J. O. P. Bland, one of the few Occidentals who know China thoroughly, declared that "only the hour and the Man are needed to restore to the allegiance of the Son of Heaven most of the men who now prudently profess and call themselves Republicans," and that "in every house throughout Peking a dragon flag lies folded away" awaiting the day when it shall again be unfolded to the breeze.

And indeed those dragon flags did wave over Peking for a week in July, 1917, when that picturesque pig-tailed general, Chang Hsun, made a serio-comic attempt to restore Pu-yi to the throne. For that brief week edicts and decrees were issued in the Emperor's name. Had Chang Hsun been actuated by a sincere desire to promote national welfare, the attempt to restore the imperial régime might have succeeded. But Chang was insincere. He was concerned with his own interests and was unwilling to agree to a fair division of the spoils of office. As a matter of fact, "nearly every high official in Peking," as Mr. Bland says, "was a party to the scheme" and was eager to see the Emperor brought back to power. Only because Chang was blinded by greed did the scheme fail.

According to Mr. Bland,* the "Western-learning section of Young China, which holds official positions at Peking, displays no violent opposition" to the restoration of imperial rule. "In the South, and especially amongst the vociferous section of students and journalists, which lives by and for political agitation in the shelter of the Treaty Ports, they will tell you that the restoration of the Throne is impossible, and that the Republic represents a genuine expression of the people's fixed will. Times being as they are, theirs are the opinions which reach and impress England and America; nevertheless, I have no hesitation in saying that they are wrong, and that the movement for the restoration of the Throne will eventually have the hearty approval of the vast majority of the people. They will welcome it, not only because the Dragon Throne has been for ages an essential part of the Confucian system, inseparable from the ideas of an agricultural race born and bred on patriarchal Theism, but also because of the callous corruption and disorder with which the present administration has become identified all over the country."

## V

Pu-yi's vicissitudes came to a tragic culmination in October, 1924, when the so-called Christian General, Feng Yu-hsiang, invaded the imperial palaces with his troops and ejected him therefrom at the point of a gun, in utter disregard of the abdication agreements of 1911. He was divested of his titles and property and was told that henceforth he would be known as plain "Mr." Though stripped of the last vestige of his imperial dignity and divested of his property, the unhappy Pu-yi was still under

* In his *China, Japan and Korea*, published by Charles Scribner's Sons. Reprinted by permission.

rigid surveillance of Feng's soldiers and was, moreover, in constant danger of assassination—so much so that Sir Reginald Johnston, his British tutor, contrived by a clever ruse to get him to the German Hospital in the Legation Quarter where no Chinese soldier or police could molest him. While Pu-yi was in the hospital, writes Mr. H. G. W. Woodhead, C.B.E., the well-known editor of the *China Year Book,* "efforts were made to find a refuge for him, and the first application was to the British Legation. It was only when it was found that there was no building there available for the Emperor's use that his tutor applied to the Japanese Legation, which agreed to place a small building in the Legation Guard Compound at his disposal. It was equally untrue that the Emperor was 'spirited to the Japanese Concession in Tientsin.' His escape from the Japanese Legation came as a complete surprise, and was an extremely hazardous adventure. For the Emperor, who had never travelled by train before, found himself *en route* to Tientsin, in a third class compartment, between two of Marshal Feng Yu-hsiang's soldiers. As soon as his flight was discovered the Japanese consular authorities in Tientsin were notified, and he was met and escorted to a hotel, on arrival. The Emperor had some personal property in the British Municipal Area, and it was his original intention to reside there. But difficulties arose in connection with adequate police protection, and it was only then that he decided to take up his residence in the Japanese Concession."

Thus did Emperor Hsuan Tung become Mr. Pu-yi, under the compulsion of a satanic general who was then in virtual control of Peking and its government. When the general's soldiers invaded the imperial sanctum they produced a document and asked the Emperor to sign it.

It declared that the Emperor renounced his title and his palaces, together with the annuity of 4,000,000 *yuan* a year, all for a solatium of 500,000 *yuan*. The Emperor refused to sign it. In an interview soon after the *coup d'état* Mr. Pu-yi said:

> I did not sign that paper, whatever may be said to the contrary. And I do not accept it. Not that I would not have agreed to a revision of the Abdication Treaty. I simply ask that the revision be done in a proper way, that I be given courteous treatment. (*North China Daily News,* November 24, 1924.)

Even a China which had, through twenty years of chaos and turmoil, become utterly callous to all sense of propriety or justice, could not but be shocked by this outrage. Tang Shao-yi, one of the negotiators of the abdication treaty on the Republican side, wondered "whether there is any sense of decency left in the land." Dr. Hu Shih, one of the best-known modern scholars in China, admitted that it was "a disgraceful proceeding, which will go down in history as the most unsavory act of the Chinese Republic."

In the light of the foregoing, it is perfectly clear why Mr. Pu-yi is now in Manchoukuo as Chief Executive. He is no interloper. This is his home. If he were to forget it, all his ancestral tablets in Mukden, former capital of Manchuria, would be a constant reminder. And, finally, there must always remain with the new Regent the memory of the 'unsavory' insult to which he was subjected by the Chinese Government. No further obligation rests upon him to respect the abdication treaty. It was torn up on his doorstep. There must be a question in Mr. Pu-yi's mind whether by that very act the Chinese had not sacri-

ficed all moral right to Manchuria. The same question
may have been in the thoughts of the outraged Chinese,
for in 1924 Tang Shao-yi said:

> The Manchus have property in China. Some of the property is
> their own; that is, they had it before they became Emperors. Some
> is family property. If a change is to be made, there must be an
> arrangement on this question. We cannot steal a man's property
> simply because he was formerly an Emperor. The moral sense of
> the Chinese people rejects that sort of treatment. (*Peking Daily
> News,* November 15, 1924.)

Was Mr. Tang referring to Manchuria? In Manchu
eyes Manchuria meets all the requirements of family property before and after the Manchus became Emperors. It
was their private estate up till 1907. It was their vice-
royalty from 1907 until 1911. It was then resigned by
treaty in return for certain rights which the Chinese stole
in 1924.

This, I think, is the view held by most of the fair-
minded Chinese and foreigners in China. And yet the
Nationalist Government declared Pu-yi a traitor to the
Republic when he became the head of Manchoukuo. "It
is preposterous," writes Mr. Woodhead in the *Shanghai
Evening Post,* "to describe Mr. Pu-yi as a betrayer of
China. The abdication decrees, signed in his name, em-
bodied a solemn pact between the Imperial Family and
the Republic. Every condition of that pact, so far as the
treatment of the Emperor is concerned, has been violated.
He has been deprived of his title and dispossessed of his
private property; the promised annuity has never been
forthcoming; the Imperial Tombs, instead of being pro-
tected, have been violated and rifled by Republican troops.

It cannot seriously be pretended that an ex-Monarch, thus treated, owes any loyalty to the nation or the government over which he formerly ruled."

## VI

There remain to be noted Mr. Pu-yi's education and training, his character and personality. From 1918 up till a few years ago he had an able British tutor in the person of Sir Reginald Johnston, one-time magistrate of the former British leased territory of Weihaiwei. According to Sir Reginald, who has genuine affection for his imperial pupil:

Mr. Pu-yi is today a young man with all the charming manners of his race and with the keenest interest in the affairs of the modern world. He speaks some English—enough for ordinary purposes—and is well-versed in English and American history; rather more in English history, perhaps, for he is greatly interested in the growth of the English constitutional monarchy. He is an admirer of the Prince of Wales, of whom he has read for many years. Mussolini is another of his heroes. . . . He is slender in build, with small, well-formed hands. His eyes are dark and his expression is thoughtful, more so, perhaps, than is usual in a young man of his age. . . . He has an inherited poetic gift and has written much classic verse and even some of the modern verse. . . . He has a taste for good literature. . . . He has also learned the art of calligraphy from his tutors. This is one of the fine arts in China and his excellence in it has repeatedly won the admiration of experts. He writes English, too, with a very bold and well-formed hand. He has never been taught to draw either in Chinese or in foreign style, but he has a native talent which enables him to produce very vivid and rapid sketches. Perhaps the most noteworthy thing about him—certainly to one who knew the tyrannical conservatism of the old imperial palace—is his readiness to listen to new ideas, his tolerance, the voracity with which he devours the newspapers and his immeasurable advance in familiarity with the social and political worlds of both East and West.

While still in his palace in Peking, Pu-yi had three other tutors—two Chinese and one Manchu. The Manchu, who was Pu-yi's guardian as well as his tutor, taught him the language and literature of his forefathers. From one of the Chinese tutors, Pu-yi learned the teachings of Confucius and the rest of the Chinese classics, while from the other he acquired the art of calligraphy. It was his wont to rise at dawn and commence his study of the Chinese classics at six o'clock. Like all Chinese imbued with classical ideals, Mr. Pu-yi assumed an attitude of reverential respect toward his tutors, and addressed them in punctilious deference.

That Pu-yi is endowed with keen intellect there is little doubt. Mr. Bland, in his thought-provoking book, *China, Japan and Korea,* tells us that "he (Mr. Pu-yi) followed the negotiations of the Versailles Conference from day to day with critical attention, studying the course of events as described in the Chinese press by the aid of the best maps procurable, and asking questions which showed a remarkable grasp of the general situation. On one occasion, for example, he complained to Mr. Johnston that the boundaries of Luxembourg were not clearly shown on his map of Europe." And he was only fourteen years old then.

Mr. Pu-yi is interested in various forms of exercise, but is particularly fond of tennis. He is also interested in modern mechanical instruments. When, some time in 1920, Sir Reginald Johnston—at the request of Hsu Shih-chang, then President of China—asked Mr. Pu-yi what he would like to have for presents on his next birthday he answered,

"Corona typewriter." He had been eager to acquire the modern art of typewriting.

Mr. Pu-yi's given name, Henry, is derived from Henry VIII, for whom he cherishes admiration. Upon his consort, a Manchu, he bestowed the name of Elizabeth, in honor of the great British queen. While they still lived in the Forbidden City, the "Empress," (or Lady Pu-yi,) had two American tutors, Misses Miriam and Isabel Ingram, daughters of a Congregational missionary from Philadelphia.

## VII

When Pu-yi left his abode in Tientsin toward the end of November 1931 and went to Manchuria, news went the rounds of the press of the world that he had been "kidnapped" by the Japanese and was spirited away to Port Arthur on a Japanese destroyer. This was a malicious piece of propaganda emanating from Chinese sources. Mr. Woodhead, generally known among the Chinese and the foreigners in China as a most conscientious and independent critic, interviewed Pu-yi on October 2, 1932, and asked the former Emperor whether he had come to Manchuria "kidnapped" by the Japanese. Pu-yi "roared with laughter," repeating, "Kidnapped? Kidnapped? No! No!" Mr. Pu-yi and Mr. Woodhead had been intimate friends, as the British writer was the editor of a British newspaper in Tientsin while the former Emperor lived in the Japanese concession in the same city. Mr. Pu-yi told Mr. Woodhead that "when he decided to leave Tientsin for Manchuria, he did not even take the Japanese Consul General into his confidence. His movements had to be kept secret for two reasons: first, because his departure from Tientsin might have been frustrated; secondly, because he would have been in considerable danger of assassination had his whereabouts been revealed."

Mr. Woodhead writes further:

"Mr. Pu-yi left Tientsin just as the trouble between the Japanese and Chinese in that city started, and travelled direct to Yinkow [Newchwang] on the ordinary steamer *Awachi Maru*. He left a letter behind to be delivered to the Japanese Consul General, informing him of his departure and asking him to afford adequate protection to the Empress (who remained in his residence in the Japanese Concession) when she followed. From Newchwang he proceeded to Tang Kung Tzu (the hot springs between Liao-yang and Tashihchao), where he remained only a couple of days, returning to meet his wife at Port Arthur. She also travelled on an ordinary steamer. The next few weeks were spent at that center where he amused himself by studying the siege operations in the Russo-Japanese War and visiting the ruins of the former Russian fortifications. He and his wife then returned to Tang Kung Tzu, where they lived quietly until he proceeded to Changchun on March 8, 1932. When he was convinced that it was his duty to go North and assume the office of Chief Executive, he went straight through to Changchun by train. At no time in Tientsin, in the leased Territory, or in Manchuria was he ever under any restraint, nor was any coercion applied to him. The former Emperor emphasized that I had seen from my own experience how nonsensical the stories told about his position in Changchun were. Here we were, talking without restriction; with only a young Chinese present, who made no attempt to direct the course of conversation, and who only interpreted my remarks and questions when Mr. Pu-yi did not understand them; with no Japanese within hearing and absolutely no restriction upon the topics discussed. Could I, he asked, really believe that he was virtually a State Prisoner under such conditions?"

Mr. Pu-yi told Mr. Woodhead that he had been actuated by a double motive in accepting the office of Chief Executive. First, on account of political reasons. The Manchu Dynasty had abdicated with the avowed intention of restoring the sovereignty to the people. Twenty years had elapsed since, but what had been the result? The political power relinquished by the Dynasty had passed into the hands, not of the people, but, of ambitious and grasping militarists. There had been incessant civil war and disorder. The welfare of the people had been entirely disregarded. They had been tyrannized over and oppressed. China's relations with foreign powers had grown steadily worse. And the pledge made in the abdication treaty that absolute equality would be maintained between the five races of China had been flagrantly violated. Secondly, he was actuated by personal motives. Manchuria was his ancestral home. It was only natural that he should feel greatly interested in what was happening in this territory. Moreover, every undertaking to the Manchu Dynasty contained in the abdication agreement had been wantonly violated. The allowance to be paid to him by the State had been cancelled. His private property had been confiscated. He had been treated with studied disrespect by the Kuomintang. And the ancestral tombs had been violated, and no serious attempt made to secure the restoration of the treasures stolen from them. It was only natural, therefore, that when trouble occurred in

Manchuria he should follow developments with great attention and wonder whether he was not destined to play some part in an attempt to improve the condition of his ancestral province. Emissaries of the separatist movement called upon him in Tientsin and urged him to proceed to Manchuria. And at last he felt that if he were ever to go he must go forthwith, or he might find it impossible to leave.

VIII

As I was motoring back to my hotel through muddy, squalid back-streets and through the narrow, crowded, ill-smelling main thoroughfare of Changchun, my thoughts, wafted upon the wings of the imagination, wandered far across the plains of Manchuria, over the majestic Great Wall and into the ancient city of Peking, whose imperial magnificence, though fast fading in the chaos that had been China for twenty years, still afforded a striking contrast to this mean, drab Manchurian city of Changchun. Pu-yi still regards the Forbidden City in Peking as his own. It was his under the abdication treaty, and it is even more so since that compact has been torn to pieces by the Chinese, thus leaving Pu-yi free to fall back upon his original status, regarding all that he possessed before 1911 as his heritage bequeathed by his great ancestors. He knows that furled away in countless homes and shops of Peking are dragon flags awaiting the day when they shall again be unfurled for the Son of Heaven. As Mr. Frank Hedges, an American journalist who lived in China for years, aptly says, "There are millions of Chinese to whom the republican form of government means nothing and who would welcome the return of their

Emperor, for they need him as a concrete symbol of sovereignty."

In the light of all this, will Mr. Pu-yi be contented to stay indefinitely in Changchun? Will his Government remain there permanently? Is he not dreaming of the grandeur that was once Peking and looking back with longing eyes to the glorious days when his illustrious sires, especially Kwang Hsi and Chin Lung, reigning in accordance with the precepts of *Wangtao,* the *Way of the King,* gave the people of China peace, prosperity, and happiness?

Yet it would be a great mistake for him to venture forth beyond the Great Wall; he would simply be following in the evil footsteps of the Changs, whose adventures in China were the chief cause of their downfall. The only sane course for Pu-yi lies in strict observance of the regional ideal of *Pao-Ching An-Min,* "Peace within the Boundaries, Security for the People."

### *Postscript*

Press dispatches, dated Peiping, February 6, 1933, reported that 3,000 cases of art treasures were hauled out of the former imperial palaces and trundled to the railway station to be shipped to a certain destination—possibly Nanking or Shanghai. That these treasures are Pu-yi's private property none will dispute. For years they have been coveted by foreign art dealers and collectors. Once they are removed from the Forbidden City, they are sure to pass into foreign hands, for China has no respect for such objects of art, as witness the deplorable neglect and decay which is the general condition of her historic structures and monuments. The announcement made by Chang Hsueh-liang, that these art treasures are being car-

ried away to forestall their possible seizure by the Japanese
in the event of Japanese capture of Peiping, is a smoke
screen too transparent to conceal the real motive. Few
nations have deeper respect for ancient treasures than the
Japanese, as is shown in the condition of historic shrines,
castles, museums, statues, etc., in Japan. In Mukden the
Japanese have a plan to establish a museum for the safe-
keeping of such of the Manchu treasures as have remained
in Manchuria, escaping the Changs' spoliations. Chang's
seizure of Pu-yi's treasures in the Forbidden City affords
a significant contrast to the manner in which the Japanese handled Chang's private property which was found
in his mansions in Mukden at the time of the September,
1931, incident. The Japanese carefully packed such property in hundreds of cases and shipped them to Chang at
Peiping. Had Chang been a gentleman or a soldier with
any sense of honor, those art treasures, which he is sending south to be sold, no doubt, for the sinews of war or
for the maintenance of his numerous wives, should have
been sent to Pu-yi, to whom they rightfully belong.

# CHAPTER VII

## THE GOVERNMENT OF MANCHOUKUO

### I

On May 4, 1932, the League of Nations Commission, entrusted with the investigation of the Sino-Japanese imbroglio, interviewed Premier Cheng Hsiao-hsu, of the Manchoukuo Government, at Changchun which, under the new name of Hsinking, meaning "New Capital," had become the seat of that Government. The Commission wanted to know how Mr. Cheng happened to become Prime Minister. The aged poet-statesman replied that when he was in Port Arthur with Mr. Pu-yi, a deputation came to invite the former Emperor to become Chief Executive of the new State, and that he became Prime Minister at the request of the Chief Executive, of whom he had been a faithful adherent for more than twenty years.

Then the Commission asked about the date when the said deputation came to Port Arthur. The Premier's memory was not clear but it was some time in February, he said. How was that deputation elected? The Premier did not know. What were the names of the deputies? Again the Premier did not know.

Was Mr. Cheng too much of a poet to remember such mundane matters? Or did he think that it was no business of the League's to nose into such details, which were

DIAGRAM OF THE ORGANIZATION OF THE MANCHOUKUO GOVERNMENT

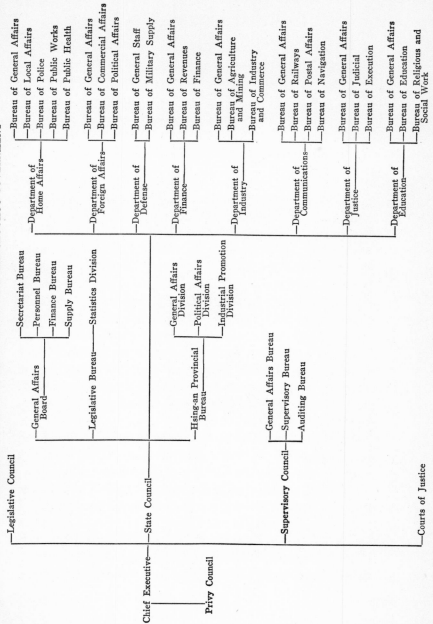

exclusively Manchoukuo's domestic affairs? The Premier, though aged, is alert and keen-witted. Surely he could have enlightened the Commission on those points had he cared to do so, for they had been matters of record. He might have been somewhat irritated by the inquisition to which he was submitted. "Are your civil laws codified?" "Your Constitution?" "What is your economic policy?" "How about your finance?" "What are the ideals of the new State?" The Premier replied that Manchoukuo had only been born; that its unhappy heritage from the old régime was financial chaos, economic dislocation, and banditry; that its first task, which had been demanding its absorbing attention, was to suppress banditry, restore order, and establish a uniform and sound currency as an initial step toward economic rehabilitation. He might have expounded *Wangtao,* the *Way of the King,* in reply to the last of the above-named questions, but he did not. Did he think that the Western "barbarians" would not understand such ideals anyway?

On the other hand, the League Commissioners might have remembered that Manchoukuo was not quite two months old. They might have remembered, too, that none of their own countries "just growed like Topsy," adopting a constitution, codifying civil laws, definitely formulating its economic and financial policies, etc., all in less than two months. But they did not. Neither did they remember that they were uninvited guests, having come to Manchoukuo only at its sufferance. Manchoukuo never asked the League to investigate Manchoukuo. The new State came into existence three months after the League had decided upon dispatching the Commission to the scene of conflict. A Manchoukuo official, a Chinese, said to me last autumn:

"If the League wants to study why Japan and China have been playing cat and dog, let it go to it. If Japan and China wish to be investigated, they can have all the investigation the League can make, at their cost. As for Manchoukuo, it has no use for investigation."

This feeling of aloofness was made all the more intense by the studied insult displayed by the Lytton Commission in refusing to communicate with the Manchoukuo Government for permission to enter its territory. But for Japanese persuasion Manchoukuo would have barred out the Commission. Personally I feel that Japan should have let Manchoukuo decide upon the question for itself.

II

To supply the apparent deficiency in Premier Cheng's memory, the delegation which went to Port Arthur to invite Mr. Pu-yi consisted of six men—Chang Yen-ching (now Minister of Industry), Chao Hsin-po (now President of the Legislative Council), Feng Han-ching (now Minister of Justice), Pao Kwang (now Vice-Minister of Civil Affairs), Ling Sheng (representative of the Barga Mongols), and Su Pao-lin. This deputation was chosen by the All-Manchuria Independence Conference held at Mukden on February 29, 1932, by some 700 representatives of the various provinces and *hsiens* (prefectures), of the Mongol leagues, of various guilds and chambers of commerce, of the Koreans in Kirin province and in Harbin, etc. It was this conference which unanimously nominated Pu-yi as Chih-Cheng, or Chief Executive, of the new State.

The above-named deputation of six waited upon Mr. Pu-yi at Port Arthur on February 30, and urged him to accept the nomination. Mr. Pu-yi replied that the proposal was too grave to be decided upon at once, and that he must have some time to think it over. On March 4 the above deputation, augmented by twenty-three new delegates, again waited on Pu-yi. This time the former Emperor agreed to head the new Government, but on condition that he should be relieved of his duties at the end of his first year of office if the people were not satisfied with his rule. Whereupon, on March 5, the Northeastern Administrative Committee, which had issued the Declaration of Independence on February 18 (see Chapter III), went to Port Arthur to notify Mr. Pu-yi of his nomination as Chief Executive. On March 6 Mr. Pu-yi, escorted by the Committee, went to Tang Kuang Tse and, after staying at this spa two days, arrived at Changchun, the seat of the new Government, on March 8. On March 9 he was officially inaugurated as head of Manchoukuo.

### III

As I see it, the goal of Manchoukuo is a constitutional monarchy. Mr. Pu-yi may not assume the title of King or Emperor. But what, after all, is in a name? Both the Chief Executive and the Prime Minister, thanks, perhaps, to Sir Reginald Johnston's influence, are admirers of the British system of government. Their espousal of *Wang-tao,* the *Way of the King,* as the guiding principle of the new State may be an indication of their desire to combine the modern constitutionalism of the Occident with the ancient ideals of China. They know, too, that even so distinguished an American scholar as Dr. Frank N. Goodnow had recommended to China a constitutional monarchy as opposed to republicanism. Furthermore, Henry

Pu-yi cherishes a fond memory of the ill-fated constitutional movement launched in 1898 by his uncle, Emperor Kwang Hsu (1875-1908), who had come under the influence of the Cantonese liberal Kang Yu-wei. Emperor Kwang Hsu issued numerous decrees which, if carried into effect, were calculated to bring about the most far-reaching reform. But the autocratic Empress Dowager Tzu Hsi, that terrible conservative who later indirectly encouraged the Boxer rebellion, took alarm at the youthful Emperor's liberal policies and, coming from behind the dragon throne, snatched the scepter from his hand and virtually made him a prisoner of state in a secluded palace. Now Henry Pu-yi is said to cherish a desire to revive Emperor Kwang Hsu's plan, which was so brutally nipped in the bud.

In the meantime, Manchoukuo is governed by a set of laws which were drafted by Dr. Chao Hsin-po (one of the principal figures in the independence movement and at present President of the Legislative Council) and his colleagues, assisted by Japanese jurists, and which were promulgated on March 9 when the new State was formally inaugurated. Taken together, these laws constitute a sort of provisional constitution. The Government's plan is to organize a Legislative Council as soon as circumstances will permit, and submit to it a permanent constitution. How soon this will be done is not as yet decided upon. The Chinese "Republic" adopted a provisional constitution in November, 1911, but its permanent constitution was not adopted till October, 1923. Manchoukuo may not wait so long, but it thinks it the part of wisdom to allow the provisional constitutional laws, now in effect, an ample period of experiment to the end that such shortcomings as may be found in them shall be remedied in the permanent constitution.

Pending the organization of the Legislative Council, provided for in the Organic Law, all legislative and budgetary bills will be enacted by the State Council and will be promulgated as ordinances with the approval of the Privy Council and the sanction of the Chief Executive. The Legislative Council is to be a unicameral body whose organization is yet to be determined by law. It will, however, probably consist of some 300 members, that is, one to each 300,000 of the population, to be elected by local assemblies, whose members will be elected by popular vote with certain property and age qualifications.

The frame work of the government as it stands may be briefly described. The Chief Executive is "nominated by" and "responsible to" the people. This is the ancient doctrine of *Wangtao* expressed in modern constitutional terms, for, according to *Wangtao,* the mandate of Heaven by which the ruler rules is a reflection of popular approval. The Chief Executive exercises legislative, administrative, and judicial powers in accordance with the law and with the approval or assistance of the various Councils. He may issue orders for the execution of laws passed by the Legislative Council, but he has no authority to revise laws, this authority being reserved by the said Council. He may, however, issue emergency mandates with the approval of the Privy Council. In such cases he is required to submit reports to the earliest session of the Legislative Council.

The Chief Executive, unless otherwise provided by the organic or other laws, determines the "organization of the administration, the appointment and dismissal of officials and their salaries." He has the power to declare war, make peace, and conclude treaties. This is more or less a legal fiction, for, as a matter of fact, this power will be exercised by the State Council, which corresponds to the Cabinet in other countries. From the above it is clear that the Chief Executive exercises all the authorities usually exercised by a constitutional monarch.

The supreme advisory body to the Chief Executive is the Privy Council, whose membership is left undetermined by the provisional constitution. At present it consists of six Manchurians (that is, Chinese) and two Japanese. The Council, when consulted by the Chief Executive, expresses its views on proposed laws and mandates, budgets, treaties and agreements with foreign nations, major appointments and dismissals of officials, and other important matters of state.

The State Council, which is practically the Cabinet of Manchoukuo, is composed of the Premier and the Ministers of Civil Affairs, Foreign Affairs, Defense, Finance, Industry, Communications, Justice and Education. In the Organic Law there is no provision for the Department of Education, because when the law was issued, educational matters were in the hands of the *Tse Cheng Chii,* or Advisory Bureau, under the direct supervision of the Prime Minister. Since then the Advisory Bureau has been abolished, and education has been assigned to an independent department. The Premier presides over the State Council meetings consisting of Ministers of Departments, the Chief of the General Affairs Board of the State Council, the Chief of the Legislative Bureau and the Chief of the Hsingan Provincial Board. The State Council has the power to deliberate and decide upon (1) laws, ordinances,

CHENG HSIAO-HSU
PREMIER OF MANCHOUKUO

military orders and the budget, (2) treaties and important diplomatic matters, (3) disputes between various Departments over their respective jurisdiction, (4) expenditures not included in the budget, and (5) other important matters of state.

Then there is the Supervisory Council, whose function is to "supervise and audit the accounts." This Council is "directly subordinate to the Chief Executive and independent of the State Council." This is to maintain independence of judgment on the part of the Supervisors and Auditors. Like judges, they are appointed for life and "shall not be subject to suspension, transfer of position and office, or reduction of salary, against their wish."

## IV

A peculiar feature of the State Council is its Board of General Affairs which has exercised, and still exercises, great powers. The chief of this Board may be called Chief Assistant to the Prime Minister. The Board consists of the Secretariat Bureau, the Personnel Bureau, the Financial Bureau, and the Supply Bureau. The Secretariat takes charge of these matters: (1) confidential matters, (2) proclamations of laws, mandates, military orders, ordinances and orders of the State Council, (3) custody of official seals, (4) dispatches and receipts of official communications, (5) publications, (6) accounting and general office affairs.

To the Personnel Bureau are assigned the following functions: (1) appointment and dismissal, promotion and demotion of officials, (2) discipline, reward, and punishment of officials, (3) salaries and treatment, (4) elections of delegates.

The Financial Bureau controls the following matters: (1) general budget and general settlement of accounts, (2) budget for special accounts and their settlement, (3) management of national resources and funds, (4) receipts and expenditure of the national treasury, (5) classification of receipts and expenditures. Finally, the Supply Bureau controls constructions and repairs and other related matters.

Over all of these bureaus the Prime Minister has direct control, but the actual work is, or was at first, done by the Chief of the General Affairs Board. From the inauguration of the Manchoukuo Government on March 9, 1932 to September, 1932, this chief was Mr. Tokuzo Komai, a civilian Japanese who had for many years been interested in Chinese affairs and who had been most actively associated with the Manchurian separatists since the beginning of 1932.

But on October 3, 1932, Mr. Komai resigned the post and was appointed member of the Privy Council, the Premier himself assuming most of the powers formerly exercised by Komai. With Mr. Komai's resignation, the office of the Chief of the General Affairs Board was abolished. Although Mr. Kiichi Sakatani, formerly Chief of the General Affairs Bureau of the Finance Department, succeeded Mr. Komai, his official title is "Secretary-General" instead of "Chief" of the General Affairs Board, and his authority is much smaller than was exercised by Mr. Komai.

The General Affairs Board is a unique office devised to meet the exigencies of the new government which had so suddenly come into existence. For the sake of efficiency and to expedite quick decision and execution, it was found necessary to institute within the government a strong central body under the direct control of the Premier and consisting of able administrators. Mr. Komai himself was not an experienced administrator, but he gathered around him a staff of able Japanese. Of 135 officials of the Board, only 35 were Chinese. Japanese were especially numerous in the Finance and Supply Bureaus of the Board. Both Premier Cheng and Mr. Komai were of the opinion that the Government of Manchoukuo must start its history with "clean hands," absolutely free from the irregularities, corruption, and peculation which had characterized the old régime under the war lords, and which marred all governments in China proper. In the initial stage of the new State the various administrative departments were not sufficiently coördinated. It was feared that the more or less confused state then prevailing might be utilized by some officials for selfish purposes. To meet this extraordinary situation was the object of the General Affairs Board, which controlled appointments and dismissals of officials in all Departments, as well as budgetary matters and purchases. Under the old régime, most appointments were obtained by bribing superior officials. This is the system which still prevails in China. From the beginning, the new Government of Manchoukuo was determined to abolish this age-long squeeze system. Furthermore, it was imperative that the Government should prevent the creation of unnecessary offices for office-seekers, and that only meritorious men should be appointed to positions in which their respective abilities could best be utilized.

But, as the various Departments are better organized and more effectively coördinated, the General Affairs

Board is prepared to relinquish some of its powers. For instance, budgetary matters and purchases will in time be transferred to the Department of Finance. In time each Department will be authorized to appoint and dismiss officials within its own jurisdiction—a power which has been exercised by the General Affairs Board for all Departments.

With the change in the status of the General Affairs Board, the powers of the Premier will also undergo a change. Formerly the Premier alone countersigned ordinances issued in the name of the Chief Executive, but since October 3, 1932 they have been countersigned both by him and by the Minister of the Department concerned. For instance, an ordinance regarding education is countersigned by the Premier and the Minister of Education. Again, a financial ordinance bears the signatures of the Premier and the Finance Minister. And so forth. This is only a step toward a wider distribution of responsibility.

Just as there is the General Affairs Board in the State Council so is there in each of the eight Departments of Government a General Affairs Bureau, which exercises controlling influence over the other bureaus in the same Department.

v

In the foregoing paragraphs the position of Japanese officials in the Manchoukuo Government has been intimated. So important is the matter that it calls for elucidation.

The central government of Manchoukuo comprises 846 officials. These are classified as follows:

I. Officials appointed by the Chief Executive; namely, Presidents of the various Councils, Privy Councillors, and Ministers of the various Departments, receiving salaries of 20,000 *yuan* to 30,000 *yuan* a year.

II. Officials by special appointment, including vice-Ministers and some of the Bureau Chiefs, receiving salaries of 16,000 *yuan* to 17,000 *yuan* a year.

III. Officials appointed by recommendation, whose salaries range from 3,600 *yuan* to 15,000 *yuan* a year.

IV. Minor officials, whose monthly salaries vary from 70 *yuan* to 360 *yuan*.

Of the first class, 15 are Manchurians (Chinese and Manchus) and 2 Japanese.

Of the second, 7 are Manchurians and 27 Japanese.

Of the third, 113 are Manchurians and 151 Japanese.

Of the fourth, 377 are Manchurians and 154 Japanese.

All in all, there are 512 Manchurians as compared with 234 Japanese. But these figures do not disclose the real nature of relative importance. As a matter of fact, the Japanese officials exercise greater influence than is indicated by the figures because they occupy most of the key positions to which are assigned the most important and responsible work.

All Ministers of Departments are Chinese, or to be exact, seven Chinese and a Manchu. So are vice-Ministers, except the vice-Minister of Foreign Affairs (who is a Japanese, Mr. Chiuchi Ohashi, formerly Consul General at Harbin). Of 27 Bureau Chiefs, 17 are Japanese and 10 Chinese.

How long the Japanese will continue to exercise such great authority in the Manchoukuo Government depends upon the degree of progress their Manchurian colleagues and assistants will make. Thus far it has been absolutely necessary that the Japanese should be placed in responsible positions, as it has been impossible to find efficient administrators in sufficient numbers to organize the government.

Nevertheless, this condition cannot continue indefinitely. If it is not gradually changed, dissatisfaction is bound to appear among the Chinese. Last autumn Mr. Ting Chien-hsiu, Minister of Communications, said to me:

If my house were on fire, I would ask firemen to put it out. I would not tell them how to fight the fire, for they would know their job better than I would. But when the fire is extinguished I should like to build a house to suit *me,* and not the firemen.

Since September, 1931, Manchuria has been on fire. We are glad that the Japanese have been here to fight the fire. But the fire will soon be extinguished and we shall begin to build. As a matter of fact, we have already begun to build. We must make sure that the new house, when completed, will be comfortable and convenient to *us,* not to the firemen.

We do not deny that in this construction work we need your help. We know we could not build without your assistance. At the same time we should like to feel that we are building our own house. Let us put it this way—we would gladly let you determine the general design of the house, but as to the details of construction work we should like to attend to them ourselves. We shall continue to call upon you for help. We shall want a Japanese adviser of big caliber in each of our Departments and our Councils; we shall need Japanese technical experts to train our officials; but, at the same time, we must be sure that the house we are now building will suit us.

With this point of view the Japanese should have no quarrel. But in order to bring about the desired change in the relative positions of the Manchurian and Japanese officials, it is most essential that the Chinese should make a radical departure from certain old traditions which have been the bane of all Chinese governments. From time immemorial it has been the practice among Chinese officials of high rank to provide jobs for their relatives and friends, regardless of their merits or usefulness. The same practice has been common among corporation officials, which explains why China has few successful corporations on a large scale. Already the capital of Manchoukuo swarms with relatives, friends, and servants of the Chinese who occupy high positions in the new Government.

Then, too, the official practice of "squeeze," so rampant in China for unnumbered ages, must be done away with. As so keen a critic of Chinese characteristics as Arthur Henderson Smith, for twenty-two years a missionary in China, observes, "The Chinese, with that practical sagacity for which they are so deservedly noted, have reduced this business [of squeeze] to a perfect system, which can no more be escaped than one escapes the pressure of the atmosphere. Vicious and demoralizing as the system is, it is not easy to see how it can be done away with, except by a complete reorganization of the empire."

Premier Cheng is fully conscious of this baneful system, which has been the curse of all Chinese governments, whether imperial, republican or nationalist, and is sincerely solicitous that it should be kept out of Manchoukuo. That is why, at the initial stage of the new Government, the Premier, with the aid of Mr. Komai, Chief of the General Affairs Board, put budgetary matters and disbursements, as well as appointments and dismissals, under his direct control. It also explains why the salaries of the Manchoukuo officials, as is shown in the above classification of ranks, are far more generous than were paid by the old régimes. They are much higher than the salaries of Japanese officials. The Prime Minister of Japan, for instance, receives 9,600 *yen* a year, while the Manchoukuo Premier is paid 30,000 *yuan*. Again, a Cabinet Minister in Japan receives 6,800 *yen* a year as compared with 25,000 *yuan* paid a Manchoukuo Minister. This ratio, roughly speaking, holds good as regards the salaries of all other officials of the Manchoukuo Government.

VI

A radical departure of the new Government from the old system is the centralization of provincial administration except in the case of the predominantly Mongol province of Hsingan. Under the old régime, provincial governors administered both military and civil affairs. They were military governors and had armies of their own which were nominally controlled by the Central Government, but whose allegiance was always uncertain. For the maintenance of their respective armies, the military governors collected exorbitant taxes in addition to the sums they were required to send to the Central Government.

Under the new régime this system has been effectively abolished. The provincial governors are now civilians and have no control over military forces. Furthermore, they are no longer permitted to collect arbitrary taxes. All funds collected must be forwarded to the Central Government, which in turn defrays all the necessary cost of administration in each province.

Troops stationed in the provinces are now a part of the National Army and are commanded by officers appointed by, and under direct control of, the Central Government.

Their cost of maintenance is borne entirely by the Central treasury. In adopting this radical innovation, the Manchoukuo Government has found it necessary to replace some of the old officers, who had been appointees of the old régime, by its own appointees for reasons of efficiency and loyalty. That is why there have been temporary rebellions and disturbances in some of the provinces. The most notorious example is Su Ping-wen, commander at Hailar, who revolted last September, but who has been interned in Siberia since his defeat in December.

The policy of Manchoukuo is to effect a radical reduction in the army and in military expenditure. Under the old régime Marshal Chang had a great army estimated at from 250,000 to 300,000 men. Of these, about 110,000 are still under the Marshal's command on the other side of the Great Wall. Of the rest, about 60,000 have surrendered to the Manchoukuo régime, while 50,000, scattered throughout the country, have been carrying on guerrilla warfare in different parts of Manchuria. When peace and order are more fully restored, the new Government will proceed to effect the military retrenchment it has in view. This, however, must be done with great caution and by degrees, lest the disbanded soldiers turn bandits. At present, the Manchoukuo army consists of some 116,000 men, mostly an unwanted legacy of the old régime. In time this will probably be cut in half.

Similar reforms have repeatedly been proposed by the Nationalist Government at Nanking in regard to the military forces of China proper. Time and again Nanking announced the nationalization of the armies, but the military chieftains in the various provinces still maintain their "private" armies, levying taxes at their own sweet will.

That explains the reason for perennial civil strife and eternal factional wrangle in China.

Manchoukuo has been able to carry out the desired reform because it had the support and guidance of the Japanese. The removal of this military curse alone is worth all the travail and sacrifices incident to independence.

VII

Finally, a word about Manchoukuo's "Bill of Rights"— namely, the Law for the Guarantee of Civil Rights promulgated on March 9, 1932, simultaneously with the rest of the constitutional laws of the new State. In other countries bills of rights were wrested by popular demand from unwilling monarchs. In Manchoukuo the Law of Civil Rights was voluntarily issued by the Chief Executive.

The law protects the liberty and property rights of the people, regardless of race or religious creed. It also guarantees equality before the law and recognizes the right of the people to present petitions to the Government. In case the rights of any subject of Manchoukuo are violated by the authorities, he is entitled to seek redress in accordance with the law. Furthermore, this law protects the people against the exaction of taxes which are not provided for by the law and "against all forms of practise for excessive profits as well as other forms of unlawful economic oppression."

The last provision is significant. It is meant to forestall any such abuses of governmental power as were perpetrated by the deposed war lord of Manchuria. Under the now defunct war-lordism Manchurian farmers were forced to sell their crops to the Government, which paid for them in worthless inconvertible paper money but sold them to foreigners at Newchwang or Dairen for gold or silver. Sometimes farmers were forced to raise poppy and to sell opium to the war lord for the same worthless currency, thus affording him a fabulous profit. The Law of Civil Rights protects the farmers and others against any such abuses.

# CHAPTER VIII

## MANCHOUKUO'S HELMSMEN

### I

On the eve of the downfall of the Manchu Dynasty in 1911, its Government at Peking was predominantly Manchu. Of the fifteen highest posts in the ministries, nine were held by Manchus, five by Chinese, and one by a Mongol. Of the eleven next highest officials, seven were Manchus, three Chinese, and one Mongol. The revolution of 1911 was in reality the rebellion of the Chinese against the Manchu domination.

Bearing this in mind, it is interesting to observe that the new Government of Manchoukuo has only one Manchu and one Mongol among its higher officials. This Manchu is Hsi Hsia, Minister of Finance; the Mongol is Chi-mo-te-se-mu-pei-le (or Prince Chi), Chief of the Board of Hsingan Provincial Affairs. Though the Chief Executive is a Manchu, he has shown no favoritism toward men of his own race, but has surrounded himself with Chinese. All Cabinet Ministers, except the above-named one, are Chinese. This is perhaps largely due to the dearth of men with administrative ability among the Manchus. At the same time, it is significant that a majority of the Chinese occupying high positions in the Manchoukuo Government are Chinese born and reared in Manchuria and naturally imbued with a strong local feeling, expressed in the well-known slogan *Pao Ching, An-Min,* "Peace within the Borders, Security for the People."

## II

Premier Cheng Hsiao-hsu is not a Manchurian but a native of Fukien province in southern China. Seventy-three years of age, the Premier was a distinguished official in the old Manchu Government at Peking. Sir Reginald Johnston, long tutor to Mr. Pu-yi, has said of him, recently:

His name and reputation stand extremely high in those scholarly circles representative of the "Old China" of the classical tradition. He is undoubtedly one of the most learned and accomplished men of his generation in China, and is perhaps the most distinguished of living Chinese poets. Cheng Su-k'an (Su-k'an is his familiar name) is not only an eminent scholar and poet, but also a great calligraphist. . . . This means that he is among the first of living artists. He is by no means a young man, for he has reached the early seventies, but he is full of vitality and intellectual energy and looks at least a dozen years less than his age. Under the Empire . . . he received various high appointments, including the post of Chief Justice, first in the Province of Anhui, then in Canton. He also held military commands in South China. Subsequently he became an associate of Sheng Hsuan-huai, the well-known administrator-general of railways. He was opposed to the revolution from the beginning, not only because of his devotion to the cause of the Imperial House—with men like Su-k'an loyalty is part of their religion—but also because as a Chinese patriot he sincerely believed, and still believes, that the revolution was a ghastly mistake and a terrible calamity for China.

In 1908 Mr. Cheng, in coöperation with Willard Straight, the late American Consul General at Mukden, and Tang Shao-yi, then Governor of Mukden, broached the plan of building an 800-mile railway between Chin-the plan of building an 800-mile railway between Chin-chow and Aigun in Manchuria, as well as a harbor at Hula Tao as the sea outlet of the projected railway. The project failed partly because of opposition by Russia and Japan, partly because of the death of E. H. Harriman, of Southern Pacific Railway fame, who was the driving force behind the scheme. What irony of fate that this man, once the initiator of a plan which was calculated to cripple the Japanese railway in Manchuria, should now be Premier in a government which depends upon Japanese support!

### III

Yu Ching-han, President of the Supervisory (or Control) Council, was born in Pei-Chi-Hu, Manchuria. When a young man, he was sent to Tokyo by the Imperial Manchu Government for higher education. In 1891 he was appointed magistrate of a prefecture in Jehol. In the first years of the Republican Government he was Governor of Fengtien province, Manchuria. After 1904, he became an adherent of Chang Tso-lin, the late war lord of Manchuria, and was given such important posts as president of the Bank of the Three Eastern Provinces, and director of the Chinese Eastern Railway.

A civilian administrator, Mr. Yu repeatedly remonstrated with Marshal Chang against his policy of carrying costly military campaigns into China proper. When his views were not accepted, he relinquished all official positions under Chang, and entered into business, identifying himself with such enterprises as the Electric Light Company at Liaoyan and the Iron Mills at Anshan. When the

Tzu-Chi-Chitao-pu, or Self-Government Guidance Society, was organized in the wake of the Sino-Japanese
clash of September 18, 1931, at Mukden, he became its
president and did much for the preparation of the popular
mind for the new régime which was bound to be born.
When the Manchoukuo Government was established the
above-named society was dissolved, and Mr. Yu became
President of the Supervisory Council. He died in December, 1932.

#### IV

Chang Ching-hui, President of the Privy Council, is also
a native of Manchuria. Although he was a bandit chief
in his younger days, he served both the Central Government at Peking and the Government at Mukden under
the late Marshal Chang Tso-lin, who was his fellow bandit. Under the Peking Government, Chang Ching-hui
was commander of the first division. When Chang Tso-
lin made himself generalissimo Chang Ching-hui became
war minister under him. From 1929 to September, 1931,
he was governor of the Special Administrative District of
Harbin.

#### V

Hsi Hsia, Minister of Finance, is not only a native of
Manchuria, but a full-blooded Manchu. He received military training at the Military Academy at Tokyo and was
for a time military instructor in the government schools
at Pao-ting-fu and at Mukden. Later he became chief
assistant to the military governor of Kirin province. He
was one of the first to declare independence against the

old régime in September, 1931, when the governor was away in Peiping.

## VI

Tsang Shih-yi, Minister of Civil Affairs, was born in Fengtien province, Manchuria, fifty-four years ago. After graduating from the government Military School at Paoting-fu near Peking, he went to Tokyo to further his military training at the Military Academy there. When Yang Yu-ting was appointed governor of Kiangsu province by the late Manchurian war lord Chang Tso-lin in 1925, Tsang Shih-yi became chief of the general staff under him. Like most Manchurian leaders, Tsang emphatically disapproved of the war lord's reckless politico-military adventures in China proper. For a time he was director of the Mukden Arsenal. From 1929 to the time of the Sino-Japanese incident of September, 1931, he was governor of Fengtien province. Under the new régime of Manchoukuo he is Minister of Civil Affairs in the Central Government and also governor of Fengtien province.

## VII

Hsieh Chieh-shih, Minister of Foreign Affairs, was born of Chinese parentage in Formosa, and studied law at the Meiji University at Tokyo. After graduating from that university, he went to China, became a Chinese subject, and was for a time Chief of the Foreign Affairs Bureau of Chili province. A consistent believer in constitutional monarchy for China, he played a part in the short-lived movement, launched in 1918 by General Chang Hsun, for the restoration of Emperor Hsuan Tung, now Mr. Pu-yi,

to the dragon throne. Although that move ended in a
fiasco, Mr. Hsieh remained loyal to the former Emperor
and never lost hope that he would some day be brought
back to power. Before the outbreak of the Mukden incident of September, 1931, he was a professor at the provincial college in Kirin. He is fifty-five years of age.

VIII

Chao Hsin-po, President of the Legislative Council, is
not a Manchurian but a Chinese who was born in Chih-li
(now Hopei) province. He was educated at the Peiyang
College in Tientsin and also studied law at Meiji University at Tokyo. He speaks and writes Japanese almost without a fault. The Tokyo university conferred upon him the
degree of Doctor of Laws upon the strength of a volumi-
nous and profound thesis which he wrote on a certain
aspect of criminal law. In 1926 he became legal adviser
to the late Manchurian dictator, Chang Tso-lin, and organized a Society of Jurisprudence. He was also a member of the committee instituted by the Chang Government for the purpose of studying the question of treaty
revision.

Dr. Chao watched with deep apprehension the policy
pursued by Chang and his son, the "Young Marshal,"
which subjected the people to the most ruthless exploitation known to history. Time and again he expressed the
view that, unless that policy was changed, popular discontent throughout Manchuria was bound to demonstrate
itself in a violent manner. To all such remonstrances the
two Changs turned a deaf ear.

Immediately after the incident of September 18, 1931,

Dr. Chao was largely instrumental in organizing a Committee for the Preservation of Order. On October 20 he became mayor of Mukden and took over municipal administration from Colonel Doihara, who had temporarily administered the city as an emergency measure. All the constitutional laws under which the Manchoukuo Government has been functioning were drafted by Dr. Chao. He is forty-six years of age.

### IX

Chang Yen-Ching, Minister of Industry, is the eleventh son of the late great Chang Chi-tung, the famous reformer-viceroy of Hupei and Hunan provinces in central China in the last years of the Manchu Dynasty. His father was an ardent advocate of constitutional government and introduced many reforms in his provinces. Believing that China would do well to walk in Japan's footsteps, the great viceroy invited many Japanese advisers to assist him and also sent many Chinese students to Japanese schools in 1906 and the following few years. Influenced by his illustrious father, young Chang, after graduating from a Chinese school, entered the Peers' School in Tokyo. Upon his return to China, he was appointed magistrate of various prefectures in Chili province. Before the September, 1931, incident, he was chief of the bureau of industry of the Kirin provincial government. He is only thirty-five years of age.

### X

Feng Kan-ching, Minister of Justice, forty-one years of age, is a Manchurian, a native of Kaiping in Fengtien province, and was educated entirely in Manchuria. After graduating from the Political Science School of Mukden, he became a judge in the provincial court of Kirin. From that time to September, 1931, he filled various important posts both in Manchuria and in China.

## XI

Ting Chien-hsu, Minister of Communications, is a Manchurian and has always been an advocate of "Manchuria for the Manchurians." Naturally, he was opposed to the policy of exploitation followed by the war lords for the purpose of satisfying their personal ambitions in China proper. When Kuo Sung-ling revolted against the war lord, Chang Tso-lin, in 1926, Mr. Ting was one of the secret sympathizers of the revolt. After the rebellion was put down, the war lord had a mind to mete out severe punishment to those sympathizers, but so numerous were they that he did not dare round them up. This is another indication of the unpopularity of the Chang régime. Mr. Ting believes that the Manchurian railways owned by the South Manchuria Railway and those owned by the Manchoukuo Government should be unified or coördinated so as to avoid unnecessary competition and to increase efficiency. He is forty-six years of age.

## XII

Yuan Chin-kai, senior member of the Privy Council, is also a native of Manchuria and was born sixty-four years ago in Liao-yang, famous as a battlefield in the Russo-Japanese war. He is, perhaps, the most famous living *literati* in all Manchuria. Although once chief of the secretariat of the Chang Tso-lin Government, he was against Chang's militarism and his policy of oppression, and was a believer in *Wangtao,* the *Way of the King,* as the guiding principle of government. Naturally, he was never liked by the war lords. For several years prior to the Sino-Japanese clash of September, 1931, Mr. Yuan was in retirement, pondering over the Chinese classics, writing poetry, and hoping all the while that the Changs would come to their senses. When, in the wake of that clash, a Committee for the Preservation of Order was organized at Mukden, Yuan became its chairman.

### XIII

Chang Hai-peng, member of the Privy Council, is a Manchurian, and is sixty-four years old. His training and career have been entirely in the military field. A graduate of the Military Academy at Mukden, he was military adviser to the Manchurian Government under Chang Tso-lin in 1922, and was made lieutenant-general. Before the September, 1931, incident he was a division commander at Taonanfu. In the new Manchoukuo Government he is both a Privy Councillor and the chief *aide de camp* to the Chief Executive.

### XIV

Finally, Tokuzo Komai, a Japanese, whose position in the Manchoukuo Government has already been discussed in Chapter VII, is worthy of a more intimate introduction. From the inauguration of the new Government to the early part of September, 1932, he was Chief of the General Affairs Board in the State Council.

At present he is serving in an advisory capacity as a member of the Privy Council. I shall let Mr. Komai himself tell how he came to be identified with the Manchoukuo Government in the following language which he used in speaking to the Lytton Commission on May 6, 1932:

Ever since my youth I have entertained the deepest interest in China and her affairs, and my intention and desire was to assist in some way to consolidate and build up China. I have held this interest for twenty-five years. As preparation for myself I first made a study of law and then entered an agricultural college for the study of agriculture so that I would be able to assist China in these two fields.

It was at the time of the downfall of the Tsing [Manchu] dynasty that I first came to China. At that time the Chinese people were beginning to plan the development of their country. In order to study the nature of the Chinese nation and people, I first came to Manchuria and spent ten years in a special study of the problems of the people of Manchuria. It was in the early stage of the South Manchuria Railway, and I was an employee of the Railway studying Manchuria and Mongolia. It was in 1914 that I made my first general study trip to Mongolia.

Then, in order to make my study of China more thorough, after completing the general study of Manchuria and Mongolia, I went to China proper and continued studying there for a year and a half. It was then that I observed the reality that at no time has China been a political unity since the revolution. I also observed that the general population of China as a whole is good, sound and wholesome, but the leaders in the political field are mostly corrupt and engaged in satisfying their own greed; and it was evident to me that as long as such men were in the upper political strata, the political unification of China was impossible.

Those observations compelled me to think further and to try to discover what would be the best means of assisting China. The very striking character of Chang Chun, once Minister of Agriculture and Commerce under Yuan Shih-kai, appealed to me.

Across the Yangtze River from Shanghai is a region called Nan-chung, where Chang Chun was an important figure. He was somewhat of a dreamer and wished to develop that region through industrialization. I was associated with him and felt that I would even give half my life to the cause in cooperation with Mr. Chang Chun. Then, as he passed away and that area was brought back to the former disorderly conditions, I lost my connection there and was compelled to return to my home in Japan. Yet I still held a hope for the realization of my dream to establish a model area in part of China, so I continued my study and gave thought to this idea.

Toward the close of the Tsing dynasty, Sir Robert Hart was adviser to the Empress Dowager and Director General of the Customs. It was he who established the customs system. It was then the only dependable administrative organization in exist-ence in China and all the foreign people trusted the reports issued by the customs authorities. Most of the employees in that organization were British, but other races were included—French, Italians, Japanese and others. Of course many Chinese were em-ployed in the service. It was very clear that the shortcomings of the Chinese people might be remedied by good foreign assistance. The customs system has really shown that it is possible. And the idea which I discovered—that it is possible to reform some admin-istrative organizations in China, as shown in the customs service —might, I felt, be applied to other phases of administration. I realized that although Manchuria had very close relations with Japan, political conditions there were no different from those in other parts of China, and I felt that some help could be given to the administrative organization in Manchuria through assisting the Manchurian people to establish an independent state.

The Manchoukuo Government prides itself on being "cosmopolitan." Its intention is, as soon as its finances will permit, to invite Americans and Europeans to work in its various departments in an advisory capacity. Natu-rally, the Japanese, for cultural, linguistic, historical, and financial reasons, will be far more numerous than other foreigners, but as a matter of principle, the doors will be open to all. Even Chinese, now serving in Peiping or Nanking, will not be discriminated against, if sufficient proof is shown that they have experienced a change of heart and are sincerely in sympathy with the cause of Manchoukuo.

# CHAPTER IX

## THE FINANCES OF MANCHOUKUO

### I

THE financial status of Manchoukuo is all that can be expected of a new State, which was born of a great politico-military upheaval, whose heritage was a bankrupt treasury, a chaotic currency, an arbitrary taxation, and which is going through a most fundamental political reorganization. The new Government came into existence on March 9, 1932. Of course, no budget had been prepared. For two months after its inauguration, its expenditures amounted to 9,100,000 *yuan*. These were met by the 9,300,000 *yuan* which had been turned over to the Manchoukuo Government by the finance offices of the old régime and the Salt Gabelle.

As the Government completed its organization and enlarged its scope of activity, its expenditure proportionately increased. Consequently, the budget for the fiscal year 1932-33, made public on October 11, 1932, shows a deficit of 12,291,055 *yuan*.

According to this budget, the estimated total revenue is 101,017,000 *yuan* (Manchoukuo silver) as against a total expenditure of 113,308,055 *yuan*. The deficit is to be met by bond issue, that is, by using a part of the 30,000,000 *yen* Reconstruction Bond recently floated in Japan. Considering all the difficulties surrounding the new Government, this deficit is rather small. The authorities are confident that by the beginning of next fiscal year the revenue system will have been so improved that the budget for the year 1933-34 will be balanced.

The outstanding feature of the current budget is a radical reduction in military expenditure as compared with a similar expenditure under the old régime of war-lordism. In 1930, Manchuria under Marshal Chang Hsueh-liang expended 115,000,000 *yuan* for military purposes, amounting to 80 per cent of its total revenue. The new Government cut this to 30,000,000 *yuan,* or less than 30 per cent of the total expenditure. This is a reduction of 85,000,000 *yuan* as compared with Marshal Chang's military expenditure for 1930.

In 1930, the old Government's total revenue was 121,-265,479 *yuan,* and its expenditure 148,116,563 *yuan*—a deficit of 26,851,084 *yuan.* This condition had lasted almost ten years. Compared with this, the new Manchoukuo Government's deficit of 12,291,055 *yuan* is small indeed.

Again in 1930, only 20 per cent of the total revenue was used for civil administration, while 80 per cent was used for military purposes. The new régime has reversed this ratio, devoting 70 per cent of its total revenue to civil administration and 30 per cent to military purposes.

In *A General Outline of Manchoukuo*—a publication of the Foreign Office at Hsinking—a glimpse is afforded of the war lord's arbitrary method of taxation. "When the old régime needed extra funds for military purposes, it imposed a heavy tax on all commodities and found little difficulty in collecting. There was no uniformity. In 1924, salt was taxed at the rate of $2.75 per picul, but during the past seven years it has been steadily increased. During this same period, the bean tax was raised 70 per cent and, in addition, the production tax was doubled. The old régime concentrated on indirect taxes. Goods were never rightly assessed. Duty was imposed on anything and everything up to the maximum that the traffic would bear, causing deep discontent and suffering among the people."

In addition, the old régime issued inconvertible paper money without limit, and used it in buying up from farmers crops which it sold to merchants for gold or silver.

The new régime, even before the formulation of the 1932-33 budget, abolished a few minor taxes and reduced the rate of some of the others. Thus, in Fengtien province, taxation was reduced by 6,448,000 *yuan;* in Kirin province by 3,530,000 *yuan;* and in Hei-lung-kiang province by 60,000—a total of 11,338,000 *yuan.*

II

According to the 1932-33 budget, the revenues of Manchoukuo are as shown in the table on page 173.

The grand total, including ordinary and extraordinary revenues, is 113,308,055 *yuan.* One of the ordinary revenues is from state monopolies and industries, amounting to 9,631,000 *yuan.* This includes 5,000,000 *yuan* from opium monopoly, a new enterprise which I shall discuss in Chapter XII. Again, the extraordinary revenues include 12,291,055 *yuan,* which is a part of the 30,000,000 *yen* bonds floated in Japan and which is the amount of the deficit. Of this total deficit, 290,000 *yuan* is for road building and 12,001,055 *yuan* for various administrative purposes.

The Maritime Customs and the Salt Gabelle are by far the most important sources of revenue. Before the inde-

*Ordinary Revenues*

1. Taxes and Duties ........................85,378,000

| | | |
|---|---|---|
| Customs duties | .......... | 40,460,000 |
| Tonnage dues | ............ | 430,000 |
| Salt tax | .................. | 16,814,000 |
| Land tax | ................ | 2,955,000 |
| Production tax | ........... | 6,213,000 |
| Business tax | .............. | 3,694,000 |
| Live-stock tax | ............ | 960,000 |
| Slaughtering tax | .......... | 50,000 |
| Deeds tax | ................ | 1,445,000 |
| Tobacco and Wine tax | .... | 2,069,000 |
| Consolidated tax | .......... | 7,172,000 |
| Stamp duty | .............. | 1,954,000 |
| Mining tax | ............... | 116,000 |
| Coal tax | ................. | 349,000 |
| Miscellaneous | ........... | 697,000 |

85,378,000

2. State Monopolies and Industries......... 9,631,000
3. Miscellaneous ........................ 2,377,000

Total, ordinary revenues ............ 97,386,000

*Extraordinary Revenues*

1. Sale of State Properties ................ 155,000
2. Miscellaneous ....................... 1,372,000
3. Receipts from Chinese Eastern Railway... 2,104,000
4. Bonds ............................. 12,291,055

Total, extraordinary revenues ........ 15,922,055

pendence of Manchuria, its Customs and Salt Gabelle were parts of the two organizations which embraced both China and Manchuria. There were certain foreign obligations of China which were secured by customs and salt revenues. Naturally, Manchurian portions of these revenues, together with those of China proper, were used for

the service of those obligations. When Manchuria declared independence, the new Government announced in
no uncertain terms its intention of respecting all foreign
obligations which were bequeathed by the old régime. In
accordance with this pledge, Manchoukuo will continue
to pay to the same service its share out of the receipts
from its Customs and Salt Gabelle.

The current Manchoukuo budget includes 40,460,000
*yuan* from the Customs and 16,814,000 *yuan* from the Salt
Gabelle. Of these sums, 11,050,419 *yuan* and 2,335,773
*yuan,* respectively, on the Customs and the Salt Gabelle
accounts, are to be paid to the service of China's foreign
obligations in the fiscal year 1932-33. These payments are
included in the ordinary expenditures of the Department
of Finance.

A word about the salt revenue. Up till about 1920, salt
tax in Manchuria was 2 *yuan* per 100 pounds. But about
that time the late war lord, Chang Tso-lin, acquired dic-
tatorial power in that region, and began to cherish territorial ambitions in China proper. To finance his politico-
military ventures, he resorted to many questionable means
of raising revenue. The salt revenue, which had ordinarily
been a little over 10,000,000 *yuan,* was one of the first to
be tampered with. Chang attempted to obtain twenty to
thirty million *yuan* from this single source. Thus, in 1925,
the salt tax was raised from the original rate of 2 *yuan* per
100 pounds to 2.75 *yuan.* In 1926, this was again raised
to 4 *yuan;* in 1927 to 8 *yuan;* and in 1928 to 9 *yuan.*
Chang's income from the salt tax was more than 45,000,-
000 *yuan* in 1927.

Nor was this all. In 1922, Chang declared the independence of Manchuria, and refused to send any portion

of salt revenue to the Chinese Government at Peking, despite the fact that a part of this revenue was for the service of foreign obligations. This lasted till about 1927.

When his son, Chang Hsueh-liang, succeeded him in 1928, he reduced the salt tax to 6 *yuan* from the preceding year's 9 *yuan*. This was still three times the original rate. Young Chang also agreed to resume payment to the Chinese Government of Manchuria's quota out of the salt revenue. In 1930, the salt income was 25,000,000 *yuan*, of which only 1,000,000 *yuan* was sent to the Inspector-General of the Salt Gabelle at Shanghai.

In Manchoukuo's budget for the current fiscal year, the salt revenue is estimated at 16,814,000 *yuan*. This is about one-third of the amount collected by the old régime in 1927. Of the above sum, 2,335,773 *yuan* is to be turned over to the Inspector-General at Shanghai. This shows that, while Manchoukuo's salt revenue for the current year is 8,186,000 *yuan* less than Chang Hsueh-liang's income from the same source in 1930, its remittance to Shanghai is 1,335,777 *yuan* more than Chang's remittance in 1930—another evidence of Manchoukuo's fastidiousness in meeting old foreign obligations, even though these obligations were incurred not by itself but by China.

Nor is this all that Manchoukuo has done for China and her creditors; it has paid even the arrears, amounting to 576,200 *yuan* owed by Chang Hsueh-liang to the Chinese Government, that is, to the Salt Gabelle administration at Shanghai.

### III

As against the revenues shown in the foregoing table, the expenditures are as follows:

*Ordinary Expenditures*

| | | |
|---|---|---|
| Chief Executive's Office ................... | | 1,150,000 |
| General Affairs Board .................... | | 37,664,697:— |
| General Affairs Board proper .. | 980,117 | |
| Privy Council ............... | 197,669 | |
| Legislative Council .......... | 256,332 | |
| Supervisory Council .......... | 362,506 | |
| Bureau of Legislation ........ | 189,098 | |
| Capital Construction Bureau... | 259,975 | |
| Tatung Academy ............ | 213,446 | |
| Provincial Governments ...... | 12,000,000 | |
| National Treasury subsidy .... | 5,196,000 | |
| National Treasury reserve ..... | 15,000,000 | |
| Others ................... | 3,009,464 | |
| | 37,664,697 | |
| Hsing-an Province Administrative Office.... | | 1,012,030 |
| Department of Civil Affairs ............... | | 4,168,175 |
| Department of Foreign Affairs ............ | | 666,892 |
| Department of Defence ................... | | 30,000,000 |
| Department of Finance ................... | | 24,458,243 |
| Department of Industry .................. | | 434,589 |
| Department of Communications .......... | | 1,547,825 |
| Department of Justice .................... | | 3,108,126 |
| Department of Education ................. | | 271,511 |
| Total ............................. | | 104,482,088 |

EXTRAORDINARY EXPENDITURES

| | |
|---|---|
| General Affairs Board ................... | 5,033,517 |
| Department of Finance .................. | 662,400 |
| Department of Defence .................. | 3,000,000 |
| Department of Civil Affairs ............... | 116,200 |
| Department of Communications .......... | 13,850 |
| Total ............................. | 8,825,967 |
| Grand Total .........................113,308,055 | |

The above shows that the General Affairs Board of the
State Council receives by far the largest appropriation,

both ordinary and extraordinary. This is due to the unique position of importance it occupies in the governmental scheme of Manchoukuo, as has been described in Chapter VII. On the ordinary account, the Board is allowed 12,000,-000 *yuan* for provincial governments. This is very significant. It shows that the Government is centralizing local administration, thus reversing the old system which allowed provincial governors—usually generals with troops—too great a power, to the detriment of the central authorities.

Again, on the extraordinary account, the General Affairs Board has an appropriation of 5,033,517 *yuan*—much larger than the sum allowed any other department. This extraordinary appropriation includes 2,500,000 *yuan* for the construction of government buildings, 1,787,600 *yuan* for the relief of the flood sufferers in the Harbin region, and 290,000 for road building.

The Department of Defence has an ordinary appropriation of 30,000,000 *yuan,* of which 28,000,000 *yuan* is for the army; 1,320,000 for the administration of the Department; and 600,000 *yuan* for the navy, consisting mostly of small destroyers and gunboats on the Sugari River. In addition, the Department is allowed 3,000,000 *yuan* on the extraordinary account, mostly for the suppression of banditry and irregulars now conducting guerrilla warfare against Manchoukuo. The authorities are confident that in two years such extraordinary expenditures will become unnecessary.

IV

In order to put Manchoukuo's finances upon a sound basis, the old system of taxation and financial administration must be radically reformed. The following quotation from *The Outline of Manchoukuo* shows the line of reform the Government is following:

Under the old régime, the provinces, prefectures, and municipalities enjoyed fiscal independence, resorting to the contract system in connection with their budgets.

The new government makes the prefectures and municipalities the units of finance, considering the provinces as mere administrative sections. The revenues of prefectures and cities are to be derived from taxes fixed by the Central Government, and their budgets are to be submitted to the Government for approval. In general, they are to draw up a budget based on their financial resources, but in special circumstances, a portion of the expenditure will be subsidized by the Government.

Both the Central Government and the Provincial Governments are to draw up a single budget that will cover the whole revenue and expenditure, but extraordinary budgets for various offices may be allowed for special purposes.

All public financing shall be transacted through the National Treasury. The revenues of prefectures and cities are to be paid into the National Treasury.

Under the old régime, the Central Government required the provincial governments to contribute a certain amount to the Central treasury. It did not matter how much the provincial governments collected in taxes, as long as the allotted sum was sent to the Central Government. In turn, the provincial governments assigned a certain sum to each of the *hsiens* (prefectures) within its jurisdiction. The tax collector of the *hsien* generally collected much more than the assigned sum and pocketed the surplus, usually allowing a "due" share to the magistrate and a few other officials of the same prefecture. This is what is meant by "contract system," mentioned in the above quotation from *The Outline of Manchoukuo*. The Central Government did not fix the rate of taxation to be collected from the people—it merely called upon each province to contribute a fixed amount, while the province called upon the *hsien* to contribute a fixed sum. The consequence was that the authorities, directly engaged in collecting taxes, levied as much as they could without risking the danger of popular revolt. That is why taxes were so high and arbitrary.

This brings up the question of China's age-long official practice of "squeeze"—a question which I shall discuss in Chapter XIII. One wonders if this practice, with all its intricate ramifications, can ever be abolished. Should the Manchoukuo Government, with the aid of Japanese experts, fix the rates of taxes (as it has already done), and see to it that no local officials would collect more than the fixed rates, it is more than possible that the local officials would make only a feint of coöperating with the central authorities. The result might be that the expected amount of revenue from taxation would not be forthcoming. That is the greatest difficulty confronting the new Government in its endeavors for financial reform.

v

In the financial reform of Manchuria, the Central Bank of Manchoukuo has played and is playing a very important part. The Bank was established on June 16, 1932, with a capital of 3,000,000 *yuan,* and took the place of the four old-régime banks, namely, the Bank of the Three Eastern Provinces, the Kirin Provincial Bank, the Heilung-kiang Provincial Bank, and the Frontier Bank. Both the assets and the liabilities of the old banks were transferred to the Central Bank.

In addition to the capital of 30,000,000 *yuan,* the Bank

has a specie reserve (gold and silver) of 82,000,000 *yuan* and a security reserve of 60,000,000 *yuan*.

The Lytton Commission's report has this to say about the Central Bank:

It is not clear how the new Manchoukuo Bank can hope to accomplish its ambitious programme of unifying and stabilizing all Manchurian currencies with the limited amount of capital at its disposal. The resources inherited from the old provincial banking institutions, with the addition of a loan from Japanese banks and a subscription to its capital from the Manchoukuo Government, seem entirely inadequate for the purpose. Moreover, it is not clear on what basis the financial relations between the Bank and the Manchoukuo Government will be established. According to the preliminary Manchoukuo budget supplied to the Commission by the Finance Minister, Manchoukuo expects to face a deficit of over 20,000,000 *yuan* during its first year of existence. According to the Minister, this was to be covered by a loan from the Central Bank (not then in existence). A government which subscribes 7,500,000 *yuan* to its bank and then borrows over 20,000,000 *yuan* from it to balance its budget is not establishing either its central bank or its budget on a sound financial basis.

Since the above was written conditions have changed. To begin with, the Manchoukuo Government not only paid 7,500,000 *yuan* in cash to the Central Bank but it loaned to the Bank 20,000,000 *yen* (Japanese), this sum having been advanced by the Bank of Chosen (Korea). Secondly, the deficit of the Government for the fiscal year 1932-33 is, as we have noted, 12,291,055 *yuan,* not 20,000,-000 *yuan*. The Bank, which has a capital of 30,000,000 *yen* (Japanese) and a specie and security reserve valued at 142,000,000 *yuan,* would have been justified in advancing temporarily 12,000,000 *yuan* to the Government, which had loaned 20,000,000 *yen* to the Bank. But the Bank did not have to advance this sum, for the Government made good the deficit by using a portion of the 30,000,000 *yen* Reconstruction Bond floated in Japan in November, 1932. This Bond was underwritten by the Banking Syndicate of Tokyo. The first installment was paid in December, the second in January 1933, and the third and last in February 1933. The Bond is to be redeemed in five years beginning on January 10, 1936. It is secured on the revenue from the Kirin-Heilungkiang Salt Transportation Office and from the Opium Monopoly. The fund obtained from the Bond is to be used mostly for the pacification of the country and for construction work, such as road laying and the erection of government buildings.

That the Central Bank has sufficient resources to cope with the task before it may be judged from the similar experience of the Bank of Japan. When the Bank of Japan was organized at Tokyo in 1882, its capital was only 10,000,000 *yen* in silver. Yet this Bank fully succeeded in unifying currencies issued by various national banks. In 1895, its capital was increased to 30,000,000 *yen* in silver. Only in 1910 was it increased to 60,000,000 gold *yen*. In the light of the achievements of the Bank of Japan, the financial authorities of Manchoukuo are confident that the Central Bank is fully prepared to meet all the requirements expected of it.

To quote from the Lytton report again:

Unless the Central Bank can obtain more actual hard money than it now appears to possess, it can hardly hope to unify and stabilize all Manchurian currencies on a *convertible* silver dollar basis. Even if it were to succeed in creating a currency which was uniform, though not convertible, it would possibly have accomplished something; but even a uniform currency, the stability of which is not guaranteed by conversion, falls short of the requirements of a sound monetary system.

This prediction has already been belied by the actual achievements of the Bank. At its opening to business on July 1, 1932, there were 140,000,000 *yuan* of fifteen kinds of old currencies to be redeemed. This total was based upon the revaluation of the old notes at the rate of exchange fixed by law (for each of the fifteen), for the purpose of redemption. From July 1 to November 30, the Bank redeemed old notes to the amount of 49,540,596 *yuan,* and issued new notes totaling 39,994,059 *yuan.* The Bank expects to complete the work of redemption in two years.

That the Central Bank is gaining in public confidence, and that the notes issued by it have been stabilized, is shown by the fact that, since the beginning of September 1932, the new notes have been at a premium over the silver dollar even in Shanghai, the current market exchange rate being 99 *yuan* of the Central Bank notes for 100 *yuan* of hard money.

This is a remarkable achievement, especially when we consider the difficult nature of the task. We have said that, on July 1, 1931, there were 140,000,000 *yuan* of old notes. But this was the total estimated on the exchange rate for redemption. As a matter of fact, there were over a billion old notes, some of which were so depreciated as to be worthless. Of these latter varieties, the Fengpiao (Mukden notes) issued by the Changs, war lords of the old régime, were the most numerous and the most depreciated. They were printed in such enormous quantities that it is impossible to even guess at their total number, but it has been variously estimated at between 700,000,000 and 1,000,000,000. They were used by the Changs in buying up crops of beans and grain, which they sold for gold or silver. The transaction yielded enormous profits to the Changs, but the farmers were left in the cold with worthless Fengpiao foisted upon them.

Besides the fifteen varieties of old bills, which have been designated as redeemable by the Bank, there were more than a hundred kinds of minor bills, official and private. These were so depreciated and valueless that they were declared irredeemable and their circulation was stopped on July 1, 1932.

Financially, Manchoukuo has a great advantage over Japan, China, or Korea, in that its exports greatly exceed its imports, while her neighbors import more than they export. In 1927 and 1928, the excess of her exports over imports was 139,122,593 haikwan taels and 131,079,520 haikwan taels, respectively. Even in the depressed year 1931, the excess was 90,359,436 haikwan taels. The steady inflow of silver consequent upon this favorable trade balance is bound to improve Manchoukuo's financial status. Furthermore, Manchoukuo is said to have a plan to develop its gold reserves, both reef and alluvial, estimated by Professor Aubert (in his book *Minerals of Manchuria*) at $2,300,000,000 gold.

# CHAPTER X

## MANCHOUKUO'S FOREIGN RELATIONS

### I

To recognize or not to recognize Manchoukuo—that is the question now before the world. Secretary Stimson, of the United States, and the "small" nations in the League of Nations are insistent that she be not recognized because she is a puppet of Japan. The "big" Powers, perhaps willy-nilly, are following them, for they are too staid to fly in the face of convention.

But whether recognized or not, Manchoukuo is here to stay, with her population of 32,000,000 strong, her vast territory 448,957 square miles in area, her well-organized Government, leaning upon the Japanese, it is true, yet hopeful of future achievements as an independent state, her budget nearly balanced even in these days of universal deficit, her export trade exceeding her imports by almost a hundred million *yuan*. Such a country is bound to challenge attention. The Powers may not *recognize* her, but they cannot *ignore* her and certainly do not. They try very hard to avert their eyes from her, but she is too big and potentially too rich to be ignored.

On March 12, the Manchoukuo Government, in the name of the Foreign Minister, Mr. Hsieh Chieh-Shih, cabled the Foreign Offices of seventeen nations, which were represented in Manchuria by consular officials, advising them of the advent of the new State and asking them to open diplomatic relations. The fifteen countries were Denmark, Esthonia, France, Germany, Great Britain, Japan, Italy, Latvia, Lithuania, the Netherlands, Poland, Portugal, the United States, and the Union of Soviet Socialist Republics. Shortly afterwards, thirty-five other nations were also similarly advised. In the cablegram, Manchoukuo enunciated the following principles:

1. That the Government will conduct the affairs of the State according to the primary principle of faith and confidence and the spirit of harmony and friendship, and pledge itself to maintain and promote international peace.
2. That the Government will respect international justice in accordance with the international laws and conventions.
3. That the Government will succeed to the obligations of the Republic of China by virtue of treaty stipulations with foreign countries, in the light of international laws and conventions, and that these obligations shall be faithfully discharged.
4. That the Government will not infringe upon the acquired rights of the peoples of foreign countries within the limits of the State of Manchuria, and, further, that their persons and properties shall be given full protection.
5. That the Government will welcome the entry of the nationals of foreign countries and their residence in Manchuria, and that all races shall be accorded equal and equitable treatment.
6. That trade and commerce with foreign countries shall be facilitated so as to contribute to the development of world economy.
7. That, with regard to the economic activities of the peoples of foreign nations within the State of Manchuria, the principle of the Open Door shall be observed.

To this communication, Japan alone made an encouraging reply. True, she was non-committal as to recognition, but she expressed the hope that the new State, adhering to the principles of the open door and equal opportunity for all nations, would achieve a wholesome progress and would secure its position as an independent state. The fact was that, in Tokyo at that time, opinion was divided as to how soon Japan should recognize Manchoukuo. A large group—including, of course, the army—was for immediate recognition. It was argued that Japan, having assisted in the establishment of the new State, should not disappoint and discourage that State by hesitating to open diplomatic relations with it, and that she would expose herself to the charge of cowardice if she were thus to evade her responsibility. On the other hand, the Foreign Office group had to consider that the League of Nations had appointed a Commission to study the Sino-Japanese situation, that Japan herself had largely been responsible for the creation of the Commission, and that the Commission had already arrived in Japan on its way to China. In such circumstances, the Foreign Office could not afford to appear in the rôle of slapping the Commission in the face by recognizing Manchoukuo then and there. Quite possibly, some in this group secretly hoped that, as a result of the Commission's investigation, Japan might be absolved of the charge of aggression, in which event she might take steps toward recognition with better grace. In any event, it was thought advisable to wait until after the Commission left the Orient for home. This view was permitted to prevail.

But the Commission did not absolve Japan. On the contrary, it accused Japan of aggression and of having set up a puppet government. That put Japan in a desperate position. She could not back out without appearing to admit the accusation. In similar circumstances, no nation with any sense of self-pride would back out; and Japan, unfortunately, happens to be one of the most sensitive and proudest nations on earth. To her, the only alternative was to recognize Manchoukuo.

Although the League Commission's Report was not published until October 1, the substance of its recommendations were known, or at least surmised, in responsible circles in Tokyo. The Commission visited Tokyo for the second time from July 4 to July 15 and held conferences with the Prime Minister, Viscount Saito, and the Foreign Minister, Count Uchida. As a result, what the Commission had in mind became fairly clear.

Meanwhile, Manchoukuo had been becoming more and more impatient waiting for Japanese recognition. A large Manchoukuo mission, headed by Ting Chien-hsiu, Minister of Communications, had been in Tokyo to urge the Japanese Government to take immediate steps for opening formal diplomatic relations between the two nations.

The League Commission left the Orient in the early part of August; and on September 15, 1932, Japan recognized Manchoukuo by concluding a protocol, the essential parts of which read as follows:

Whereas Japan has recognized the fact that Manchoukuo, in accordance with the free will of its inhabitants, has organized and established itself as an independent State; and

Whereas Manchoukuo has declared its intention of abiding by all international engagements entered into by China in so far as they are applicable to Manchoukuo;

Now the Governments of Japan and Manchoukuo have, for the purpose of establishing a perpetual relationship of good neighborhood between Japan and Manchoukuo, each respecting the territorial rights of the other, and also in order to secure the peace of the Far East, agreed as follows:

1. Manchoukuo shall confirm and respect, in so far as no agreement to the contrary shall be made between Japan and Manchoukuo in the future, all rights and interests possessed by Japan or her subjects within the territory of Manchoukuo by virtue of Sino-Japanese treaties, agreements or other arrangements or of Sino-Japanese contracts, private as well as public;

2. Japan and Manchoukuo, recognizing that any threat to the territory or to the peace and order of either of the High Contracting Parties constitutes at the same time a threat to the safety and existence of the other, agree to cooperate in the maintenance of their national security; it being understood that such Japanese forces as may be necessary for this purpose shall be stationed in Manchoukuo.

The protocol was signed at Hsinking, the capital of Manchoukuo, by General Nobuyoshi Muto for Japan and by Premier Cheng Hsiao-hsu for Manchoukuo. Simultaneously, the Japanese Government issued a statement which, in part, said:

The Protocol confirms the fact that Manchoukuo is an independent state organized in accordance with the free will of its inhabitants, and it stipulates that all rights and interests which Japan and her subjects possess within the territory of Manchoukuo by virtue of treaties and other agreements are to be confirmed and respected, thus doing away once and for all with all pending disputes concerning these rights and interests. Recognizing the fact that any menace to Manchuria constitutes at the same time a threat to the safety and existence of the Empire, the Protocol further provides that Japan and Manchoukuo are to cooperate in the maintenance of their national security and that Japanese forces necessary for this purpose are to be stationed in Manchoukuo. It is the object of the Protocol thus to establish a perpetual relationship of good neighborhood between the two countries and to secure the peace of the Far East.

On several occasions, the Japanese Government has declared that it harbors no territorial designs in Manchuria, and the preamble of the Protocol reaffirms that both Contracting Powers will mutually respect each other's territorial rights. As regards the economic activities of foreigners, the Manchoukuo Government made clear in their communication of March 10 above alluded to that they would observe the principle of the Open Door. What Japan desires in Manchuria is to do away with all anti-foreign policies there so that the region may become a safe place of abode for natives and foreigners alike, while, at the same time, guaranteeing her legitimate rights and interests there; and therefore, it is hardly necessary to repeat the assurance that Japan sincerely hopes that all the peoples of the world will pursue their economic activities in Manchuria on a footing of equal opportunity and will thereby contribute to the development and prosperity of that region.

Shortly afterwards, Japan appointed General Muto Ambassador to Manchoukuo, Commander-in-Chief of the Kwantung Army (Japanese forces stationed in Manchuria), and Governor of the Kwantung Leased Territory. By thus combining three offices in one person, Japan thought that her Manchurian policy could be unified, avoiding the issuance of conflicting orders from three different sources, as had often happened when there was little coördination between the Consul General at Mukden, the governor of the Kwantung territory, and the commander of the Kwantung army.

General Muto's position in Manchoukuo is similar to that occupied by Prince Ito as Resident General in Korea from 1904 to 1909. Muto, though a military officer, is said to be endowed with qualities of statesmanship. Just as Ito labored against the annexation of Korea, so is Muto expected to work for the establishment of a really independent Manchoukuo. His success or failure must, of necessity, depend largely upon the ability and endeavors of the Manchoukuo leaders. If these leaders, instead of bending their energies to internal rehabilitation in hearty coöperation with the Japanese, should waste their efforts in insidious intrigues among themselves and, what is worse, revive the age-old Chinese diplomacy of setting this, that, or the other Power against Japan, Japan, in spite of herself, might be forced to a course which she does not now anticipate. Such a regrettable eventuality may not happen in Muto's time, just as Korean annexation did not take place in Ito's time; but it is a potential danger which both Manchoukuo and Japan must bear in mind.

Meanwhile, there are potent reasons why Japan does not want to annex Manchuria but would do her utmost to avoid being forced to take the course that she took in Korea. We may mention only two of such reasons. The first is that Japan has had to take cognizance of the repeated Korean attempts to assassinate her leaders, not excepting the Emperor himself. With Japanese reverence for the Emperor being what it is, she would stop and think many times before she were forced to take in Manchuria the same course as she did in Korea. If the Koreans, obviously effete as a race and nation, prize independence so highly and could cause Japan so much uneasiness for the loss of it, what would not the more virile Chinese in Manchuria do to keep the independence for which they are toiling?

The second reason which dampens any Japanese desire that may exist for the eventual annexation of Manchoukuo is fear of unrestricted Chinese immigration. The spectre has been haunting Japan for some years, for the Korean laborers, lured by high wages prevailing in the industrial regions of Japan, have been coming there in ever-increasing numbers. Not only do they replace Japanese laborers, especially of the unskilled class, but they live in squalid and unsanitary quarters and often become public charges. Japan, having made the Koreans her own subjects by annexation, cannot logically or justly exclude them. Should she annex Manchoukuo, she would, in effect, invite Chinese immigration from that region, and this is something she would avoid if she possibly could. As long as Manchoukuo is independent, Japan can treat Manchurian Chinese as aliens and can find some way to keep out their laborers.

II

Next to Japan, Soviet Russia has, for various reasons, been most friendly to Manchoukuo. As soon as Manchoukuo was inaugurated on March 9, 1932, the Soviet Consul General in Harbin and the Soviet manager of the Chinese Eastern Railway signified their intention of co-operating with the new authorities. A more concrete example of Russian good will toward Manchoukuo was her denial to the Chinese Consul at Blagoviestchensk (on the Amur River) the use of the Russian telegraph service in his secret-code communication with General Ma Chan-shan and Marshal Chang Hsueh-liang, soon after Ma rebelled against the Manchoukuo Government and set up his headquarters at Heiho (on the Manchurian side of the Amur River just opposite Blagovestchensk) on April 7, 1932. The Soviet Government went so far as to notify China that she must recall her Consul from Blagoviest-

chensk if he would continue to render clandestine assistance to the forces hostile to Manchoukuo, because Russia,
it said, wished to be strictly neutral. For the same reason,
the Soviet authorities declined to assist the League Commission in its investigations in North Manchuria. Russia
knew that the Commission, though permitted to enter
Manchoukuo, was far from welcome to the Government
which it came to investigate.

Moscow further indicated its friendliness toward Hsinking by consenting to the establishment of Manchoukuo
consulates at Blagoviestchensk, Khabarovsk, Vladivostok
and Chita. The Consulate at Blagoviestchensk, where
there are 7,000 Manchurians, was opened toward the end
of September, 1932, when the Manchoukuo Foreign Minister, Hsieh Chieh-Shih, issued a statement saying, in part,
as follows:

> We have realized the urgent need of affording proper protec-
> tion and offering the necessary facilities to our nationals residing
> outside our domain. Following negotiations with the representa-
> tives of the U.S.S.R., an agreement was reached whereby Man-
> choukuo is permitted to open and maintain a Consulate at Blago-
> viestchensk. In due course of time, Vladivostok, Khabarovsk, and
> Chita will also witness the establishment of our Consulates.
>
> On this occasion, we wish to declare to our fellow countrymen
> residing in the neighboring country that strict discipline among
> all of our officials and the efficient discharge of duties by our
> Consular officers, as well as the maintenance of friendly relations
> with the U.S.S.R., will undoubtedly combine to ensure them
> safety and well-being, just as to their fellow countrymen at home.

Another indication of Russia's good will toward Manchoukuo was the disarming and internment of General Su
Ping-wen and his followers who fled into Siberia after
they were defeated by the Japanese and Manchoukuo

army. She had also succored the Japanese who had been held at Manchuli by the rebel general as hostages—a mark of kindness which was deeply appreciated by Japan. This incident will be more fully described in Chapter XIII.

Last, but not least, Russia agreed to hand over to Manchoukuo, and not to Marshal Chang or the Nanking Government, one-half of the profits of the Chinese Eastern Railway, which is under the joint ownership and management of China and the Soviet Union in conformity with the Moscow-Peking treaty and the Moscow-Mukden treaty of 1924. This means that the Soviet Government has, in effect, repudiated China's authority and recognized Manchoukuo's control over the railway.

Thus Moscow, while still withholding recognition *de jure,* perhaps for some trading purposes, has accorded Manchoukuo recognition *de facto.* In the summer of 1932, rumor was abroad in the Far East that Moscow intimated to Tokyo a willingness to recognize Manchoukuo if Tokyo would sign a mutual non-aggression treaty with the Soviet Union. As a matter of fact, a non-aggression pact was suggested to Mr. Kenkichi Yoshizawa, then Ambassador to France, when he passed through Moscow on December 31, 1931 (when there was yet no independent Manchoukuo) on his way back to Tokyo. Japan's reply to this suggestion was handed to the Russian Ambassador at Tokyo, M. Troyanovsky, only on December 13, 1932. In it Japan expressed the view that, before any general non-aggression pact could be concluded, certain problems, which are likely to cause serious difficulties, should be discussed and, if possible, settled. Pending the consideration of such problems, Japan might enter into an exchange of views with the Soviet Government as to the means of ensuring peace along the Manchurian borders, possibly by establishing a Japan-Soviet-Manchoukuo Committee. The Japanese reply also stated that "Japan and the Soviet Union are each prepared scrupulously to respect the sovereign rights of the other, and to refrain strictly from violating in the slightest degree the boundaries of the other."

What Japan considers the outstanding questions affecting her relations with Russia are "Red" propaganda, the fishery and lumber concessions on the Russian coast, and matters relative to the oil concession in northern Saghalin. Here we need to note only the question of "Red" propaganda. Japan asks the Soviet to agree to stop communist propaganda as a prerequisite to the conclusion of a non-aggression treaty. The Soviet replies, as usual, that its Government, as such, is not responsible for, nor is it in a position to stop, such propaganda, because it is a matter entirely within the jurisdiction of the Third International, over which it has no control. But Japan believes, as do most other nations, that there is reason to believe that the Moscow Government and the Third International maintain a close relationship of coöperation.

Although it is not entirely clear that the Soviet Government proposed formally to recognize Manchoukuo in exchange for Japan's acceptance of a non-aggression treaty, it is true that it signified the intention of concluding a similar treaty with Manchoukuo. It also signified its willingness to have Manchoukuo represented at Moscow, although the title of such a representative might not be "minister" nor "ambassador."

The substance of the non-aggression treaty proposed by Russia is said to be as follows:

1. Each of the high contracting parties agrees to respect the territorial integrity and political independence of the other.

2. Should either of the high contracting parties be attacked by any third power or powers, the other should remain strictly neutral.

3. Should there arise between the contracting parties any controversy which could not be settled by the usual diplomatic means, they should endeavor to seek a solution by conciliation and other peaceful means.

On the face of it, the proposal is reasonable. Even in Japan it is countenanced in influential circles. Even though the question of "Red" propaganda stands in the way, the eventual conclusion of such a pact between Tokyo and Moscow, and between Hsinking and Moscow, is considered not entirely impossible. It is true that the sudden announcement of a Sino-Soviet treaty, signed by M. Litvinoff and Dr. W. W. Yen at Geneva on December 12, 1932, has caused Japan to doubt Russia's good faith, and has momentarily set back the improvement of relations between the two nations. Nevertheless, the question of non-aggression may be regarded as still on the tapis, and will again be taken up in earnest at some opportune time.

### III

The most delicate international problem which Manchoukuo has so far handled is that of the maritime customs. This problem was complicated by reason of the fact that the Chinese Maritime Customs, of which the Manchurian

Customs was a part, was controlled by foreigners, and that its receipts were deposited in certain foreign, mostly British, banks in Shanghai for the service of certain of China's foreign obligations. These foreign obligations, outstanding on January 1, 1930, were as follows:

| | |
|---|---|
| Boxer Indemnity, approximate... | $200,000,000 (gold) |
| Franco-Russian Loan of 1895.... | £ 1,571,000 |
| Anglo-German Loan of 1896 .... | £ 2,633,000 |
| Anglo-German Loan of 1898 .... | £ 8,538,000 |
| Reorganization Loan of 1913 .... | £ 22,326,000 |
| French Indemnity Bonds, 1925... | $ 41,326,000 (gold) |
| Belgian Indemnity Bonds, 1928... | $ 4,628,000 (gold) |

As far as the foreign creditors are concerned, the independence of Manchuria makes no difference, for the new Government, in its declaration of independence and in the Foreign Minister's announcement, quoted in this chapter, pledged itself to shoulder its share of the foreign obligations secured on customs revenue. Under the old régime, the Maritime Customs of Manchuria was a part of the general customs administration of China, of which Sir Frederick Maze, a British subject, was, as he still is, the Inspector-General, who is assisted by a large staff of foreigners, largely British. The entire customs receipts collected in Manchuria, as well as in China, were sent to the Inspector-General at Shanghai, where the funds were deposited in foreign banks. If customs receipts exceed, as they of course do, the annual payments required on these obligations, the surplus is turned over to the Chinese Government for its own use.

The new Manchoukuo Government is willing to remit to the Inspector-General, not the entire customs receipts of Manchuria, but the sum necessary to meet its quota of the annual payments on the above-named obligations, thus retaining for its own use any amount over and above the requisite remittance. As we noted in the chapter on Manchoukuo's finances, its customs revenue for 1932-33 is estimated at 85,378,000 *yuan,* out of which Manchoukuo proposes to remit 11,050,419 *yuan* to the Inspector-General of Customs at Shanghai. The surplus of some 74,328,000 would have gone to the Chinese treasury had Manchuria remained under the Chinese flag. But now this surplus goes to the Manchoukuo treasury. Therefore, it is only China, not foreign creditors, who loses by the independence of Manchuria.

Soon after Manchoukuo became independent, it proposed to solve the customs question substantially on the following terms:

1. Manchoukuo respects the integrity of the Maritime Customs administration, that is to say, it will not disturb the present personnel of the Manchurian Customs offices, and is willing to place them under the supervision of the Inspector-General of Customs at Shanghai provided, however, that their ultimate control rests with the Manchoukuo Government, just as the ultimate control of customs in China proper rests with the Nanking Government.

2. Manchoukuo will remit to the Inspector-General the requisite sum to meet its share of annual payments on the foreign obligations secured on customs revenue.

3. Manchoukuo will keep for its own use the residue after the above obligations have been met.

The first term was, of course, acceptable to China. But China objected to the second and third terms, and proposed that Manchoukuo remit to Shanghai the entire amount of receipts of the Customs at Dairen and one-third of receipts of all other customs under its jurisdiction. This would give Manchoukuo practically no revenue from

the customs. Dairen is by far the largest part of Manchoukuo, and takes the lion's share of the entire trade of
that country. To Manchoukuo, therefore, China's proposal was devoid of sense.

The controversy lasted for almost three months with no
hope of amicable settlement. To cut the Gordian knot,
Manchoukuo, on June 12, 1932, peremptorily ordered the
Customs Commissioner at Dairen, Mr. J. Fukumoto, a
Japanese, and the Dairen offices of the Bank of China and
the Yokohama Specie Bank, the depositaries of Dairen
customs receipts, to discontinue remittances to the Inspector-General at Shanghai, warning them that unless remittances were stopped at once, Manchoukuo would set up
its own customs offices outside the boundary line of the
Kwantung Leased Territory (in which Dairen is located)
to collect duties on goods which had already been taxed
upon their entry at Dairen. To avoid this double taxation,
the Japanese Commissioner refrained from transmitting
money to Shanghai. At the same time, he urged upon the
Inspector-General, Sir Frederick Maze, the advisability
of settling the dispute amicably upon the basis of Manchoukuo's terms (as outlined above), which would at
least keep the customs administration of both China and
Manchoukuo intact. No doubt, Sir Frederick recognized
the wisdom of adopting Mr. Fukumoto's suggestion; but
he was not free to act alone. Sir Frederick, acting, no
doubt, under instructions of the Nanking Government,
summarily dismissed Mr. Fukumoto as Commissioner at
Dairen. Whereupon, all the Japanese staff of the Dairen
Customs, 65 in number, indignant at the unreasonable
dismissal of their chief, who had served the Chinese customs for twenty-seven years with uncommon loyalty

MANCHOUKUO CENTRAL BANK

HSINKING

and ability, wired their resignations to the Inspector-General.

Thus did the Nanking Government and Sir Frederick Maze force a showdown, and played, perhaps unwittingly, into the hands of Manchoukuo. For Manchoukuo lost no time in opening its own Customs Office in Dairen, and in reinstating Mr. Fukumoto as its Customs Commissioner there. On June 27, Mr. Fukumoto, with his former staff of 65 Japanese, took charge of the new customs.

Simultaneously, that is, between June 26 and 29, Manchoukuo took over all the maritime customs offices under its jurisdiction. These numbered forty, including branches. While the foreign commissioners at the various offices declined to serve under Manchoukuo, many of the Chinese staffs remained at their respective posts.

The importance of Manchurian customs revenue may be seen in the following table comparing the amounts of duties (in Haikwan *taels*) collected in China proper and in Manchuria in 1929 and 1930:

|      | *China*     | *Manchuria* |
|------|-------------|-------------|
| 1929 | 130,090,000 | 22,400,000  |
| 1930 | 155,691,000 | 24,553,000  |

## IV

A word about the Dairen Customs. While Czarist Russia was the master of Manchuria, she permitted no Chinese customs house to be established in Dairen. She took the stand that, within the Leased Territory of which Dairen was a part, she was free either to allow or to prohibit the establishment of a Chinese customs house. But when Japan succeeded to Russian rights in South Manchuria, she, out of a desire to develop Manchuria's foreign trade, decided to let China open a customs house in Dairen. For that purpose the Japanese Minister at Peking, Mr. Gonsuke Hayashi, and the British Inspector-General of Chinese Customs, Sir Robert Hart, signed (in May, 1907) an agreement, of which the first three articles were as follows:

1. The Commissioner or the Chief of the Maritime Customs Office at Dairen is to be of Japanese nationality. The Inspector-General of Customs will come to an understanding with the Japanese Legation at Peking in case of appointing a new Commissioner.

2. The members of the staff of the Maritime Customs Office at Dairen shall, as a rule, be of Japanese nationality; in case, however, of a suddenly occurring vacancy or of temporary requirements of the service, members of other nationalities may be provisionally sent to Dairen.

3. The Inspector-General of Customs will inform the Governor-General of the leased territory beforehand about the change of the Commissioner of Customs at Dairen.

These provisions were but an emulation of the examples set by other Powers in their respective leased territories in China. Thus the Chinese Government and the Inspector-General of Customs bound themselves to consult the Japanese Legation and the Governor-General of the Kwantung Leased Territory before changing the Commissioner at Dairen. This agreement was plainly violated when Sir Frederick Maze, acting under the pressure of the Nationalist Government, dismissed Commissioner Fukumoto without even notifying the Governor-General of the Leased Territory.

Japan was even more anxious than Manchoukuo to obtain an amicable settlement of the Dairen Customs question. It was reported that her plan of compromise was virtually the same as that of Manchoukuo, which has already been outlined in this chapter. The Manchoukuo Government, as soon as it was organized, ordered all customs offices under its jurisdiction, except the Dairen office, to stop remitting customs receipts to the Inspector-General at Shanghai. Not until June 12, as we have noted, was a similar order given the Dairen Customs Office. This delay was in deference to Japan's hope of effecting an amicable adjustment. This hope was blighted through China's refusal to consider any practicable plan of compromise.

Technically, the Dairen Customs question had remained unsolved until Japan formally recognized Manchoukuo on September 15, 1932. The recognition changed the whole situation. By it, the sovereignty of the Kwantung Leased Territory, in which Dairen is locatedw, has been transferred from China to Manchoukuo, though its administration, as heretofore, remains in Japan's hands. Both as a legal question and as a practical matter, China can no longer send her own Customs Commissioner to Dairen, now a foreign territory to her. China may refuse to recognize the independence of Manchuria and insist upon appointing her own officials to the Dairen Customs Office, but if Manchoukuo, invoking her sovereignty over Dairen, asks Japan (the lessee of that territory) to bar out Chinese appointees, Japan will be legally obliged to comply with the request, and there is nothing China can do about it.

Knowing this, China threatens to collect duties on goods destined to Dairen at the customs houses at Shanghai, Tsingtao, or Tientsin, when ships carrying such goods stop at such Chinese ports *en route* to Dairen. But Manchoukuo thinks that this retaliatory measure will have little effect upon the import trade of Dairen; it is at least confident that a way can be found to counteract it.

v

In the chapter on Manchoukuo's finances, we have noted that the new Government has been far more generous than the old Chang régime in remitting its quota of salt revenue to the Inspector-General of the Salt Gabelle at Shanghai. This has international significance, because the income of the Salt Gabelle has been hypothecated to certain of China's foreign creditors. Chief among the foreign obligations thus secured are the following, the figures being as of January 1, 1930:

Anglo-French loan of 1908................. 2,500,000
Hukuan Railway Loan, 1911 (British, German, French, American) ................ 5,501,000
Crisp (British) loan, 1912 ................ 4,584,000

We have seen that the late Marshal Chang Tso-lin appropriated all the income of the Salt Gabelle for several years, sending no part of it to China. We have seen that his son, Chang Hsueh-liang, did a little better, but was far from paying his full quota to China. Finally, we have noted that the new Manchoukuo Government has not only been paying its own quotas in full, but has even paid up the arrears left by Chang Hsueh-liang.

Finally, we shall see how Manchoukuo is going to settle the old régime's foreign debts on goods bought on credit or on contracts which had remained unexecuted.

Soon after the establishment of the new Government, a special commission was organized for the liquidation of such foreign claims. The chairman was Mr. K. Sakatani,

Japanese adviser to the Department of Finance of the Manchoukuo Government. It was found that the creditors of this class included Americans, Japanese, British, French, German, Norwegian, Swedish, Netherlanders, Czechoslovakians, etc. These had been approaching the Manchoukuo Government for settlement through their respective consular representatives in Manchuria. The cases involved were more than 1,100 in number, and the total sum of claims amounted to some 12,000,000 *yuan* in the new Manchoukuo currency. Most of the claims were in connection with the famous Mukden Arsenal, for which the old-régime war lords had bought machinery and supplies from all quarters of the globe, with no regard for the coördination essential to so vast a plant.

After a careful study, the liquidation commission, on December 14, 1932, made public the following plan:

1. The claims whose contracts were concluded since 1930 and whereby goods were duly delivered amount to approximately 7,110,000 *yuan*. Of this amount, 35% or approximately 2,500,000 *yuan* will be paid in cash during the fiscal year July 1, 1932-June 30, 1933, and 20% or approximately 1,500,000 *yuan* during the next fiscal year, in uniform ratio to all creditors. The balance of this sum will be paid in 3% bonds, redeemable in 20 years, whose total face value shall be equivalent to the sum to be paid.

2. In regard to the contracts agreed upon prior to and including 1929, as well as those whose goods were not delivered, totalling 5,410,000 *yuan* or thereabouts, the sum of the contracts or damages incurred in each case will be reasonably decided upon after careful investigation, and will be paid in similar bonds with face value equivalent to the sum so decided.

The above plan has already been accepted in principle by the British traders concerned, on January 12. The Americans interested are reported to be in favor of a plan which will allow foreigners, who will receive the above-mentioned bonds, to use these bonds in paying customs duties on their future shipments to Manchuria.

Such is the record of Manchoukuo's dealings with foreign governments and foreigners. It is an honorable record. No fair-minded critic can fail to recognize it. It stands out in striking contrast when compared with the foreign dealings of Soviet Russia or of Nationalist China. If Manchoukuo keeps up this record unwaveringly and consistently, paying no attention to the sinister criticisms of the prejudiced, nothing in the world can prevent her from receiving the recognition due her.

# CHAPTER XI

## JEHOL AND BARGA, HOME OF THE MONGOLS

### I

WHEN Henry Pu-yi, the last of the Manchu Emperors, agreed to head the new Government of Manchoukuo as Chief Executive, few other racial groups under his prospective jurisdiction were so jubilant as were the Mongols. This was natural. The Mongols were the allies of the Manchus when the Manchus were waging war against the Chinese almost three centuries ago. When the war ended in Manchu victory and in the establishment of a Manchu Government at Peking, the Mongols were generously rewarded. In the words of Mr. Owen Lattimore (Foreign Affairs, January, 1933), the Manchu Dynasty "granted to the Mongols privileges, honors and a degree of tribal autonomy which made them, in their own estimation, peers of the Manchus and superiors of the Chinese. There is no doubt that princes and church would rally to a Manchu Emperor if they were convinced that he had come to stay and could give them real support."

Contrary to the deep sense of affinity that has always existed between the two races of the north, the Mongols' feelings toward the Chinese have been anything but friendly. They looked, and still look, upon the Chinese as marauding squatters sneaking into their territory only to exploit and expropriate them. This enmity is deep-seated and fundamental. It comes from the essential difference in the respective economic schemes of the two races—the Mongol irrevocably wedded to the life of a herdsman, the Chinese a son of the soil, ever making inroads into lands which the Mongol would preserve for grazing purposes. Since "Cain killed Abel because Abel's sheep trespassed on Cain's cornfields," farmers and shepherds have never been friends. To this eternal conflict of interests the Great Wall, which stands a barrier between China and the land of the Mongols and Manchus, is a fit monument.

Unfortunately, even this barrier did not prevent the northern "barbarians" from carrying periodic invasions into China, nor did it keep the Chinese from making inroads into Mongolia and Manchuria. Brave in war, the Mongols are no equals of the Chinese in the art of barter and bargaining. Pitted against the business acumen of the Chinese, the Mongols invariably go to the wall. That is why there has always been much enmity between the two races. The Manchu Dynasty, in order to protect the Mongols and Manchus, prohibited Chinese immigration into Mongolia and Manchuria from 1740 to the beginning of the present century. There was also a law forbidding Chinese women to pass beyond the Great Wall. Moreover, Manchu women were allowed to marry no Chinese except those who had served in the Manchu army and had been made "bannermen."

But before the ban was put upon Chinese immigration, Chinese had already settled in Manchuria in large numbers. When the Tang and the Ming Dynasties, both Chinese, had invaded Manchuria as a measure of self-protection against the recurrent "barbarian" assaults, many of the Chinese who had followed the invaders as soldiers or hangers-on remained in Manchuria. Meanwhile, the Manchu Dynasty, impelled by the necessity of maintaining order and preventing possible rebellion in China (which it had subjugated), drafted most of the Manchu men for garrison duty inside the Great Wall. Moreover, by the beginning of the present century the Manchu Dynasty, though still opposed to Chinese immigration into Manchuria, had been obliged to lift the ban in the hope of counteracting the increasing Russian inroads into that country.

For these reasons Manchuria, though regarded as a Manchu reservation, has become predominantly Chinese in population. The Chinese interlopers have become the majority as against the minority of Mongols and Manchus, who consider themselves the rightful owners of the lands north of the Great Wall.

While the Manchus have been assimilated by Chinese culture and adopted Chinese customs, the Mongols have to this day maintained an attitude of sullen aloofness toward the Chinese. So strong is this Mongol antipathy that "the majority of their [Mongols'] leaders," as Mr. Lattimore tells us, "are resigned to almost any amount of Japanese control if only they are guaranteed against Chinese colonization."

II

There are about 2,000,000 Mongols in Manchuria. Of this total, half a million is in Jehol and the remainder in Fengtien, Kirin, Hei-lung-kiang and Barga provinces, but mostly in Barga. Let us first consider Jehol province.

Jehol is a province of 60,550 square miles, with a population consisting, roughly, of 3,600,000 Chinese and

500,000 Mongols. The province is famous as the birth-place of Chin Lung (1736-95), the greatest emperor of the Manchu Dynasty which ruled China and Manchuria from 1662 to 1911. In 1703 Emperor Kwang Hsi built in Chengteh, commonly known as Jehol City, a magnificent palace which was maintained until the Dynasty's fall in 1911 as a summer palace and a place of refuge in case of serious disturbance within the Great Wall. Twice did the Manchu Court take flight to this palace—once in 1860 when the British and French forces entered Peking and again in 1911 when Emperor Hsuan Tung, now Mr. Henry Pu-yi, abdicated in favor of the "republican" régime. What wonder that Mr. Pu-yi, having returned to power as the ruler of Manchuria—his homeland and ancestral domain—should place Jehol under his jurisdiction?

Under the Manchu Government, as we have seen, Jehol had been regarded as a Mongolian reservation. For this reason, Jehol had been kept separate from the three original provinces of Manchuria—Fengtien, Kirin and Hei-lung-kiang, which together had been called the Three Eastern Provinces. There was not the slightest doubt as to the Manchu intention of keeping Jehol outside the pale of China proper but as part of Manchuria. When China became a Republic in 1911, she was desirous of establishing closer relations with Jehol, and conferred upon it the new official name of the "Special District of the Eastern Provinces." For a short time its governors were appointed by the Chinese Government at Peking. But when Chang Tso-lin, the late war lord of Manchuria, became powerful, no appointee of Peking who was not acceptable to him could hold office.

From the foregoing it is clear that historically, traditionally, and legally, Jehol belongs to Manchuria. The Great Wall is a line of demarcation between it and China. Its natives, the Mongols, are hostile to the further inroads of the Chinese, though they seem to tolerate those already settled in their province. The Mongols in Jehol are grouped in various Mengs, or Leagues, the chief of which are known as the Chosoto League and the Chaouda League. These leagues seem to maintain certain relations with the Cherimu League, an organization of the Mongols in other provinces in Manchuria. Contrary to a statement in the Lytton Commission's report, there is no Cherimu League in Jehol.

According to Mr. Lattimore, "some of the Mongols in Jehol have lost their language, but the majority preserve it; none have forgotten their nationality. Though they are not nomadic, and live like the Chinese, they cherish the memory of their Mongol race and rarely intermarry with Chinese." The intensity of the antipathy of nomad Mongols toward the Chinese may be judged from the fact that they look upon the non-nomadic Mongols in Jehol with mingled suspicion, pity, and contempt. Indeed, the Jehol Mongols are sorry figures. On one hand, they are out of touch with the main stock of Mongols living in Barga and the Inner and Outer Mongolias, and, on the other, they keep aloof from their Chinese neighbors whom they think are cunning, treacherous, and grasping.

When the delegates of the various provinces met at Mukden, in February, 1932, to consider the establishment of the new State of Manchoukuo, the Mongols were represented by two representatives, Chi Wang and Ling Sheng. The Mongols all over Manchuria saw in the new

State a new hope for their regeneration and their eman-
cipation from Chinese oppression. From the beginning
of Manchoukuo, the incorporation of Jehol in its territory
was a definite plan.

Since 1924, Jehol has been governed by General Tang
Yu-lin, who, like Chang Tso-lin, the late war lord of Manchuria, rose from the ranks of bandits. Close friends at
first, Chang and Tang later fell out for reasons of personal interest. When the separatist or independence movements cropped up in various sections in Manchuria, in the
wake of the Sino-Japanese clash at Mukden on September
18, 1931, Tang seems to have maintained an attitude of
friendly neutrality toward them. When these movements
culminated in an All-Manchuria Independence Conference held at Mukden on February 16-17, 1932, Tang did
not attend the meeting in person, but was represented by
one of his lieutenants, Hsieh Lu-sih. Moreover, he put his
name to the Declaration of Independence adopted by the
Conference, and thus signified his intention of casting his
lot with the new State of Manchoukuo.

Nevertheless, General Tang was not free to act as he
pleased, for Marshal Chang Hsueh-liang had sent emissaries, "volunteers," and even regular soldiers into Jehol,
for the double purpose of restraining General Tang from
coöperating with Manchoukuo and of establishing a base
of operation against the new régime. Thus General Tang
became a virtual prisoner in his own province. Though
he is, at heart, sympathetic toward Hsinking, he is compelled to feign a friendship with Peiping. That is why
he has appeared to be carrying water on both shoulders.

Jehol is the key to the peace of Manchoukuo. It cannot

be left in the hands of Marshal Chang's volunteers and regulars, if Manchoukuo is to restore and maintain order within its jurisdiction. As Mr. Lattimore says, "Jehol is an obvious base for Chinese guerrilla warfare against Manchoukuo," and "if the new State is to survive, a struggle between it and China for the mastery of Jehol is inevitable."

Marshal Chang derives much of his war fund from Jehol opium. His illicit income from this source is estimated at 40,000,000 *yuan* a year; some put it even as high as 1,000,000 *yuan* a month. If Manchoukuo expells Chinese forces from Jehol and establishes a firm hold upon it, Marshal Chang will lose both a base of operation and a rich source of war revenue used against the new Manchurian régime. Furthermore, Manchoukuo has established an opium monopoly conceived to put all opium production and consumption under rigid governmental control. Unless Jehol, the largest opium-producing province in Manchoukuo, is controlled by the Hsinking Government, this new policy, which, it is hoped, will solve the noxious opium question, cannot effectively be carried out. This matter is more fully discussed in Chapter XII. In Chapter XIII an account will be found of how the so-called "volunteers" in Jehol are organized.

### III

One of the novel features of the Manchoukuo Government is the Hsingan Province Board, instituted within the State Council and under the direct supervision of the Prime Minister. The function of this Board is to look after the affairs of Hsingan province, the new administrative district which was, under the old régime, a part of

Hei-lung-kiang province—a vast region covering almost the entire northern half of Manchuria.

The new province of Hsingan covers the mountainous regions on either side of the Hsingan range and also vast and thickly settled plains west of these mountains. The province is essentially Mongol land, though Chinese are found in considerable numbers on its fringes. That is why the Manchoukuo Government separated it from the eastern half of hei-lung-kiang, where the population is mostly Chinese.

The new Government, headed by a former Manchu Emperor, and professing the humanitarian principle of *Wangtao,* the *Way of the King,* considers it one of its missions to put an end to Chinese exploitation of the Mongols, and to accord the Mongols the protection for which they had been crying. The Mongols look upon Mr. Pu-yi, whose forefathers were their allies and protectors, as the one man who can deliver them from the sad fate to which they seem to have been condemned.

Discussing Manchoukuo's creation of Hsingan province and a special Board for its administration, Mr. Lattimore makes these significant observations:

Ever since the fall of the Manchu Dynasty, when Russia made good a claim to "special interests" in Outer Mongolia, the world has assumed that the Mongols were no longer a force in controlling their own destiny. It has been taken for granted that Russia on the north and China on the south would gradually devour Mongolia, while the majority of the Mongols would die out and the negligible remnant become absorbed among Russians and Chinese. No one has thought that the Russian device of setting up a Soviet Republic in Outer Mongolia, and the Chinese formula of calling the Mongols one of the "five constituent races" of the Chinese Republic, were anything but convenient temporary fictions.

The attempt to create a new Manchurian state, the recognition of the Mongol element within it, and the setting apart of a large frontier province which is virtually a Mongol reserve, have totally changed the situation. The Japanese have long claimed a special interest in "Manchuria and Eastern Inner Mongolia," but the geographical limit of this claim has never been properly defined. It must in fact be based on the three eastern "Leagues" of Inner Mongolia, Cherim, Chao-ude and Chosotu, which lie within the administration of modern Manchuria; but little attention has been given to defining "Eastern Inner Mongolia," because there was a great stretch of Chinese-colonized territory between the sphere of immediate Japanese activity and the nearest Mongol nomads; and Mongol affairs, considered as affairs of the Mongols themselves, were in any case held to form an academic question.

The recognition of a regional Mongol interest by the creation of Hsingan province is important because it means that instead of two nations, each treating its Mongol subjects as auxiliaries or victims as seemed expedient, three nations are now bidding for power. This in turn means that the Mongols can no longer be disposed of arbitrarily; they must be courted, and thus they have once more become to a certain extent agents of their own destiny. Until a year ago they had only the choice of extinction under Chinese rule or drastic social revolution under Outer Mongolia, affiliated as it is with Soviet Russia. Now they have at least a margin of bargaining power, for any concerted action, or even the action of a determined minority, can profoundly affect the policies and strategic positions of Russia, China and Japan.

The Mongols of Barga are, in certain respects, different from their fellow tribesmen in Outer Mongolia and those in Jehol and Fengtien provinces. For some reason, Barga was affected comparatively little by the great migrations which took place among the Mongol tribes, in the twelfth and thirteenth centuries, and the tremendous upheavals which attended them. Thus more or less isolated from the rest of the Mongol tribes, the Mongols of Barga have maintained a certain spirit of independence. They are uncompromisingly anti-Chinese and have, in the face of great odds, resisted Chinese inroads more effectively than have their fellow men in other parts of Manchuria.

Being anti-Chinese, the Barga Mongols are also anti-railway, for, to them, the Chinese are the inevitable concomitants of the railway. It was the Chinese Eastern Railway, built by Russia toward the end of the past century, which has brought Chinese colonists in increasing numbers into their country. Naturally, they think that any new railway extended into their domain is a menace to their existence, for the Chinese "invaders," never pastoral herdsmen, are bound to apply the plough to the land which the Mongols are determined to reserve for their herds. If Manchoukuo, with Japanese advice, is to build new railways in Barga, it must first convince the Mongols there that the purpose of the railway is not to bring Chinese, or Korean or Japanese agriculturists, into their midst, but rather to develop the forestry and pastoral industries by facilitating the marketing of wool, lumber and meats. This is a very difficult task for the new Government, which is controlled by Chinese and which would naturally put the interest of the Chinese majority before that of the Mongol minority. Whether the Japanese advisers are far-seeing enough to formulate a sane Mongol policy, and influential enough to carry it out in the teeth of Chinese opposition, we have yet to see. The creation of the separate Mongol province of Hsingan and the establishment in the Central Government of a special board, presided over by a Mongol prince, for the administration of Mongol affairs seem to show that the Japanese advisers are keenly alive to the great importance of the question so long neglected by the Chinese. At least it is a step in the right direction. If it is followed by wise measures allowing the Mongols the autonomy they desire, yet giving them an opportunity for advancement along modern lines, it is quite possible that Outer Mongolia, now under Soviet tutelage, will veer toward Barga and eventually even merge with it, thus accepting the suzerainty or sovereignty of Manchoukuo. For Outer Mongolia, though it was forced to accept Red protection by the sheer necessity of guarding itself against Chinese oppression, still cherishes a certain sense of kinship toward Manchuria in general and Barga in particular, especially now that Manchoukuo is ruled by a Manchu. The Mongols of Outer Mongolia will not easily forget the brutality with which the Chinese treated them in 1919-20, when China sent an expedition into that country. So horrible was it that the Mongols were at last stirred to fury and massacred most of the Chinese invaders, thus bringing to a culmination the intense hostility which had long existed between the two peoples. Outer Mongolia, hating China and feeling not entirely at home with Soviet Russia, may yet reorientate its policy in favor of Manchoukuo. That, of course, presupposes a wise, generous, yet firm, policy on the part of Manchoukuo.

# CHAPTER XII

## SOLVING THE OPIUM QUESTION

### I

WHEN the Manchoukuo Government promulgated the opium law on November 30, 1932, it took the first step toward the solution of the opium evil, which had been leading China on the road to degeneration for more than a century. The law, as it stands, leaves much room to be desired. Evidently it was hastily drafted to meet the exigencies of the period of transition from the old régime, which encouraged the production and use of opium, to the new, which aims at the eventual eradication of the age-long curse. Before a more comprehensive law can be framed, a scientific investigation must be carried out as to the number of addicts, the volume and varieties of opium produced in Manchuria, the number of opium dens and retailers, etc. The present law, therefore, may be regarded as a stop-gap.

Under this temporary law, "no person shall be allowed to smoke opium." Only to those adults who had already acquired the habit before the law was issued will a special permit be given. No juvenile, whether an addict or not, shall be given permission. The government is to undertake directly the manufacture and sale of prepared opium. No one shall be permitted to cultivate opium poppy without a government license. All raw opium obtained by poppy growers shall be purchased by the Government

Monopoly Bureau. From my conversations with them it is evident that their intention is to adopt, eventually, a system similar to that in Formosa, as well as a system of hospitals for the cure of addicts. The nucleus of this latter system already exists in Manchuria, for the South Manchurian Railway Hospital at Mukden and two private hospitals in Dairen, also helped by the Railway, have for some years been treating addicts.

II

It is, then, pertinent to take a glance at the Japanese system of opium-control as practiced in Formosa. The essential features of that system are the registration, licensing, and rationing of addicts, and absolute prohibition of opium-smoking among non-addicts. In Formosa no one without a license issued by the proper authorities is permitted either to sell or to obtain opium. An addict can obtain a license only when the fact of his addiction is established by examination by an authorized physician. The quantity of opium for daily consumption is determined by the degree of addiction and is designated on the license, as well as in the pass book with which each licensed addict is provided and which he must produce whenever he wishes to obtain his ration from the licensed dealer. The quantity of opium the dealer is permitted to sell an addict at a time shall not exceed his (the addict's) ration for three days. The dealer is required to enter in his retail book the names and addresses of the addicts who have obtained opium of him, together with the quantities and prices of opium sold to each. Should the entries in the dealer's retail book disagree with the entries in the addict's pass book, the police authorities might investigate the discrepancy, thus minimizing the chances of the addict's purchases exceeding his prescribed ration.

This Japanese system, is, contrary to popular understanding, widely different from the system which is in effect in all European colonies in Asia—India, Ceylon, the Straits Settlements, the Federated and Unfederated Malay States, British North Borneo, Sarawak, Brunei, Mauritius, Hongkong, Iraq, the Netherlands, East Indies, and French Indo-China. Under the Japanese system both opium dealers and addicts are licensed; under the European system dealers are licensed, but addicts are not. In practical operation the two systems bring about vastly different results.

India furnishes the best illustration of the European system. There the addict neither is licensed nor has his ration regulated by the authorities. The only restriction is that no licensed dealer may, to quote from *The Truth about India Opium,* published by the India Office of the British Government, "sell to any one person at one time more than the quantity of opium which an individual may lawfully possess." Note the language used in designating an opium buyer. This document significantly uses the term "any one person" or "an individual," instead of "a licensed addict." Any one in India, whether an addict or a non-addict, may obtain opium from any licensed druggist or vendor. True, the quantity he may buy at a time is limited to something between 360 and 540 grains according to locality, but as there is no rationing system enforced by means of license and purchase book, he may make repeated purchases at different shops by disposing of the amount of one purchase between times. In India not even minors are prohibited from smoking opium, while in Formosa no minor is permitted to smoke.

In order to put the license and ration system into effect, the Formosa Government had to ascertain the number of addicts. This was no easy task, as Formosa, under the old régime, had never taken a census. But without waiting until the enumeration was completed, the government, in 1898, licensed 95,449 addicts. In 1900, as a result of a more thoroughgoing survey, the number increased to 165,752. During the following ten years 50,000 more addicts, who had escaped the previous enumerations, were given a license. Yet, in spite of this addition, the total of addicts decreased year by year. In 1900 total addicts, as we have seen, numbered 165,752. By 1926 these had decreased to 33,755. As the government issues no license either to non-addicts or to minors, the majority of the licensed addicts at present are over fifty-five years of age. Only a few, less than twenty, are between twenty-one and thirty years of age, while about 24,000 are of various ages between fifty-one and seventy. Therefore, in twenty years hence, the opium-using population will become a negligible quantity.

Such is the Formosa system, the goal aimed at by Manchoukuo. It will be noticed that in Formosa, the opium monopoly was inaugurated in 1898, that is, three years after the island was taken over by Japan. Even then the number of addicts had not been fully ascertained. Not until 1900 was the administration prepared to carry out the law in all its details. Manchoukuo adopted an opium monopoly within eight months after its independence. It is, therefore, only natural that the law is considered merely a step in the right direction.

### III

As Mr. Owen Lattimore, in his illuminating and schollarly *Manchuria: Cradle of Conflict,* tells us, "Opium has been cultivated openly, under official license and land tax, in the oldest settled regions of Manchuria, in years when the large revenue thus available was imperatively needed for the financing of Manchurian armies participating in civil wars in China." It is commonly known that the war lords, in order to finance their military adventures, compelled farmers to give up cultivating grain or beans and to grow the poppy instead, not only for the high land tax imposed upon poppy farms but also for the fabulous profits obtained by the miiltarists through various schemes in connection with the retail of opium. Under war-lordism, Manchuria maintained the so-called "Opium Suppression Bureaus," but the real business of these bureaus was to raise an enormous revenue by imposing a heavy "fine," namely a license, upon the poppy farmers and opium dealers. In Hei-Lung-Kiang province, says the *China Year Book,* "it is estimated that $2,000,000 can be raised yearly from planting only, and several times this amount from the tax of 50 cents an ounce on opium and $20 a year for a smoking license." This means a revenue of some $15,000,000 (silver) in this single province. The *China Year Book* further says that in Kirin and Fengtien provinces the condition was much the same.

Jehol province is more extensively planted with the poppy and is, according to the *China Year Book,* "the source of the bulk of the opium supplied to Manchuria." Indeed, Jehol is the largest opium-producing province in Manchuria. Including poppy-land tax and planting license, tax on opium, license for smokers, and tax on the transportation of opium, etc., the annual opium revenue of Jehol must amount to 50,000,000 silver dollars.

From the above, it is fairly clear that the aggregate opium revenue of the four provinces under the old régime must have amounted to almost 100,000,000 silver dollars. It is also fair to assume that most of this total went into the coffers of the Changs, former war lords of Manchuria.

The above figures are obtained upon the basis of taxes and license fees levied in the high-sounding name of "suppression." But under the Chang régimes there were other opium revenues whose amount could not be ascertained, or even conjectured, because these were collected not through regular tax offices but by underhand methods such as are commonly employed by the "racketeers" of Chicago or New York in the illicit handling of liquor under the prohibition law. Every one knows that the Changs themselves were directly interested in the opium traffic, buying opium in large quantities and retailing it at a fabulous profit. Of course, this was done by the war lords' henchmen, who, in America, would be called "gangsters" or "racketeers." In addition to regular license fees, these gangsters extorted "hush" money from opium-den keepers. They could do this because nominally, or legally, opium was prohibited, which furnished the "gangsters" with effective means of preying upon their victims. And the biggest of all the gangsters were the war lords themselves, though they hid themselves behind the smoke-screen of conventionality.

The Manchoukuo Government, with Japanese advice, is determined to root out this "racketeering" system. As a principle, it prohibits opium, but it openly makes exceptions for the addicts who cannot get along without opium. Its budget for the current year includes an estimated revenue of only 5,000,000 silver dollars from the opium monopoly. The sum is insignificant as compared with the revenue raised by the old régime both openly and clandestinely from the same source.

IV

We have seen that Jehol is the largest source of opium supply in Manchuria. That is one of the reasons why the Manchoukuo Government is anxious to control it. If the new opium monopoly system is to work effectively, opium production in that province must be regulated so that Jehol opium will not be secretly dumped upon the market throughout Manchuria.

V

Opium has an important bearing upon agriculture, the transportation system, and banditry. In the localities where the farmers are compelled by militarists to grow the poppy, food shortage, and even famine, is often the consequence. "The most serious abuses," to quote Mr. Lattimore again, "is the forced cultivation of the poppy. The normal form of overproduction is that found in territories where land taxation is enforced at a rate which can only be met by poppy growing; the revenue usually being spent in the maintenance of armies. Production on such a large scale brings down the price and increases the consumption; but, more than that, it weakens the economic structure by reducing the area under food crops. In heavily populated agricultural communities in China this is very serious, for the average farmer, even in normal times, not only lives poorly and eats poorly but is unable to hold more than a very small food reserve. . . . In a region, therefore, in which the land tax has enforced poppy growing widely enough to reduce food crops to a bare subsistence level, one bad season can precipitate a famine, even when other parts of the country have an ample reserve."

In Manchuria, as elsewhere in China, banditry is almost an inevitable concomitant of opium culture. Where farmers raise the poppy without paying the high land tax and license fees, bandits are hired to protect them from the officers of the law. Naturally, banditry is a profitable business in opium-growing regions. Many of the bandits are themselves opium-growers on the side.

Lack of transportation facilities is an indirect cause of opium cultivation. Along railways, good cart roads, or navigable rivers, the farmers have facilities to ship heavy crops such as beans and grain. But the pioneers settling on the fringes of cultivated areas encounter great difficulty in transporting their crops. If, on the other hand, they raise the poppy they have no transportation problem to worry about. Raw opium, even to the tune of thousands of dollars, is small in volume and can easily be shipped even where there are no good roads.

If Manchoukuo, in cöoperation with Japan, extends its railway system into the rich but as yet undeveloped regions, the poppy culture now popular in such regions will gradually give way to the legitimate business of growing food crops.

## VI

In 1923 Sir Francis Aglen, Inspector-General of the Chinese Maritime Customs, advocated an opium monopoly as the only practical means of solving the opium question in China. No doubt Sir Francis had in mind the British system in India. If so, the suggested plan, for the reason already explained in a foregoing paragraph, would not have solved the problem. The plan, which is now in the minds of the Manchoukuo authorities, is the Formosa system, which is materially different from the India system.

Should Manchoukuo succeed in carrying out the plan, that alone would be worth the independence it has achieved from China. Think of the opium peril in China. That country today produces within her borders something like 30,000 tons of opium a year. As the *China Year Book* tells us, "So complete is the reversion to the old opium days of unrestricted indulgence that secrecy is not required. In the provinces, taxation removes all semblance of legal infraction, and thereby encourages an openness of use which renders the act perfectly legitimate. Governers, generals, and magistrates smoke in their offices, and offer it to their visitors; hotels and restaurants supply the pipe publicly; the majority of country inns do likewise; trains and steamboats permit smoking and literally the atmosphere is everywhere filled with the pungent fumes of the burning drug."

Nor is it among the wealthier or high classes alone that the evil practice is so rampant. The condition is equally bad, perhaps worse, among the lower classes. This is particularly so because the masses of people, oppressed and exploited by the militarists, are so disheartened and hopeless that they seek a doubtful and fleeting comfort in opium. "In an era of social change, of strife without end, lack of economic security and hopelessness all too often seemingly without horizon," writes Mr. Lattimore, "it is in the lower strata that the greatest damage is done" by opium. The poorer people in China take more and more to swallowing opium or drinking it dissolved in water, thus evading the pipe tax and satisfying their want by using a smaller amount of opium.

Not only do the Chinese authorities everywhere encourage, even enforce, poppy cultivation, but high officials, both military and civil, national and local, are personally and privately interested in the traffic, deriving fabulous fortunes therefrom. Although the transactions are done under cover, they are of such magnitude that they cannot entirely or always be kept secret. I shall describe a few which are highly illustrative of the traffic.

In 1916 a party consisting of seven members of "parliament" at Peking, the newly appointed Minister of Justice, and General Tsai Ao, arrived in Shanghai from Yunnan province, noted for opium production. At a certain stage of their journey by sea, a telegram was sent to the Maritime Customs at Shanghai requesting the usual facilities accorded to high officials. On arrival at Shanghai, the baggage of the party was bowed past the inspecting officers without examination and joyfully removed to a native hotel in the International Settlement. There then followed a quick distribution of the baggage to the far corners of the city. The municipal police, however, arrived just in time to catch the last four trunks, and to arrest the M. P.'s in charge. These gentlemen bitterly opposed the examination of their belongings and swore that the trunks contained nothing but official papers. But the foreign policemen, being without bowels, forcibly opened the boxes and found them filled to the brim with opium. They obtained other evidence which enabled them to trace twenty more trunks to the official residence of the Chinese city magistrate. These, being found in an adjacent house, were given up, and on examination were also found to contain "official papers"! The opium seized was valued at $750,000, and there were thirty-six trunks missing, believed to contain opium worth $1,125,000.

In 1924 Fukien militarists arranged with their confreres of the neighboring province to land about $20,000,-000 worth of opium at a small seaport north of Ningpo, and the militarists of Hunan, Kweichow and Szechuan transported tons of it to Hanyang for the purchase of arms and ammunition. About the same time, 150 tons of Yunnan opium was brought out through Tonkin and found its way to Tsingtau where it was disposed of to raise funds for certain military and naval cliques. In 1925 certain ships of the Chinese Navy landed an enormous quantity of opium at Shanghai. In November, 1928, Shanghai was agog over a scandal of unprecedented magnitude. An opium cargo worth $50,000,000 Mexican, brought down the Yangtse River from the interior by a military faction, was seized by an opposing faction. The trail of the scandal, it was said, led to the very gate of the office of President Chiang Kai-shek, and Marshal Feng Yu-hsiang, the so-called "Christian general," was anxious to expose it to discredit the President, his avowed political rival. The whole affair was "whitewashed."

Finally, let me cite a most interesting case which came under my personal observation and which furnishes a most apt illustration of the subtlety of opium dealings in which Chinese dignitaries are involved. On February 2, 1931, the Japanese captain of a Chinese steamer named *Ejinnoun* was arrested by the Japanese Consul at Canton on the ground that the ship under his command brought a large quantity of opium from Persia. The nominal owner of the ship was the Yung Hsian Company, which was the dummy for the Tung Yung Company, the capital of which was 2,000,000 *yuan* and whose leading members were Chen Ming-shu, Ou Yang-chu, Pan Chi-wu and other prominent politicians then in control of the Canton Government. Its secretaries were Chen Tsu, commander of the naval fleet at Canton, and Weng Kuei-ching, an inspector of the Maritime Customs of the same port. The steamer *Ejinnoun,* owned by this company, cleared from the harbor of Bushire, Persia, on January 2, 1931, with two large cases of opium, but, before sailing, the ship assumed the Japanese name of *Sagara Maru.* When the ship was sailing through the Malacca Straits, she was stopped by the Dutch Opium Monopoly Administration's ship, *Valk,* whose captain suspected that the Chinese ship with a Japanese name carried a contraband cargo. Then the Japanese captain raised the Japanese flag, and replied that the ship was of Japanese nationality. The Dutch captain permitted the ship to proceed, but at the same time cabled the Dutch Consul at Canton, advising him to notify the Maritime Customs that a suspicious-looking ship was headed for Canton.

When the "Chinese-Japanese" ship arrived at a point five miles below Canton, she was met by a lighter to which the cases of opium were transferred and immediately taken to an unknown destination without going through customs inspection. The lighter was escorted by two Chinese destroyers. Although the Maritime Customs, whose chief inspector was an Englishman, had been advised by the Dutch Consul of the suspicious nature of the ship, the officers did nothing, because they knew that practically all the "higher ups" of Canton were interested in the smuggling business.

But when the ship, having disposed of the opium, docked at Canton, her Japanese captain, a Seitaro Matsushita, was arrested by the Japanese Consul, who had also been advised by the Dutch Consul. Ordinarily, he would have been tried at the Japanese Consulate at Canton, but in view of the delicate nature of the case, the trial was transferred to the Japanese court at Taihoku, Formosa, where he was sentenced to a month's imprisonment on the charge that he had abused the Japanese flag, a violation of the merchant marine law. He confessed that he had been promised a compensation of 200,000 *yuan* for the voyage by the Chinese smuggling ring, although the actual amount paid, he said, was only 15,000 *yuan*. It was generally said in Canton that out of the total proceeds of that smuggled cargo the National Government at Nanking received, or was to receive, $2,000,000 and the Canton provincial government $1,000,000. Needless to say that the gentlemen who were directly interested in the enterprise pocketed a fabulous profit.

While China imports foreign opium of finer quality, Chinese combines export native opium and smuggle it, as the *China Year Book* informs us, into Hongkong, the Straits Settlements, and Malay States, Indo-China, the Dutch East Indies, Borneo, Formosa, the Philippines, Japan, the United States, Canada, and South America— practically all countries where Chinese are found in large numbers. Thus Chinese opium is not only sending millions of Chinese to their moral and physical doom, but it has become a menace to other countries. And in this problem America is vitally interested, for in the last thirty years opium smuggling into this country has been growing more and more serious.

### VII

Of all Asiatic countries, Japan alone has steered clear of the opium evil. Though she is hemmed in by opium-ridden countries, though her people have been in constant contact with addicts in China and Formosa, she has not been contaminated. The only regret is that some of her traders walk in the footsteps of Western and Chinese traffickers in opium and dabble in the smuggling of the contraband into China.

Miss Ellen N. La Motte, in her *The Ethics of Opium*,* says, "Japan has committed a crime which is hard to forgive; she has disproved the contention that Oriental races need opium as part of their daily bread. At the time when the European nations were loading themselves up with the White Man's Burden, Japan was considered too insignificant a burden to be worth picking up. This oversight has had far-reaching consequences, the end of which is not yet."

* Published by The Century Company. Reprinted by permission.

# CHAPTER XIII

## "VOLUNTEERS," REBELS, BANDITS, "SQUEEZES"

### I

IN Manchuria today Japan is repeating much the same experience as she went through in the early stage of her occupation of Formosa. In Formosa, from 1896, when the island came under the Japanese flag, to the first years of the present century, banditry was rampant everywhere, head-hunting savages were running amuck, rebels were waging guerrilla war, and there were only a few miles of railway and no roads worthy of the name. The condition was so bad that the world thought this colony a white elephant on Japan's hands.

Yet by 1905, only a decade after her occupation of the island, Formosa had become financially independent and had ceased to receive any subsidy from Japan. Today Formosa is a new land where the old order has been completely reversed. The Japanese administration has laid modern roads where there were only footpaths, and has built railroads equipped with up-to-date rolling stock. It has constructed or improved harbors to advance and facilitate foreign trade, and has encouraged agriculture by inaugurating an extensive system of irrigation and reclamation. It has established colleges in the larger cities, and has opened schools all over the territory, even in many of the villages inhabited by the savages. In 1897 the revenue of Formosa was only 11,283,000 *yen*. In 1925 it was

119,560,000 *yen,* as against an expenditure of 87,770,000 *yen,* leaving a surplus of 31,790,000 *yen.* Even in 1930, when the effect of the general depression was severely felt, Formosa's ordinary revenue was 101,739,000 *yen* and its ordinary expenditure 81,996,000 *yen,* a surplus of 19,743,000 *yen.* In 1897 its foreign trade amounted to only 31,000,000 *yen;* in 1928 it reached 439,072,000 *yen.*

Whether as bright a future is in store for Japan in Manchuria as well, we have yet to see. Meanwhile no one realizes more keenly than does the Japanese himself that Manchuria offers him no bed of roses and that his path there is strewn with thistles and thorns. Troubles are thick around him, due to the activities of "volunteers," rebels, bandits, and last but not least, the officials still preying upon the masses of people. For one thing, however, he is thankful namely, that in Manchuria there is no blood-thirsty, head-hunting savages, as there were 120,000 of such aborigines in Formosa.

## II

In the last year or so the world has heard so much of the Chinese "volunteers" fighting the Japanese and Manchoukuo armies. What are these volunteers? In answer I introduce two of the secret notices which have been distributed in towns and villages and in the lairs of bandits in Manchuria by the emissaries of Marshal Chang Hsueh-liang, the deposed war lord of Manchuria. When I was in Manchuria last autumn I saw these two notices found on the bodies of "volunteers" killed and in the pockets of those captured by the Japanese or Manchoukuo army.

In one of the notices the "Young Marshal" offers prizes for various sanguinary services as follows:

1. A town or village, whose inhabitants organize themselves into an anti-Japanese army, shall be exempted from all taxation for three years following the restoration of Manchuria by Marshal Chang.

2. Any one who heads an army so organized, and who succeeds in capturing a *hsien* [prefecture], shall be formally appointed the magistrate of the captured prefecture in the event of the restoration of Manchuria by Marshal Chang.

3. A civilian wounded while serving in an anti-Japanese army shall receive from 20 to 500 *yuan*. The family of a civilian similarly killed shall receive 500 to 1,000 *yuan*.

4. In the event of the restoration of Manchuria the leaders of the above-mentioned armies shall be formally appointed officers in the regular army. Those who do not wish to become officers shall receive cash rewards.

5. The parents, wives, sons, brothers and sisters of those who betray the volunteer armies, and divulge their secrets to the enemy, shall be put to death.

Tempted by these alluring offers and still more or less skeptical about the permanence of the Manchoukuo Government, not a few villages and towns have espoused the cause of the expelled war lord, and have hindered or resisted by violence the administrative activities of the new régime.

The second notice offered prizes as follows:

1. For capturing one Japanese, or for breaking a leg of a Japanese, 100 *yuan* (silver dollars). For killing more than 10 Japanese, 1,000 *yuan*.

2. For killing one foreigner, especially an Englishman or an American, 1,000 *yuan*. For capturing and holding one foreigner as hostage, 50 *yuan* per day.

3. For a pistol or rifle captured, 100 *yuan;* for a machine gun, 200 *yuan;* for a field gun, 500 *yuan;* for an airplane, 5,000 *yuan.*

4. For derailing a train, 500 *yuan.*

5. Following prizes for killing Japanese army officers; a gen-

eral, 30,000 *yuan;* a lieutenant-general, 20,000 *yuan;* a major-
general, 10,000 *yuan;* a colonel, 5,000 *yuan;* a major or a lieutenant, 2,000 *yuan.* One-half of the above sums for wounding the
officers named.

6. For killing the head of a council of the Manchoukuo Government, 20,000 *yuan.* For killing a cabinet minister of the same
Government, 10,000 *yuan.*

The encouragement offered for the capture of Europeans and Americans is a clever method of embarrassing
Manchoukuo and the Japanese. No doubt the capture of
Mrs. Muriel Pawley and Mr. Charles Corkran, both
British subjects, at Newchwang on September 7, 1932,
was in response to that encouragement—an incident
which created a world-wide sensation at the time. They
were held as hostages for fifty-six days, but were finally
rescued by the combined efforts of the Japanese gen-
darmes and the Manchoukuo police.

In the earlier days of the new Manchoukuo régime, the
"volunteers" were more widely scattered. This was possible because among the magistrates of one hundred sixty-
three *hsiens,* or prefectures, in Manchuria, quite a few had
remained adherents of the old Chang régime and acted
as Marshal Chang's emissaries. But toward the end of
1932 the "volunteers" were concentrated in Jehol province,
from which base of operation they descended upon the
plains of Fengtien province—another reason why the
Manchoukuo and Japanese forces are pressing forward to
Jehol.

### III

Of the few rebel leaders who, for one reason or another,
took field against the Manchoukuo régime, Ma Chan-
shan was most notorious. His frequent changes of front

and his final defeat and death in July, 1932, have been fully told in Chapters II and III.

Toward the end of September General Su Ping-wen, a division commander at Hailar, north Manchuria, revolted and held as hostages some 366 Japanese at Manchuli and Hailar. In this he was actuated entirely by personal grudge. He was an old-régime man, and when the new Manchoukuo Government was known to have decided to replace him with another officer, he revolted. Because of the large number of hostages he held, the Japanese forces had to proceed with the utmost caution. But, early in December, they defeated the rebels, and on December 6 entered Hailar. Whereupon the rebel chief, General Su, and his staff, instead of offering resistance, commandeered a train and fled into Russian territory, where they were disarmed by the Soviet authorities. Prior to this fiasco, most of the Japanese hostages had been released. Those who had remained in captivity were found unharmed when the Japanese forces reached Manchuli.

Perhaps the most tenacious rebel leaders were Li Tu, Ting Chao, and Wang Te-lin, all of whom had been division or regiment commanders in Kirin province under the old régime. They, too, were actuated by personal reasons. Li Tu had received military training at the Military Academy in Tokyo, and had been known to be friendly to Japan. So was Ting Chao. But neither relished the thought of taking orders from General Hsi Hsia, who had formerly been his colleague but who was appointed governor of Kirin province and Minister of Finance by the Manchoukuo Government. Wang Te-lin was inspired by much the same motives. All three operated in the northeastern part of Kirin, which is mountainous and inaccessible.

From the beginning, the cause of the Kirin trio was a forlorn one and was doomed to defeat. By the beginning of January, 1933, they had been forced back to the region adjacent to the Russian territory of the Maritime province. On January 9, Li Tu crossed the Russian border to Iman where he was disarmed by the Soviet authorities, while Ting Chao offered to surrender, disarm his troops, and proceed to Hsinking, the capital of Manchoukuo, to swear allegiance to the new government. Wang Te-lin is still holding out near the Russian border, but his fate is sealed.

Thus have the rebel leaders, one after another, succumbed or bowed to the inevitable. Those who are fighting in Jehol against the new régime are not rebels, but are soldiers sent there by Marshal Chang and the natives who have been tempted by the prizes offered by him.

IV

Now we come to the old problem of banditry. In China, organized banditry, like the organized "squeeze" system, has a history of unnumbered centuries, with the result that bandits have long been a fixed social stratum, almost as much as the gentry, the peasantry, or the trading class. In Chinese eyes, to join the bandit brotherhood is not necessarily criminal. Often whole villages or towns join the brotherhood in self-defense against official extortion. Centuries of maladministration are to blame for the existence of the organized social stratum of bandits.

Under the old régime in Manchuria, the war lords somewhat alleviated the situation, at least momentarily, by the questionable means of enlisting bandits into their armies employed in the civil war in which they were perpetually engaged. These armies were defeated and dispersed by the Japanese following the "incident" of September 18, 1931. No doubt many of the defeated soldiers have taken to banditry. Now Manchoukuo, acting upon Japanese advice, has abolished war-lordism, centralized military administration, and reduced the army to something like 100,000 men as compared with 300,000 under the old régime. The plan is a good one, but what about the bandits who are no longer to be accommodated in the army?

The work of suppressing banditry has been made immeasurably difficult by the inefficiency of the Manchoukuo soldiers, most of whom were themselves bandits and who could not quite bring themselves to fight their former comrades in earnest. This peculiar attitude of the regular soldiers toward the bandits is nothing new. Mr. Owen Lattimore, in his *Manchuria: Cradle of Conflict,* says:

> The common soldier has no great stomach for fighting bandits. He would far rather come to a sensible arrangement by which the bandits withdraw when the patrols come around, and the patrols, as they make their rounds, do not look over their shoulders at the bandits coming back. Even when, under orders from above, it is necessary for the troops to make a definite effort to clear a given territory, the private soldier will often give the game away. He will have one signal by groups of rifleshots which means "We are on patrol, but nothing serious," and another which means "Look out! We'll fight you if we find you!" This is because, in a generation of unscrupulous violence, the soldier is far from regarding the bandit as his natural enemy. The soldier, like the bandit, is a professional. The bandit wants to take villages and loot them; the soldier waits for his chance in a civil war to take towns and get either loot or promotion and power. Neither sees any point

in a stand-up fight, when the prisoners and the dead are not likely to have anything on them but arms. Moreover the bandit may some day be a soldier and the soldier a bandit. Consequently they regard themselves as colleagues with a certain professional rivalry, but not enemies unless personal quarrels arise.

Many of the Manchoukuo soldiers, being remnants of the old army, maintain the same sympathetic feeling toward the bandits. To make a really efficient army of such old materials is a difficult task and will require years of training under Japanese officers. Meanwhile, the burden of suppressing organized banditry must be shouldered largely by the Japanese troops. Yet the gentlemen at Geneva think that these bandit-soldiers can be organized into an efficient gendarmerie!

For the reason I have already intimated, it is perhaps unwise to attempt an immediate suppression of banditry. A social stratum, so old, so well-established, so vast, cannot be abolished on short order, as the Japanese military evidently thought it could be. The old régime admitted its inability to cope with the task and seldom did anything but cajole bandit chiefs into holding their men in leash. The old method of "buying" bandit chiefs is, to say the least, reprehensible. It must be abolished sooner or later. At the same time, it is well to bear in mind that repressive warfare alone would not accomplish the elimination of banditry. The Japanese military now fully realize this, and are prepared to temper their past strategy of repression with some conciliatory measures whereby such bandits as are willing to earn an honest living will be given an opportunity to work. To this end Manchoukuo will launch a program of road-building and other construction work. At the same time, it would be wise to encourage the old system of self-protection as was developed among villagers and townsfolk, until the time when this system is rendered unnecessary by the progress of Manchoukuo.

v

In the age-old "squeeze" system of China the Manchoukuo Government and its Japanese advisers have the most difficult problem to solve, if it ever can be solved. There are American and European authorities without number on this question, but I shall quote only one—the late Dr. Arthur H. Smith, whose penetrating *Chinese Characteristics* * still remains an outstanding work on China. "It is almost impossible," he says, "for any enterprise, however good or however urgent, to escape the withering effects of the Chinese system of squeezes, which is as well organised as any other part of the scheme of Chinese government. It is not easy to possess one's self of full details of the working of any regular Chinese charity, but enough has been observed during such a special crisis as the great famine, to make it certain that the deepest distress of the people is no barrier whatever to the most shameful peculation on the part of officials entrusted with the disbursement of funds for relief. And if such scandals take place under these circumstances, when public attention is most fixed on the distress and its relief, it is not difficult to conjecture what happens when there is no outside knowledge either of the funds contributed or of their use."

The above observation was made thirty years ago. To-day the same still holds true. If the American Government looks into the disposition of the wheat sold to the Nationalist Government at Nanking in 1931-32 by the

* Published by Fleming H. Revell Company. Reprinted by permission.

American Farm Board at a very special price for the relief of the great famine area in Central China, it will discover a most amazing fact. In Shanghai everybody knows that most of that wheat never reached the famine sufferers. A few years ago the American Red Cross sent to China a special commission to investigate how the funds which it had contributed toward the relief of various disasters there had been disposed of. The commission, for reasons intimated in the above quotation from Dr. Smith's book, recommended against any further contribution until the American Red Cross could convince itself that funds donated would not be abused.

Such is the system with which the new Government of Manchoukuo must grapple. In Chinese official circles, squeeze takes many forms, but the commonest ones are bribery and misappropriation of tax money. Provincial governors secure their appointments by bribing their superiors. They, in turn, receive bribes and tributes from the heads of districts known as *hsiens,* while the district heads not only recoup but amass a handsome fortune by pocketing a considerable part of taxes that they collect. Much the same practice prevails among the officials in the central government.

In China the quickest way to get rich is not to plunge into Wall Street, but to creep into the official ring. The common saying is that "an honest *hsien* magistrate amasses one hundred thousand *yuan* (Chinese dollars) in three years"—this in spite of his meager salary of four hundred *yuan* or so a month. There is no telling how much dishonest ones make. For centuries this official practice has been so general and so open that few think it criminal or even immoral.

Now came the Japanese advisers to Manchoukuo with

the new-fangled notion that official squeeze must cease, and cease at once. They did not remember that what was irregular in other modern countries was quite regular in China. Worse, they forgot that so universal, so deep-rooted, so old a system could not be got rid of on short notice. Surely the abolition of such a system must be preceded by a long period of preliminary work such as education and propaganda in the right direction.

But the impetuous Japanese preferred revolutionary change to gradual evolution. So they sent forth into *hsiens* and towns overseers, Chinese and Japanese, charged with the supervision of tax collection and with the disposal of funds collected. Most of them were young men with little experience in the administration of human affairs. Puffed up with a sense of the authority so suddenly given them, they no doubt acted arrogantly toward the district heads and town masters, who were suave, smooth-tongued, often venerable gentlemen. By their insolence and impetuosity they made themselves obnoxious to all who came in contact with them.

The local officials, fearful that their enormously profitable industry of "squeeze" was doomed to abolition, were up in arms against the new régime. Immediately they started a whispering campaign, spreading rumors that the Japanese came to exploit the people of Manchuria; that Manchoukuo would soon be annexed to Japan, and so on.

Here, then, is a dilemma for both Manchoukuo and its Japanese advisers. If they connive at the old system, the noble ideal of *Wangtao,* government by benevolence, will not be realized. If, on the other hand, they make honest and serious efforts to suppress it, the whole army of provincial and local officials, high and low, will resort to a conspiracy of sabotage which will render it very difficult for the central government to obtain the requisite revenue, for tax cannot be collected without the coöperation of local functionaries.

That the squeeze system must be abolished none will gainsay. But every one wonders how it can be abolished. It would be the miracle of miracles if Japan could ever succeed in eliminating it in Manchoukuo.

### Postscript

After this chapter was written, the *New York Times* of January 23, 1933, published an illuminating article dated Mukden, December 15, 1932, from its well-informed correspondent in China, Mr. Hallet Abend. The following passages from that article seem to tally with the views expressed in this chapter:

Japanese leaders in Manchuria now admit, though with tardy reluctance, that their own misunderstanding of Chinese customs and Chinese psychology has contributed greatly to lengthening the period of Chinese resistance. For a time the Japanese made lenient offers, outlining generous terms to the leaders of volunteer and brigand bands if they would surrender. This policy the Chinese interpreted as a sign of weakness, just as they have always interpreted such offers in their own civil wars.

Those who accepted the Japanese offers confidently expected that, as soon as they had submitted to the formality of surrendering and of being disarmed, their arms would be returned to them and they would be made "peace guardians" over their own areas. When the Japanese did not follow out these time-honored Chinese tactics, those who had surrendered felt that they had been cheated, and immediately departed for fresh fields to organize new forces of resistance.

Later, when some of the larger bands of irregulars began to

actually make terms with the Japanese, the liberal terms offered made pacification of the country enormously costly. Suppose a band of 500 irregulars in an inaccessible mountain fastness begins to parley with a representative of the Japanese Army, or of the Manchoukuo Government. Likely as not immunity is offered if arms are surrendered, free allotments of land are promised to landless farmers, transportation to their homes is guaranteed to men who already own farms, and clothing, food and a small amount of money is guaranteed to each man who gives pledges of good behavior.

News of this dickering spreads quickly over the countryside, and by the time the actual surrender occurs the original band of 500 irregulars frequently increased to 4,000 or 5,000 men, each one of whom must be taken care of.

As soon as a contingent of the Japanese army clears a given area of volunteers or of soldiers that have been in rebellion against the Manchoukuo Government, the old form of Chinese local government by magistrates is immediately reëstablished. Organizers employed by the Manchoukuo Government follow close upon the heels of the Japanese soldiers, as do small contingents of Manchoukuo troops who become garrison forces of the principal towns.

As a rule, from six to ten Japanese soldiers remain in every village in order to guard against plots or the disaffection of Manchoukuo troops, and invariably at least two Japanese civilians— employees of the Manchoukuo Government—remain as permanent advisers to the new magistrate. These advisers do not interfere with the Chinese mode of administration, except to check corruption and make certain that the proper share of local revenue finally gets to the central government at Hsinking.

The new administrative officials are nearly always chosen after consultation with chambers of commerce, merchants' guilds or farmers' associations, but of course former loyal supporters of Chang Hsueh-liang are automatically debarred from office.

# CHAPTER XIV

## THE OPEN DOOR—IS IT CLOSED?

### I

EVER since Secretary John Hay proclaimed the open door doctrine for China at the turn of the century that doctrine has been regarded as one of the axioms of American diplomacy. No American, be he an intellectual or the man in the street, can think of China without recalling the Hay doctrine. Even the American navy considers the upholding of the open door as one of its first functions.

And yet, to the American mind, the meaning of the open door is far from clear. To know what grotesque meaning is often, one might almost say usually, read into the famous doctrine one need only to glance at newspapers now and then and read therein dispatches from the Far East or speeches or statements of "experts" and "authorities" on the subject. If a Manchurian farmer at Ssupingkai or Paiyantala swaps his beans, which are about the only thing he has to sell, for coarse cheap cotton goods from Osaka instead of paying cash, of which he usually has none, for finer goods from South Carolina or Fall River, that is a violation of the open door. If General Ma or Colonel Pa, of the Manchoukuo army, prefers Japanese-made rifles to American firearms, that is the closing of the open door. If a coolie up in Heilungkiang —the province along whose long borderline the great Black Dragon River winds its way—refuses to chew Mr.

243

Wrigley's gum from Chicago or brick tobacco from Virginia, but sticks to abominable but cheap Japanese cigarettes, that, too, is an encroachment upon the open door. If His Excellency Mr. Henry Pu-yi, Chief Executive of Manchoukuo, prefers rice cake from Tokyo to Dr. Kellogg's corn flakes from Battle Creek, Mich., U. S. A., why that is putting an official seal of approval upon the closed door! In short, if Japanese trade in China steals a march upon American, that is a grave offense which justifies even the use of the American navy as a punitive measure.

Of course, our American defenders of the open door do not speak exactly in this language, but their utterances, when paraphrased and boiled down, often sound like the above. Thus has the open door become a fetish before which incense never ceases to burn.

It, therefore, behooves us to inquire into the meaning of the Hay doctrine. If the doctrine is meant to throttle legitimate competition, if it frowns upon honorable winner and countenances ill-natured loser, if it insists upon ignoring natural economic laws, then the sooner it is discarded the better.

II

The meaning of the "open door," as defined by Mr. Secretary Hay himself in his notes addressed to the various Powers between September 6 and November 17, 1899, is as follows:

First, that no power will in any way interfere with any treaty port or any vested interest within any so-called "sphere of influence or interest" or leased territory it may have in China.

Second, that the Chinese treaty tariff of the time being shall apply to all merchandise landed or shipped to all such ports as are within said sphere of influence (unless they be free ports), no matter to what nationality it may belong, and that duties leviable shall be collected by the Chinese government.

Third, that no power shall levy any higher harbor dues on vessels of another nationality frequenting any port in such sphere of influence than shall be levied on vessels of its own nationality, or any higher railroad charges over lines built, controlled, or operated within its sphere on merchandise belonging to citizens or subjects of other nationalities transported through such sphere than shall be levied on similar merchandise belonging to its own nationals transported over equal distances.

To appreciate the real significance of the above proposals, it is necessary to understand the international situation prevailing in China toward the end of the nineteenth century. It was the perilous period when China was on the verge of dismemberment. In Manchuria, Russia had seized the Kwantung peninsula. In the South, France had obtained a lease of Kwanchou Bay and declared the vast provinces of Yunnan and Kwangsi her sphere of influence. England had leased the Kowloong peninsula, and proclaimed the entire Yangtse valley her sphere of interest. She had also entered into an agreement with Russia and with Germany whereby she recognized, respectively, the Russian domination of Manchuria and the German preponderance in Shantung and in the territory north of the Yellow River; while these two continental Powers had assured England that her vested rights in the Yangtse valley would not be disturbed. Germany had seized Kiaochow Bay in Shantung. To counteract this German move and the Russian fortification of Port Arthur, England had established a naval base at Weihaiwei, a strategic point between the new German and Russian bases. Italy, too, had demanded a lease of Sammun

Bay, though this demand was not "followed through" largely because the bay afforded no promise of becoming a desirable naval base.

The United States, justly alarmed by this universal scramble for Chinese territory, had herself cast about for a naval base on the Chinese coast as an auxiliary to her base in the Philippines, and had fixed her eyes upon the Samsah Inlet north of Fuchow, as witness Secretary Hay's instructions to the American Minister at Tokyo under date of December 7, 1900. But the American Government desisted, at least temporarily, from carrying out this contemplated naval project partly because Samsah Inlet, like Sammun Bay once coveted by Italy, was far from satisfactory as a naval base, and partly because the United States did not wish to antagonize Japan by occupying any Chinese territory directly across the strait from the Japanese island of Formosa. Parenthetically, the above American project was revived by the secret agreement of October 21, 1911, between the Chinese navy and the Bethlehem Steel Corporation though this, too, is in abeyance.

In the light of the foregoing delineation of the international situation, the motive behind the Hay doctrine is fairly clear. Contrary to popular belief, Mr. Hay did not challenge the existence of foreign leased territories, foreign "spheres of influence," or foreign naval bases in China, but acquiesced in these alien existences as a *fait accompli,* inevitable and unalterable, and even tried, if possible, to obtain for America herself a base calculated to maintain the balance of power with the other nations. What he wanted to accomplish was the preservation and promotion of American trade on the basis of legitimate competition. This is evident in the phraseology of his open door proposals quoted in an earlier passage in this

**HSIEH CHIEH-SHIH**
MINISTER OF FOREIGN AFFAIRS

chapter. From this standpoint, he objected to the imposition of discriminatory customs duties, harbor dues, or railroad charges in the leased territories or spheres of influence against merchandise or vessels belonging to subjects or citizens of countries other than those which had established the said spheres of territories. In other words, he insisted upon equal treatment and equal opportunity for the commerce of all nations. He also insisted that customs duties leviable be collected not by the foreign authorities in the leased territories or spheres of influence, but by the Chinese Government. Mr. Hay was prompted to make this last proposal by the fear that the Powers might brush aside the Chinese customs authorities and set up their own customs houses in their leased territories or spheres of influence. Russia, for one, had hoisted her own flag over the customs house in Newchwang, South Manchuria, and showed an intention of usurping customs authority from the Chinese. Had this been permitted to pass unchallenged, other Powers, in their respective spheres in other sections in China, might have followed suit.

In the light of the inception and intentions of the open door doctrine as set forth above, the following appraisal of the doctrine by Professor Tyler Dennett in his *Americans in Eastern Asia* seems fairly correct:

Based on sixty years of history and on the circumstances as well as the text of the notes the definition was as follows: The United States still adhered to the policy, to which Seward alone had made exception, of independent rather than allied action. This independence was not, however, to preclude cooperation. The American Government relinquished the right to lease a port in China like Kiaochow or Port Arthur, for all the good ports were either leased or preempted by non-alienation agreements. The United States was making no specific demand for the open door for in-

vestments; there was not enough American money seeking investment to make it worth while to quarrel about the preferential
rights to construct railways or operate mines which had already
been given to the other powers. The United States merely demanded an open door for trade in that part of China in which
American merchants were already interested, viz., the area west-
ward from Kwangtung on the south to Manchuria on the north.

### III

The Hay doctrine, innocuous as it was, did not have
smooth sailing either at home or abroad. At home Hay
was criticized as committing his country to a policy "impossible of attainment by our own independent action,
and if pursued in common with other Powers fraught
with the gravest possibilities of those international en-
tanglements with European nations, which it is our historic policy to keep out of." How similar to the criticism
now directed against Mr. Stimson's "non-recognition"
doctrine! Yet the open door doctrine was destined to be
apotheosized as one of America's greatest diplomatic
coups, though its actual accomplishments are open to
doubt.

Abroad the Hay doctrine met with greater obstacles.
Japan and Italy were the only nations which welcomed it
unconditionally. Great Britain, while accepting it in general, exempted her leased territory of Kowloong from
the application of the open door principle. Russia de-
mured and quibbled, and in August, 1901, the Imperial
Russian Controller of Newchwang (in South Manchuria)
issued the following proclamation which was in direct
contravention of the Hay doctrine:

As this port has now reverted to the control of the Imperial
Russian Government, all you who have matters in dispute and the

like should bring your petition to the superintendents or other
government officers, where redress can be obtained and cases
settled in perfect justice and impartiality. . . . If after the issuance of these presents there be any person disobeying this proclamation, I will punish the delinquent severely and will exercise
no mercy.

Remember that Newchwang was not a Russian leased
territory—it was Chinese territory under Chinese jurisdiction. If Russia would issue such a proclamation even
in Newchwang, what would she not do in the Kwantung
Leased Territory which was under her own administration? Furthermore, Russia, on November 18, 1903, demanded of the Chinese Government that no new port be
opened to foreign trade; that no new foreign consulates,
other than Russian, be established; that no foreigners
other than Russian be employed in administrative capacity in the whole of Manchuria. The *London Times* of
September 13, 1901 reported that the Russian administration at Dalny (now called Dairen) had refused to let
Americans build warehouses for the storage of American
kerosene, and had announced the intention of excluding
American oil altogether from Manchuria. In the face of
such grave obstacles the open door was powerless, because
it was meant to be a moral influence dissociated from
physical force.

IV

So much for history. How does the open door doctrine
fare in the present situation in Manchuria? All customs
houses are under the direct control of the Manchoukuo
Government which has inherited them from China. In
Dairen, which is within the Kwantung Leased Territory,

the customs office is organized in accordance with the 1907 agreement between China and Japan, or, more accurately, between Japan and the Inspector-General of Customs on behalf of the Chinese Government, which agreement has been recognized by Manchoukuo. Manchoukuo has also repeatedly pledged itself to uphold the principle of the open door and equal opportunity. Nor is this a mere profession. As we have noted in Chapter X, the new Government has most fastidiously observed the foreign obligations for which it is not itself responsible but which were bequeathed by the old régime of war lords or by the Chinese Government. It is paying the war lord's debts to foreign commercial firms. It is paying to China not only its own quota of Salt Monopoly revenue but also the arrears left by the war lords. It has made no change in customs tariff. It has reversed the railway policy of the old régime under which foreign shippers were as often as not obliged to pay higher rates than native shippers. This Chinese practice of discrimination in the matter of railway rates was so common that even the Washington Conference of 1921-22 at the instance of the British delegation, included the following article in the Nine-Power Treaty:

China agrees that throughout the whole of the railways in China she will not exercise or permit unfair discrimination of any kind. In particular, there shall be no discrimination whatever, direct or indirect, in respect of charges or of facilities on the ground of the nationality of passengers or the countries from which or to which they are proceeding, or the origin or ownership of goods or the country from which or to which they are consigned, or the nationality or ownership of the ship or other means of conveying such passengers or goods before or after their transport on the Chinese railways.

In China proper, even today, in spite of the above provision, railway discrimination against foreign goods or foreign shippers still prevails. In Manchoukuo, under the new régime, all shippers, native or foreign, are required to pay uniform rates. Nowhere and in no respect has the principle of the open door been encroached upon. Thus trade in Manchoukuo has become a matter of legitimate competition, unhampered by governmental interference or the iniquities of war-lordism.

### v

The question of railway rates calls for further elucidation. What we have just noted refers specifically to the Manchoukuo-owned railways. Besides, there is the Japanese-owned South Manchuria Railway. What is its policy? This question is pertinent, because the South Manchuria Railway has often been the subject of malicious criticism on the part of the uninformed or those with an axe to grind.

Let us begin at the beginning. When, in the few years immediately following the Russo-Japanese War of 1904-05, Japanese cotton goods entered Manchuria in large quantities in competition with American and British goods, foreign merchants joined in a chorus of accusation against the South Manchuria Railway. They suspected that the Railway discriminated against their goods. Perhaps this accusation was not entirely groundless. When the Russian war, upon which Japan had staked her very existence, came to an end, she found that, besides the lease of Port Arthur and Dairen, her only important gain was a battered, narrow-gauge railway equipped, not with Russian, but with her own rolling stock brought from Japan. In the wake of the war, this broken-down, narrow-gauge railway was clogged with the transportation of the evacuating army and its military stores to such an extent that it could not satisfy all civilian shippers clamoring for car space. The Japanese, with the memory of their appalling sacrifices in the war still fresh on their minds, yielded to common human weakness if they were sometimes inclined to favor Japanese shippers. They would have been inhuman, or superhuman, had they acted otherwise. What nation, under like circumstances, would not have acted likewise? As a matter of fact, however, no higher rates were charged on foreign goods than on Japanese. Nor was there any organized, wilful discrimination.

Fortunately the American suspicion or resentment gradually subsided, as it became known that the Japanese cottons imported into Manchuria were manufactured from American raw material, and that American loss in the cotton goods trade was made up many times by the phenomenal increase of American trade in other lines, notably steel and other railway materials. For more than ten years beginning in 1908, steamer after steamer arrived at Dairen bringing American rails, locomotives, Pullman coaches, passenger and freight cars, bridge material and so on.

In 1914 the question of freight rates on the Manchurian railway again came to the fore. In March of that year, the Japanese Government Railways, in conference with the Korean Railway and the South Manchuria Railway, adopted a measure by which all goods, Japanese and foreign, entering Manchuria *via* the Antung-Mukden line, were to be carried at rates thirty per cent less than the regular rates. The underlying motive was to make the Korean and the Antung-Mukden railways the main artery of trade and communication between Japan and Manchuria and thus bring the two countries into closer touch. When this schedule for the Antung-Mukden route became applicable, American merchants complained a great deal, not because the new rates were not applicable to their goods but because American goods, on account of more convenient steamship service, were accustomed to enter Manchuria through the port of Dairen, and not through Korea and thence by the Antung-Mukden Railway. The Japanese railway authorities argued that the new schedule did not discriminate against American merchandise, and that it was through no fault of theirs that the Americans could not avail themselves of the advantages equally afforded to all traders. Yet the Americans continued to protest, urging that the South Manchuria Railway should adopt the same low rates for goods imported into Manchuria through the port of Dairen or Newchwang *via* foreign ships, so that such foreign goods should not have to compete at a disadvantage with goods entering Manchuria from the Korean side. In March, 1915, the American merchants won the point. Since then there has been no occasion for complaint on the part of foreign trading interests.

## VI

Contrary to foreign assumption generally based upon hearsay, Japanese enterprise always brings in its train a signal increase in foreign trade. For the sake of brevity and because the Americans are usually the loudest complainers about the closing, real or imaginary, of the open door, we shall illustrate the point with reference to the trade of the United States only.

A good example of this is Shantung. Under the German régime, not an American nail was used on the Shantung Railway. Under the Sino-German agreements of 1898 and 1911, both the Chinese Government and merchants forfeited the right of buying in the open market foreign materials and machinery to be used in Shantung, but promised to purchase them from Germany. It was but natural that American railway materials and American machinery were completely barred from this province.

Japan, in the brief period from 1916-1922 inclusive when she operated the Shantung Railway, entirely reversed the German policy. In the five years from 1916 to 1920, the Japanese management expended $10,397,000 gold on materials and machinery for the Shantung Railway—a sum almost equal to the original cost of the line. Of this sum, about one-third or $3,047,000 went to American manufacturers. In 1921 the same management ordered from abroad, mostly from America, 18 locomotives, 293 thirty-ton coal cars, 11 passenger cars, and 12 cabosses. Since Japan quit Shantung in 1923, the Railway has been a pawn in the game of war lords, and the American rolling stock for which Japan paid so much has been either carried away or reduced almost to a state of wreckage.

Turn now to Korea. Here we see the same progress achieved by American trade because of the advent of Japan's enterprise. In the decade following the inauguration of Japanese rule in Korea in 1903, American exports for that country increased twenty-fold. In 1903, that is, the year before the establishment of the Japanese protectorate, American exports to Korea amounted to only $199,188. In the next year, when Japan became the mistress of the peninsula, American exports to the same country suddenly swelled to $906,557 gold. By 1913 they reached the handsome figure of $3,920,000. Since then American exports to Korea have progressed steadily. In 1929 they amounted to $5,000,000 gold.

In Manchuria we see much the same phenomenon. Under the Russian régime the Manchurian railways were essentially military roads and contributed little toward commercial development. Moreover, they were built and equipped exclusively with Russian materials. Russia even barred out American oil. About the only American imports were cotton piece-goods.

The advent of the Japanese changed that condition at once. In the twelve years from 1907 to 1919, the South Manchuria Railway alone bought American materials to the value of $93,790,000 gold. In addition, American machinery and materials to the sum of $60,000,000 gold were imported to Manchuria in the same period by other Japanese firms. In 1920 alone the Railway Company expended $20,000,000 for American materials. In that year the Company adopted a five-year improvement program involving an expenditure of $200,000,000, much of which was expended in the United States. In the twenty-two-year period ending March 31, 1929, the Railway Company alone bought from abroad $251,000,000 (gold) worth of materials, of which the United States supplied 26 per cent, exceeded only by Japan's 38 per cent. Of the entire rolling stock now owned by the Company,

482 locomotives, 6,574 freight cars, and 440 Pullman
sleepers are of American origin. Practically all the steam
shovels, cranes, and dredges are also of American origin,
while no less than 90,000 tons of American steel rails have
been used for its tracks.

Speaking more generally, the entire foreign trade of
Manchuria, which was 25,000,000 Hailkwan *taels* in 1907,
increased to 755,000,000 Haikwan *taels* in 1929. In 1930,
owing to the world-wide depression, it fell off to 703,-
000,000 Haikwan *taels*. In the twenty-three years
1908-1930, Japan's trade (including Korea) with Manchuria increased seven times. This, it must be remembered, consists largely of Japan's imports from Manchuria.
In the same period British trade (including Hongkong,
India and other British colonies) has increased more than
thirteen times. This, however, includes non-British
products which are trans-shipped from Hongkong.
American trade (including the Philippines) has more
than quadrupled. The following two tables show the
relative progress of Manchuria's imports from and exports
to Great Britain, Japan, and the United States from 1908
to 1930:

### IMPORTED INTO MANCHURIA

| Countries | 1908 | 1930 |
|---|---|---|
| England, Hongkong, India, and colonies | 2,594,000 | 24,681,000 |
| Japan, Korea | 14,691,000 | 120,409,000 |
| United States, Philippines | 6,776,000 | 20,775,000 |

### EXPORTED FROM MANCHURIA

| Countries | 1908 | 1930 |
|---|---|---|
| England, Hongkong, India, and colonies | 1,208,000 | 17,883,000 |
| Japan, Korea | 17,192,000 | 159,332,000 |
| United States, Philippines | 411,000 | 8,702,000 |

The above tables bring out the important fact that Japan buys of Manchuria much more than she sells to it, while exactly the reverse is the case in regard to American and British trade, especially American. In 1908 America's sales to Manchuria exceeded her purchases from it by 6,365,000 Haikwan *taels*. In 1930 the excess was 12,073,000 Haikwan *taels*. Yet American trade with Manchuria has increased four times in twenty-three years. Surely America has no reason to complain in this respect.

On the contrary, Japan, in 1908, bought of Manchuria 2,501,000 Haikwan *taels* more than she sold to it; and in 1930 the excess of her purchases over her sales was 38,923,000 Haikwan *taels*. In no year has Japan sold to Manchuria more than she bought from it. On the other hand, the excess of her imports from Manchuria over her exports to it has increased year by year. From 1910 to 1920, seventy to eighty-five per cent of Manchuria's total exports went to Japan. Although, since 1920, this percentage has somewhat decreased, by far the largest portion of Manchuria's export trade is with Japan. This is an all-important factor which should always be borne in mind. For, in normal circumstances, the country which consumes the major portion of the exports of another country holds the most advantageous position in supplying its necessary imports. The real basis of Japan's commercial success in Manchuria, then, is the above fundamental economic law and has, contrary to popular notion, little to do with the open or closed door.

## VII

Japan's commercial advance in Manchuria, which has time and again raised the question of the open door, is so closely bound up with the bean industry of that country that it is essential to discuss it at length. Indeed, the humble bean has been, and still is, the factor which determines the fortunes of the nations interested in Manchurian trade. Before this modest product, even high diplomacy, bidding for trade supremacy in Manchuria, has had to admit defeat. Here, then, is a great romance worthy of the pen of a Kipling.

Let us go back to the Sino-Japanese War of 1894, when Japan "discovered" the Manchurian pulse as a valuable food stuff. Prior to that war, the farmers of Manchuria had barely eked out a living by planting small areas in beans. The country had had no manufacturing industry, while its agricultural products could be enumerated upon five fingers. Of these, beans were the most important. No foreign nations cared for them. Even the natives did not want them, for their staple food, as well as their animal feed, was millet.

Then came the Sino-Japanese War, and the Japanese, having, during their occupation of the Liao-tung Peninsula, realized the value of the Manchurian produce, became its most liberal purchaser. So rapidly had Japanese purchases of the pulse and bean-cake multiplied that by 1899 they exceeded the total export of Southern China. The Japanese knew how to utilize beans and bean-cake. The white, red, and small green beans—for there are six varieties of beans—they manufactured into various foodstuffs; from the yellow, black and large green beans they made bean-cake and bean-oil. The bean-cake they used as fertilizer and animal feed, and the bean-oil for culinary and other purposes.

Unfortunately the Sino-Japanese War was followed by a decade of Russian domination of Manchuria, during which no foreigners were permitted to go into the interior for trade or any other purpose. Under the circumstances, no Japanese could deal directly with the bean-producers. Nor could the Americans sell their cottons to the natives except at the port of Newchwang, where the Chinese traders brought beans from the interior and sold them to American and British merchants, receiving in exchange cotton and other piece-goods. In turn the Americans and British sold these Manchurian products to the Japanese, taking a profit on the turnover, plus the storage charges, lighterage, and freight. Naturally the Japanese made little profit in the transactions, but they accepted the inevitable, for they had to have beans for culinary purposes and bean-cake for fertilizer.

With the termination of the Russian War the situation was suddenly reversed. The Japanese buyers of beans, under the new open door principle enforced by their Government, penetrated into the interior and bartered their cottons for native products. No longer were they obliged to buy beans from Americans and British at Newchwang. And the Americans and British, having lost Japanese customers for the beans and bean-cake they bought from the Chinese in exchange for their cottons, were now forced to sell their goods for cash. But cash was the one thing the natives did not have, and as the Americans and British could not barter cottons for beans, the natives dealt with the Japanese who came to their doors to sell cotton goods for beans, not for cash. As Mr. George Bronson Rea observed in his *Far Eastern Review,* a Shanghai monthly, at that time:

Under these conditions the foreign merchants and their agents in the interior were placed at a disadvantage from the outset. As they could not penetrate into the interior and purchase beans by an exchange of commodities, they were reduced to selling their wares for cash—the one thing the native was short on. If they attempted to follow the lead of the Japanese and barter merchandise for beans, they were handicapped by their various charges at Newchwang, and having to ultimately sell to the Japanese at their price, which of course was unprofitable under the then existing conditions. The decadence of American and European imports followed as a natural consequence. A few venturesome American and British piece goods agents established themselves in the interior, firmly determined to win back their lost trade, but acting solely as sellers and unable to reciprocate by purchasing the products of the farmers, results were discouraging, and they finally had to abandon the field as unprofitable. This, in short, is the real reason for Japan's success in Manchuria.

How much Japan depends upon Manchuria for her food supply may be judged from this table showing her agricultural imports from Manchuria in 1931:

|  | Tons |
| --- | --- |
| Soya beans | 498,578 |
| Bean-cake | 1,152,685 |
| Kaoliang (millet) | 93,552 |
| Maize | 26,225 |
| Wheat bran | 23,175 |
| Mixed grain | 32,777 |
| Other grains | 176,258 |
| Total | 2,003,250 |

The real extent of Japan's contribution toward the phenomenal development of Manchuria's bean trade cannot be estimated unless we also consider the enterprise of her merchants who created a great market in Europe for the beans. Says a report of the Maritime Customs of China:

It was in November, 1908 that Messrs. Mitsui & Company made the first considerable trial shipment to England. The result was so satisfactory that an order for a large consignment followed, and in March, 1909 the first large cargo—5,200 tons—was landed in Hull. Contracts were at once made, as the suitability of the new oil seeds for many purposes became known and the good condition in which they arrived. During the season 400,000 tons were exported, almost all to England, and many of the large oil-crushing mills set their entire plant to work on the crushing of the beans, to the exclusion of cotton seed, linseed, and other oleaginous seeds. The supposed shortage of the flax and cotton crops in the United States and the anticipated shortage of linseed in the Argentine, with the resultant scarcity of cotton and linseed products, found the English market comparatively unperturbed, for the reason that soya oil and cake can supply most of the requirements as well.

In recent years some 830,000 tons of beans have been annually shipped to Europe. The annual shipments of bean oil from Dairen alone amount to 200,000 tons.

### VIII

Most assuredly the open door does not, and should not, mean that all trading nations in a given area shall have an equal amount of trade. It is inevitable and logical that a nation which is more favorably situated than others, as Japan is in Manchuria, should have a relatively larger trade. Japan's position in Manchuria is a result of great sacrifices, both in blood and treasure, made in two wars. Besides, she has made investments in Manchuria estimated at 1,900,000,000 *yen,* or 77 per cent of the total foreign investments there. British and American investments amount to 39,600,000 *yen* and 26,000,000 *yen* respectively. With all the advantage Japan enjoys in Manchuria by

reason of her geographical propinquity, her vast investments, her great contribution to the development of the
bean industry, it would indeed be strange and unnatural
if she were not to forge ahead more rapidly than other
nations interested in Manchurian trade.

Americans can appreciate this situation if they stop
to think how their trade with the Philippines has developed since they annexed the islands. The following passages from Senator Harry B. Hawes's book, *Philippine
Uncertainty,** give a clear picture of how the trade of
other nations in the islands declined while American trade
advanced:

In 1899 Philippine exports to the United States were less than
$4,000,000, and Philippine imports from the United States
$2,347,000. The United States furnished to the Philippines only
9 per cent of Philippine imports, and the Islands sent to the
United States only 18 per cent of their total exports. Philippine
imports to the United States in the period from 1909 to 1914
jumped from a previous average of $4,927,000 to $21,056,000.
In the five-year period previous to 1909, the Islands purchased
from us only 17 per cent of their total imports; but in the 1909-to-
1914 period they purchased 42 per cent of their imports from us.
The exports of the Islands to the United States jumped from 18
per cent in 1901 to 35 per cent for the five-year period 1905-1909,
and increased to 43 per cent for the five-year period 1909-1914.
They have continued to increase until, for the year ending January 1, 1929, about 75 per cent of Philippine exports come to the
United States, while 62 per cent of Philippine imports come from
the United States.

Of course, as trade with the United States developed Island
trade with the rest of the world diminished. In the period of 1899
to 1901, Philippine imports from the rest of the world outside of
the United States constituted 91 per cent of their products to the
rest of the world, exclusive of the United States. At the present

* Published by The Century Company. Reprinted by permission.

time only 25 per cent of Philippine exports go to all the world outside of the United States, and less than 38 per cent of her imports, come from all the rest of the world. However, while Philippine exports to the United States increased from $3,800,000 to $115,500,000 in the thirty-year period, the exports to the rest of the world increased from $16,900,000 in 1899 to only $39,460,-000 for the year ending January 1, 1929.

According to Senator Hawes, American investments in the Philippines amount to $166,245,000. This is not very large, but still by far the largest as compared with investments by the nationals of other countries. Considered from this point alone, and ignoring America's political influence in the Philippines, it is logical that America should take the lion's share in the trade of the Islands. I have never heard any Japanese make ado about the "closed door" of the Philippines, though many wonder if Mr. Hay, had he been Secretary of State after America adopted the rigid policy of Oriental exclusion, would have had the courage to demand the open door in the Orient.

IX

President A. Lawrence Lowell of Harvard University, speaking before the Foreign Policy Association of Boston on January 3, 1933, took exception to Secretary Stimson's non-recognition doctrine. In the course of his speech, he said:

Our merchants may, of course, trade there at their own risk, but can we protect them? We shall have no diplomatic relations with Manchoukuo, and can have none without recognition; and an attempt to urge the claims of our citizens through our embassy at Tokyo is essentially recognition. Would not refusal to recognize the actual conditions, the de facto government of the region, lead to friction that would soon become dangerous, if not intolerable? And would not the only way to avoid it be for the nations to forbid their people to trade there, thus leaving to the conqueror the whole fruit of aggression? Japan appears to foresee the friction that will arise, and hence to contemplate leaving the open door only for those countries that recognize the situation she has created.

There is little danger of President Lowell's apprehension becoming a reality. Manchoukuo, as long as it heeds Japanese counsel, will not be petty. It will be generous enough to accord equal treatment to all who come to trade within its confines.

Of course, in the period of radical readjustment which Manchoukuo is going through, complaints will be heard in certain foreign quarters interested in its trade—all the more so as foreign trade with the old régime of war lords was abnormal and must give way to new trade. Take, for instance, the purchases made by the Mukden Arsenal maintained by the Changs at the inordinate cost of 80,000,000 silver dollars per year. Such an arsenal was absolutely unnecessary if the Changs' object in maintaining it was the preservation of peace and order in Manchuria. Yet most of the old régime's transactions with foreign firms were for the Arsenal. With the advent of the new régime, foreigners who had come to Mukden from many countries to share in the Arsenal business lost their trade. Also foreign experts and workers who had been employed in the Arsenal were dismissed. Manchoukuo has made rather generous provisions to meet the claims of these foreigners. Nevertheless they are disgruntled, and are longing for the return of the "good old days."

Again, the old Manchurian Government bought considerable quantities of rails from America to build new lines. Japan protested against the construction of these lines on the ground that it violated the agreement of 1905 whereby China obligated herself not to build any line parallel to and competitive with the South Manchuria Railway. When the protest interrupted this construction work, the interested Americans denounced Japan as violating the open door principle, and the denunciation still resounds in certain circles. And yet no one, who has taken the trouble to look into the matter, can fail to see that trade of this sort is neither wholesome nor desirable. The old Mukden Government, which bought these American rails, paid for them with the money which should have been set aside to meet the service of the Japanese loans which had enabled the same Government to build several hundred miles of railways. Instead the Mukdenites diverted the receipts of these Japanese-financed lines and expended them on parallel lines, buying rails from America for the purpose. From the American standpoint, the transaction was legitimate and justifiable. But the Mukdenites knew very well that the deal, as far as they were concerned, was "tainted," depriving the Japanese creditors of money due them in interest and sinking-fund. Indeed, they never paid a cent to the service of the Japanese railway loans.

But the period of readjustment in Manchoukuo will not last long; it will soon be followed by a period of reconstruction, growth, and development, when its trade will follow a normal and wholesome course. The best illustration may be seen in the recent readjustment of Japan. In the early days of New Japan, when Europeans and Americans enjoyed extraterritoriality and estab-

lished foreign settlements, Japan's international trade was
mostly in foreign hands. When the Japanese abolished
extraterritoriality and foreign settlements, and gained
control of her foreign trade, there were outcries abroad
denouncing the Japanese as tricky, dishonest, and what
not. But the outcries were bound to be short-lived, as
Japan's foreign trade in her own hands achieved a signal,
even phenomenal, progress. What Japan has eliminated
is not foreign goods but foreign agencies. More and more
foreign goods enter Japan, only their salesmen are not
foreigners, as they once were, but Japanese.

The major American exports to China, including both
China proper and Manchuria, are petroleum products,
raw cotton, tobacco, wheat flour, steel, machinery, and
automotive products. In any of these lines Japanese exports to China are either absent or extremely insignificant.
Roughly speaking, American exports to China amount
to $100,000,000 gold a year, if we base our estimate upon
figures for 1930 when the Haikwan *tael* was down to 46
cents gold. Of this total $45,000,000 (or almost fifty per
cent) is for American oil and American tobacco which
practically monopolize the market. The next important
American export to China is raw cotton amounting to
$24,000,000. Who buys and pays for this cotton, Chinese
or Japanese? It is generally agreed that at least 50 per
cent of the above total is purchased by the Japanese cotton mills in China, and that an additional 25 per cent is
shipped to Chinese-owned mills through Japanese firms
which pay and assume entire responsibility for the shipment. Then there is $8,000,000 of American machinery
and $7,500,000 of American steel imported into China.
Here again it is important to note that much of this trade
goes through Japanese agencies who assume entire respon-

sibility to the American exporters. The advantages of utilizing these Japanese intermediaries is, I believe, fully appreciated by American firms which have dealt with them.

Normal American export trade in Manchuria, as in China, consists mostly of petroleum, tobacco, wheat flour, automotive products, and machinery. In these lines America has practically monopolized the Manchurian market. This condition will not change, except for the possible dumping of Russian oil. If Manchoukuo lays good roads throughout the country, as it proposes to do, there will be a larger demand for American automotive products. Up to a few years ago the South Manchuria Railway bought, as we have seen, enormous quantities of American rails and rolling stock. Of late, materials produced in the Railway's own works have to no small extent taken the place of American imports. But if Manchoukuo launches, as it surely will, an extensive railway project, a large part of the necessary materials will have to come from abroad. For the moment, the depreciation of the *yuan* and the *yen* militates against the importation of American goods; but this is a passing phenomenon.

After all has been said and done, the open door, as a practical matter, can be enforced only where law and order are maintained by stable and honest government. As Lord Charles Beresford said in 1899, the open door would be of no use "unless the room inside is in order." Should Manchoukuo, under Japanese tutelage, fulfill the promises it made to its own people and to the foreign nations, it is difficult to see how it could fail to advance the cause of the open door. Manchoukuo's first task, then, is to put the "room inside in order," and that is what it is doing.

# CHAPTER XV

## THE RED SHADOW OF MOSCOW

### I

MANCHURIA's contiguity to Russia along unnumbered miles of boundary line extending from the Japan Sea to Outer Mongolia is a factor which all students of its problems, past, present and future, must keep steadfastly in view. It was this factor which played no small part in the molding of Manchuria's destiny. But for it Japan would not have been forced to face Czarist militarism in the Manchurian arena. We may go further back and say that, in the absence of the same factor, even the Sino-Japanese War of 1894 might not have been fought in the same arena, for, in the last analysis, it was the Russian horse stalking behind China which caused Japan to cross the Rubicon.

As in the past, so, perhaps, in the future. True, the old masters of the Kremlin are no more. Its new tenants profess peace and disavow imperialism, but so did the Czar and his *entourage* who forced war upon Japan. Whether Czarist or Bolshevist, White or Red, Russia moves eastward, with the weight of her 155,000,000 square miles of land and her 150,000,000 inhabitants behind her. Under Czarism this movement was like a mighty glacier, obvious to all eyes; under Bolshevism, it is like a tremendous undercurrent, more dangerous because it is invisible. In Soviet Russia today Japan sees the singular spectacle of a Power, not only armed as no other nation has ever been, but also marshalling forces of disruption and disorganization against those institutions which, right or wrong, the other Powers hold essential and even sacred. On one side is a nation believing in private property and cherishing traditional loyalty to an Imperial régime tempered by constitutionalism. On the other side is a nation believing and advocating universal revolution, whose objective is the abolition, all over the world, of capitalism, private property, and most of the things which are still considered necessary in all other countries. It is this relative position which has caused Mr. Owen Lattimore to believe that "Manchoukuo, after all, is only an experimental buffer between Russia and Japan." If Manchoukuo is a buffer against Red Russia, it is also one *vis-à-vis* the chaos and civil war of China which no one thinks will come to an end in the conceivable future. Should Manchoukuo, with Japanese tutelage, become stable and keep out Chinese chaos, Red inroads into its territory would also be checked, for Communist propaganda finds the most receptive soil in chaos and anarchy.

## II

It is not here pretended to determine the relative merits or demerits of Communism and Capitalism. It may be that Communism is in the right and Capitalism in the wrong, but that is beside the mark. In this connection there is no use in laboring over the point. The point to be remembered is that Japan and Manchoukuo, with most of the world, are convinced that the Russian doctrine and the Russian methods of propagating it are dangerous and derogatory to their existence.

As an indication of Japan's official opinion and her national sentiment about Soviet Russia, we may quote two Japanese diplomats—one Viscount Ishii, who has served successively as Foreign Minister, Ambassador to Washington and Paris, and Privy Councillor; the other, Mr. Tokichi Tanaka, one-time Ambassador to Moscow.

Writes Viscount Ishii in *Foreign Affairs* (New York) for January, 1933:

From the standpoint of our security, the Russian revolution has not materially changed the situation. We still must look to the north with apprehension and a certain sense of danger. M. Jules Cambon, in his article in Foreign Affairs entitled The Permanent Bases of French Foreign Policy, said: "The policy of the Soviet Government in the Far East may differ in method from that which the Czarist Government followed; but it does not differ from it in spirit or in objective." Sir Austen Chamberlain and Dr. Richard von Kuhlmann, both writing also in this review, have expressed much the same feeling in different language. I am not prepared to say whether these expressions are entirely correct, but I only state what is common knowledge when I say that the vast region known as Outer Mongolia has, under Soviet tutelage and protection, been closed to all but Russians; that even China is not permitted to preserve contact with that region, over which her suzerainty has been formally recognized by the Soviet Government itself; that hundreds of Chinese students, trained in communist schools in the Soviet Union, are yearly sent back to China to promote the communist movement there; and that increasingly large regions in China have become the prey of communist risings.

With the internal political system of the Soviet Union we are not seriously concerned. We are on friendly terms with the Union, and are prepared to deal with it in a conciliatory spirit on all problems affecting our mutual relations. But I should be guilty of insincerity if I were not to confess our misgivings as to the activities of the Third International. Its deliberations and plans are most jealously guarded. No one is permitted to get an inkling of them. But one may say without fear of contradiction that most, perhaps all, of the civilized nations outside Russia look upon the deliberations of the Third International, and the activities apparently emanating from it, as disturbing to the general peace and welfare of the world. There is no means of ascertaining the exact nature of the relations existing between the Soviet Government and the Third International, but it is strange, to say the least, that the former, whose avowed foreign policy is peace and friendship, does not seem to exercise any restraining influence upon the latter, whose headquarters are located in the very shadow of the Kremlin.

Viscount Ishii's casual reference to Mongolia calls for elucidation. Russian ambition in that country is an old story. In 1911 the Czar, taking advantage of the Chinese revolution, established a suzerainty over Mongolia. The Soviet Government, so far from renouncing this Czarist policy, has tightened its hold upon that territory. Under the aegis of clearing the country of "White" forces, the Soviet Government in 1921 sent an army into Urga, the capital of Mongolia, and for four years refused to withdraw it, in defiance of repeated Chinese protests. By 1925, when the Soviets at last removed the Red army from Mongolia, the Mongolian army had already been drilled and officered by the Reds, and had been provided with "Red" arms and munitions. There had been established an autonomous Mongolian Government which no longer recognized China's authority, but which sent its "diplomatic" representatives to Moscow. A Mongolian national bank had been organized under "Red" management, giving the Soviets a financial control over the country. The "Constitution" drawn by the "Reds" proclaims Mongolia to be a republic of independent people, its entire administrative power belonging to the working people of the country. Article 13 of the Constitution boldly declares:

In view of the efforts being made by the working people of various countries in the world for the destruction of capitalism and realization of communism, the Mongolian Republic of the working people shall exert its utmost to cooperate with them for the promotion of the fundamental object common to small nations diplomatically tyrannized, and to revolutionary working people throughout the world.

The Soviets, to set up a "republic" of workers in a country still in the pastoral or nomadic stage, must indeed be extraordinary humorists. But the humorous scheme has serious aspects. Great Britain views with apprehension the growing sovietization of Mongolia, for that spells a menace directly to the British position in Tibet and indirectly to British rule in India. The British expedition to Tibet under Colonel Younghusband in 1912, and the various British enterprises that followed, were undertaken to counteract Czarist encroachment upon Mongolia in 1911. England is just as fearful of "Red" control as it was of "White" suzerainty over the land of the "Living Buddha." Viewed in this light, England's renewed activities in Tibet since 1932 have a deeper significance than is apparent.

Japan is even more directly concerned with "Red" supremacy in Outer Mongolia, for Outer Mongolia, like the Russian territory of Siberia, is contiguous to Manchuria. Thus Manchoukuo's line of juxtaposition with "Red" domain extends not only from the Japan Sea to the very upper reaches of the Argun River, but also along the southeastern border of Outer Mongolia—a distance, altogether, of more than two thousand miles.

Now let us note what the former Japanese Ambassador to Soviet Russia, Mr. Tanaka, has to say. Like Viscount Ishii, he is particularly concerned with the activities of the Third International. Writing in *Contemporary Japan,* a highly illuminating English quarterly review published in Tokyo, Mr. Tanaka says:

The Japanese are generally aware that the guiding thesis which inspires the Third International is not the sole creation of the Soviet régime, nor is every display of its activities necessarily to be ascribed to any organs or agents of the Soviet Union. They believe, however, that the existence of the Union is a great impetus to the organization of the International. They go a step further, and believe that the hand of the Union, be it called Government, party, or a complex of unofficial institutions, is collaborating with, if not directing, the International's activities. They see with particular misgivings that the headquarters of the Third International are situated in Moscow, the capital of the Union, and that its deliberations are carried on behind closed doors— deliberations which, judging from what we are allowed to see in the world outside the Union, are, to say the least, derogatory to the general peace and welfare of the majority of the civilized nations. That the power of the Soviet Government, whose avowed foreign policy is peace and friendship, does not seem to exercise a salutary influence on deliberations which are highly injurious to its avowed policy and are carried on under the very eyes of the Kremlin, is something which my compatriots can hardly comprehend.

### III

Is the apprehension voiced by Viscount Ishii and Mr. Tanaka, and generally shared by his compatriots, justified? The nature of the question precludes any definite and final answer. We can only adduce some of the relevant facts upon which the apprehension is based.

In December, 1925, M. Boubonov, then Chief of the

Political Department of the "Red" army, addressing the annual meeting of the Communist Party in Moscow, declared:

The Nationalist movement in the Far East, awakened by us in 1925, has reached its climax. The population of Russia, India, China, and other colonial countries combined is larger than the population of the rest of the world. The organization of the colonial revolution has consequently become the chief task of the Soviet Government, especially because the revolutionary wave in Western Europe has receded. On this point no divergence of opinion is possible; everything must be concentrated for the development of the revolutionary movement in the Far East.

These words were a straw showing which way the "Red" wind was blowing. About the time these words were spoken General Bluecher of the "Red" army, under the assumed name of Galen, was sent to Canton to train the Nationalist army and to assist in, or rather lead, the Nationalist advance toward Nanking, sweeping before it British concessions and British influence along the Yangtse River. The same General is now in the Maritime Province of Siberia just across the border from Manchoukuo, commanding a large army there.

On July 15, 1928 the Third International issued a declaration, in which it said:

The Communist International is a union of Communist Parties in various countries; it is a World Communist Party. As the leader and organizer of the world revolutionary movement of the proletariat and the advocate of the principles and aims of communism, the Communist International strives to win over the majority of the working class and the broad strata of propertyless peasantry, and fights for the establishment of the world dictatorship of the proletariat, for the establishment of a World Union of Socialist Soviet Republics, for the complete abolition of classes, and for the achievement of socialism—the first stage of Communist society.

The Communist International does not show its own hand in Manchuria, but works through the Chinese Communist Party, and every one knows that the latter is financed and directed by the Communist International. The Communist program for Manchuria was set forth in an instruction (marked No.C 1836M.44) addressed to the Executive Committee of the Manchurian Provinces by the "Center" of the Chinese Communist Party under date of October 25, 1930. The salient features of the instruction were:

1. Party organizations should absorb workers of the Chinese Eastern Railway, the South Manchuria Railway, the Pei-Ning Railway, the Fushun coal mine, Harbin, Mukden, Dairen, and of other large towns, as well as agricultural laborers, poor peasants, Korean communists, wives of laborers and peasants, and youths. For propaganda purposes such magazines as the *Manchurian Red Flag* and the *Manchurian Workers,* pamphlets and leaflets are to be published.

2. The establishment of a Soviet government by armed riots must be the chief aim of the activities.

3. Red labor unions should be extensively organized, as workers in Manchuria are more concentrated than in other parts of China. The Chinese Eastern Railway is very important; labor unions of Chinese workers have to cooperate with the professional unions of the Soviet Union in and along the Chinese Eastern Railway, and to protect the Soviet labor code. In Mukden strikes should be instigated in the Northeastern University, among employees of the municipal public utility service, the Mukden Cotton Mill, the Arsenals, the Pei-Ning Railway, and factories.

4. The Party should incite peasants to disturbances, and start a land revolution. In North Manchuria white Russians and rich farmers are to be done away with.

5. Mutinies have to be instigated and white Russian "partisans" should be stamped out. Peasants are to be united into the Red army.

6. The Anti-Imperialistic League, which should have Koreans and Russians as its chief members, must invite revolutionary students to join it. The League has a mission to prevent Imperialistic oppression against the Soviet Union.

For the purpose of promoting Communist propaganda in China, Manchuria, Korea, and Japan, there have been established in Moscow two schools—one called the Chinese Laborers Communist University, the other the Oriental Toilers' Communistic University. The first, especially for the Chinese, enrolls 300 to 400 Chinese students every year. The second is for the training of students from all Oriental countries, but particularly Korea. These two institutions turn out hundreds of agents every year for field work in the Far East. On March 2, 1931, the Chinese Police at Mukden caught a Chinese named Chou Huai-jui, twenty-five years of age. From the buttons, made of string, on his Chinese clothes were found lists of names of people whom Chou was to approach in Shanghai, and names of medicine which were quite unintelligible to outsiders. Chou confessed that he had been a laborer in the Tangshan factory of the Peiping-Mukden Railway, entered the Oriental Toilers' Communistic University in 1925, and became a member of the Communist International. At the time of his arrest, he was on his way to Shanghai as an agent of the Communist International. He also said that thirteen Chinese were dispatched from Moscow together with him, and there were thirty other Chinese who were to be sent to China as laiason agents.

## IV

The influence of the Third International began to be felt in Manchuria as far back as 1920. When the late war lord of Manchuria, Chang Tso-lin, concluded a treaty with the Soviet Union in 1924, he, conscious of the potential danger of "Red" inroads, caused the following article to be inserted in the treaty:

The Governments of the two contracting parties mutually pledge themselves not to permit within their respective territories the existence and activities of any organizations or groups whose aim is to struggle by acts of violence against the Government of either contracting party.

The Governments of the two contracting parties further pledge themselves not to engage in propaganda directed against the political and social systems of either contracting party.

This provision, however, was not, and never has been, of any practical use, because the Moscow Government claimed, and still claims, that it was never interested in propaganda abroad, and that if there was any evidence of Communist propaganda in Manchuria it was the work of the Third International over which the Soviet Government had no authority. This profession of innocence convinces no one in any country. Every one in every country takes it for granted that the Soviet Government at Moscow is clearly identified with the Third International, and *vice versa.*

For a few years after the conclusion of the 1924 treaty, Communist propaganda in Manchuria was not so pronounced. This was not due to Moscow's deference to the anti-propaganda provision of that instrument but because the Soviet was absorbed in the revolutionary movement it had started with the Nationalists in the south of China, and also because of the vigilance of the Japanese authorities along the railway zone in Manchuria. But the increasing conflict of interests between Japan on one side, and the Manchurian and Chinese Governments on the other afforded the Soviet Union—or the Third International if you will—an opportunity to fish in the troubled waters of Manchuria. Moreover, the Soviet's temporary break with the Nationalists in 1927, and the consequent setback suffered by the Red movement in Central China, caused the Russian masters of propaganda to fix their eyes upon Manchuria.

In the summer of 1928 the sixth conference of the Communist International defined its Manchurian policy, which was to regard Manchuria as a semi-colonial part of China under the oppression of capitalistic Powers, that is, the Communist movement in Manchuria was to be carried out by the members of the Chinese Communist Party. The Chinese Communist Party was entrusted to organize the movement in Manchuria, and was required to coöperate with the Koreans who had been engaged in Manchuria in the movement for the independence of Korea. Since then, propaganda leaflets bearing the name of the Executive Committee for the Manchurian Provinces of the Chinese Communist Party and of the Young Communist Group have been found frequently in large towns of Manchuria. The leaflets were chiefly in the Chinese language, and often in Korean.

At first, the Chinese Communists were not very active in Manchuria. Among them there was a group who maintained that the conditions in Manchuria were not so favorable as in Central China, and that the Communist movement could not be carried out in Manchuria in the same form as in other parts of China. This "opportunistic" view was termed the "outside-the-Great-Wall" policy.

This view was rejected by the advocates of the so-called "Li Li-san course" in 1930. Li Li-san was an influential leader of the Chinese Communist Party at that time. As the result, the activities of the Chinese Communist Party became vigorous, manifesting themselves very remarkably in the disturbances in Chientao and along the Kirin-Tunhua Railway in June, and October, 1930, and in the organization of a "Red" labor union in Fushun coal mine in the summer of 1930, as well as in the mutiny of Chinese soldiers at Pokotu along the western section of the Chinese Eastern Railway.

The riot policy of Li Li-san, however, was not approved by the Communist International. On November 16, 1930 it dispatched instructions to the Chinese Communists, which said in part as follows:

The Chinese Communist Party should avail itself of the irreconcilable complicacy of interests of Imperialistic Powers, and weaken their connection with anti-revolutionary elements. Until the Party develops to a certain degree, it should desist from attempts for a decisive clash. In the meantime, the Party should make deadly efforts in anti-Imperialistic movements.

Since then, the Communist movement in Manchuria has been largely subterranean. Communist agents have been particularly active among the Koreans, of whom there are almost a million in Manchuria. A majority of these Koreans are hard-working farmers who worry about nothing but their daily bread. But there are also malcontents and agitators who readily become Communist propagandists, not necessarily because they believe in Communism but because of the material support offered by the Communist organization. The same may be said of Chinese Communists both in Manchuria and in China. Few of them are Communists in the real sense of the term. Even their leaders know little about Communism. All that they want is the sinews of war which they know they could obtain by calling themselves Communists and by making a feint of espousing the cause of Leninism or Marxism, though in reality they know no more about Lenin or Marx than they do about the man in the moon. I entirely agree with Mr. J. O. P. Bland when he describes the Communist movement in China in his penetrating new book, *China, the Pity of It,** as follows:

The movement itself, the forces behind it, and the phenomena which it produces, represent, in fact, ideas and objectives wholly different from those commonly implied by the word Communism; in no part of China does there exist a force of opinion capable of creating the type of social organization produced in Europe by the economic doctrines of Karl Marx or the political principles of Lenin. The Socialist ideas propounded in Sun Yat-sen's "Three Principles" were, like his conversion to Christianity, an imported *article d'occasion,* an opportunist faith, unmistakably influenced by his personal ambitions and necessities; since his death, his formulæ for the modernization of China have been invoked by the Kuomintang for tactical purposes, but they have never appealed to the Chinese mind as rational, nor visibly affected its political thoughts. The principles which determine the workings of a revolutionary or rebellious movement remain unchanged. Behind them lie the two paramount instincts of Chinese social life, i.e., the desire for posterity and that of family enrichment at the expense of other families. The two Chinese characters usually displayed on the banners of the Red armies mean, in plain English, "Divide Property," an economic doctrine which has appealed to landless and lawless members of every community from time

* Reprinted by permission of the author.

immemorial; but the idea of a division of property for the benefit of the community, and not of the individual, is one which could never enter the Chinese mind. Every Chinese of the "have-nots" class, every desperate victim of the present anarchy, is a "Communist," in the sense that he is ready to support any faction which promises him a chance of transferring other people's property to himself, and the landless survivors of civil war, flood and famine are naturally disposed to support a "revolution for the protection of land." But their conception of Communistic principles begins and ends with the individual and the family. In this sense there have always been Communists, and to spare, in China.

The real menace of Communism in China is not any possibility of her four hundred millions, or even a comparatively small number of them, marching hand-in-hand with the Bolshevik multitudes of Russia on the road to world revolution, but rather the prolonged period of chaos and anarchy which is certain to follow in its train in a country which has already been harassed long enough by civil wars, militarist feuds, organized banditry, and all that works for disintegration and dislocation. Only benevolent despotism, with powerful military support, such as appeared at long intervals in China in the past, can save the situation for the suffering millions.

# CHAPTER XVI

## CHINA AT HOME

### I

So much has already been written on the chaos and anarchy which have gripped China since the revolution of 1911 that it seems hardly necessary to add another tale of woe. The world has come to regard chaos as China's normal condition and anarchy her traditional state of government. If China breaks treaties by the score, the Western world treats her much as an indulgent grandmother would treat a spoiled grandchild whose daily pranks could seldom disturb her. Even if her innocent civilians are butchered in civil strife, not by the hundred or even the thousand but by the hundred thousand, the Western world takes little notice of it, but dismisses it with sublime indifference, saying, "Oh well, life is cheap in China."

But this condition in China cannot go on indefinitely without disturbing even the Western world. It has already caused serious complications with her immediate neighbor, Japan. One would think that the Manchurian trouble might at least have the effect of inducing China's militarists and political cliques to bury the hatchet and work for national unity. Such is far from the case. While the militarists and politicians are crying from the housetops that they have cast aside their feuds and differences and are making common cause against Japan, they are acting exactly the opposite, scheming against one another for the unholy purpose of self-aggrandizement or self-enrichment, usually both. When they say that they will go east, they will more likely than not go west. While they are talking harmony they are plotting discord. Of this the internal developments of China during the last two years, when she has been in greater need of national unity than ever, furnish an apt illustration.

## II

In March, 1931, Chiang Kaishek, actual head of the Nanking Government, arrested and incarcerated Hu Hanmin, his political rival and president of the Executive Council of the same government, for fear that Hu, recognized leader of the Cantonese faction, might become too powerful to suit his convenience. This incident brought to a head the long-standing enmity between the two factions, and culminated in the setting up of a separatist Cantonese government at Canton. By September, the Cantonese army had advanced into Hunan province to wrest Central China from Chiang Kaishek's rule when Chiang was engrossed with the onerous task of fighting the Communist forces in Kiangsi province. Naturally, Chiang was anxious to reconcile with the Cantonese to forestall probable grave developments in Central China, but he was at a loss to know how he could take the initiative without impairing his prestige.

Fortunately for him, the Japanese intervention in Manchuria, which began on September 18, 1931, furnished Chiang Kaishek with a plausible excuse to approach Canton on the ground that the national calamity precipitated by the Manchurian situation demanded immediate union of all factions to make common cause against Japan. To this overture, the Cantonese reply was that Chiang Kaishek should resign his post as head of the National Government as a prerequisite of the dissolution of the separatist government at Canton and the union of Nanking and Canton in a new and reorganized government. Chiang Kaishek accepted this Cantonese proposal gracefully, though he never intended to abide by it, as his later acts clearly showed.

With a tentative agreement thus arrived at, Cantonese leaders, including Wang Ching-wei, Sun Fo, C. C. Wu, and Eugene Chen, went to Shanghai. But to ensure themselves against any possible intrigue on the part of Chiang Kaishek, they were accompanied by General Chen Ming-chu, commander of the Cantonese eleventh division known as the "Iron Army," with the understanding that General Chen would be asked to take charge of the Shanghai area with his Cantonese soldiers. (It was a part of this Cantonese army which came into collision with the Japanese in January of the following year, as we shall presently see.)

On October 21, Chiang Kaishek met the Cantonese leaders at Shanghai and again told them that he would resign as soon a new government was organized. With this promise, he retired to Nanking. And yet the Cantonese, still suspicious of Chiang Kaishek, did not proceed to Nanking. They remained in Shanghai and there wasted days and weeks intriguing, arguing, dickering for objectives and purposes so involved and subtle that no outsider could understand them.

The upshot of it all was that, on December 15, 1931, Chiang Kaishek definitely resigned and retired to his na-

OFFICE OF THE CHIEF EXECUTIVE

tive village in Chekiang province. Meanwhile he had taken care to concentrate his soldiers in Honan province, with the intention of retiring there with his military power intact and undiminished. Thus were the Cantonese given the coveted opportunity of organizing a coalition cabinet in which they would have a preponderant influence.

But the new government which appeared upon the heels of Chiang Kaishek's resignation was so unwieldy, unworkable, and feeble that it lasted only two weeks. On January 22, 1932, General Chiang Kaishek, who had so lately been forced to resign, returned to Nanking and was requested to resume his power. This time, General Chiang, in order to avoid the criticism that his government was a military dictatorship, invited Wang Ching-wei, a veteran nationalist politician, to become president of the Executive Council of his government. That Wang accepted this invitation with alacrity was but another illustration of the opportunism which is generally the motive of the Chinese politicians. Had he, long regarded and posing as the leader of the radical wing of the Nationalist Party, been actuated by principle or conviction, it is difficult to understand how he could have allied with General Chiang Kaishek, whom he and his associates had looked upon as an arch-reactionary. Before this misalliance, Wang had flirted even with Chang Hsueh-liang, the now deposed war lord of Manchuria. Needless to say that the politicians, who have any considerable following, are used merely as pawns in the game of military chieftains, who hire them as a sort of "window-dressing" designed to deceive their followers and clamorous students. Of course, the politicians know this, but permit themselves to

be so hired merely for the honor and material gain proffered by the militarists.

Chiang Kaishek's return to power made it impossible
for the Cantonese—Sun Fo, Eugene Chen, C. C. Wu, etc.
—to remain in Nanking. Of course, they did not resign
graciously. As soon as they retreated to Shanghai, they
began to stir up anti-Japanese agitation, not from patriotic
motives but simply to embarrass Chiang Kaishek. They
called Chiang a pro-Japanese traitor, knowing that such
epithets would incite student mobs and ignorant masses
against him. For the same purpose, the Cantonese instigated anti-Japanese boycotts of a violent nature, encouraged the press to publish seditious matters, and inflamed
the public mind to such an extent that, by the middle of
January, Japanese lives and property in Shanghai had
ceased to be safe.

On January 18, a party of Japanese civilians was wantonly attacked and wounded—one fatally, two seriously—
by Chinese mobs on the streets of Shanghai. For all such
outrages the Cantonese leaders, who then constituted an
invisible government, in Shanghai, were directly responsible. Their object was to discredit and embarrass Chiang
Kaishek by showing up that the Nanking generalissimo
sat with folded arms while the Japanese were entrenching
themselves in Manchuria. They, no doubt, hoped that the
anti-Japanese agitation which they had kindled would
soon embroil Chiang with Japan, who would resort to
armed intervention in Shanghai just as they had in
Manchuria.

In other words, they deliberately and purposely courted
Japanese intervention. Their insincerity and the infamy
of their intentions are the more flagrant as they them-

selves, while out of power, had advocated a policy of conciliation toward Japan—so much so that, at a meeting at
Nanking in December, 1931, the venerable Wu Chih-hui,
"elder statesman" of the Nationalist Party, had attacked
the Cantonese leaders for their "flirtations" with Japan.
Indeed, in the summer of 1930, the Cantonese, while still
maintaining a separatist government at Canton, sent to
Tokyo an emissary in the person of Eugene Chen, and
tried hard to convince Baron Shidehara, then Japan's
Foreign Minister, that they were the only party in China
which would deal with Japan on a liberal and rational
basis to settle the Manchurian question. Of course Baron
Shidehara gave Mr. Chen no encouragement, knowing
that the Cantonese represented no authority which any
foreign government could trust. Now the same Cantonese
faction, which had courted Japanese friendship at the
price of a "substantial concession" in Manchuria, would
instigate anti-Japanese violence for the expediency of
domestic politics. It was the old game constantly played
by all the opposing factions in China. Chiang Kaishek
himself, in the early stage of the Manchurian trouble,
came out for a declaration of war and immediate mobilization against Japan. Of course he never meant it; he
simply thought it expedient to put forth a bold front to
silence his critics who would harp upon what they called
his "pro-Japanese" sentiment.

To come back to Shanghai, the Cantonese scheme of
humiliating Chiang Kaishek by provoking the Japanese
did not work as they had expected it to. They had had
two alternative thoughts. First, they had not thought that
the Japanese would dare to launch an armed intervention
in an area where interests of so many nations converged

as in Shanghai. If the Japanese would face the music without resistance, the Cantonese could take the glory of humiliating not only Chiang but also Japan. That was their first thought. If, on the other hand, the Japanese would land bluejackets and even an army, Chiang Kaishek would be forced to send his forces to Shanghai to coöperate with the Cantonese. Should the Japanese be defeated by force of superior numbers, the Cantonese, with their Nineteenth Route Army fighting in the forefront, could claim the glory of victory for themselves. The Nineteenth Route Army had, for more than a month, been busily engaged in digging elaborate trenches and well-protected dugouts reminiscent of the battle fronts in the World War, and was fully prepared to repulse any offensive that might be launched by the Japanese.

The first thought did not materialize. The Cantonese, having sowed the wind, were destined to reap the whirlwind. They played the anti-Japanese game once too often, and the Japanese, unable to sit quiet any longer, landed sailors for the protection of their lives and property. But a small contingent of sailors, unaccustomed to fighting ashore, was no match for the well-prepared Cantonese army far superior both in numbers and in equipment. The sailors were soon reënforced by land forces sent from Japan, with the result that, by the first days of March, the Cantonese army had completely been dislodged along the entire front from Woosung to Chapei.

Meanwhile, what had Chiang Kaishek done? Had he come to the aid of the Nineteenth Route Army, as the Cantonese had hoped? Not at all. Knowing, as he did, that the foremost motive of the Cantonese in instigating anti-Japanese agitation was to humiliate him, he saw no reason why he should coöperate with them and thus play into their hands. After all, Chiang proved to be a shrewder strategist and turned the tables against Canton.

On January 30, two days after the landing of Japanese sailors, Chiang Kaishek issued a proclamation which was substantially as follows:

> Japan has attacked China at Shanghai and other places. She is trying to overpower us by force of arms. But we shall never surrender our national rights even if Japan overruns the whole of China. We declare before the whole world that we will defend our country until the last man. But as we believe in peace, we shall not meet force with force. Therefore, we are moving our Government from Nanking to Loyang in the interior province of Honan. We ask the people to repose full confidence in this Government and support it in this hour of national crisis.

With this ambiguous proclamation, Chiang retired to Loyan, many hundred miles from Shanghai. His next step was to divide the whole country into four defense units. The first unit, comprising Canton and other southern provinces, was to be commanded by Chen Chi-tang; the second, comprising the provinces along the Yangtse River, by Ho Ying-chin, Chiang Kaishek's favorite lieutenant; the third, consisting of Shantung and the adjacent provinces, by the notorious "Christian general," Feng Yu-hsiang, and Han Fu-chu; and the fourth, including Hopei and Shansi, by the deposed Manchurian war lord, Chang Hsueh-liang, and Yen Shih-shang. This grandiose paper organization was nothing short of comical. Most of the "commanders" named were Chiang's avowed enemies. None, except Ho Ying-chin and Chang Hsueh-liang, even took the trouble to answer Chiang's appeal. As a matter of fact, Chiang never expected any reply, for he never

intended to take any military move against the Japanese
while the Cantonese were plotting to embroil him in the
conflict they had deliberately started at Shanghai. His
sole motive was to make a grand gesture to beguile the
public into believing that he was just as anxious as any-
body else to defend China against Japan, but that he was
planning to mobilize the entire army throughout the
country, for that, he said, was the only effective means of
defense. And so, while the Cantonese Nineteenth Route
Army under Tsai Tieng-kai in Chapei, was hard pressed
by the Japanese, Chiang Kaishek never sent an army to
its rescue. All that he did was to place some three divisions under Ku Chu-tung at Suchow and Chinkiang, near
enough to Shanghai to make it appear that these divisions
were ready to help the Cantonese army, but too far from
it for them to be actually drawn into the fray if the commander only took discreet precaution.

On March 1, when the Cantonese army had all but collapsed before the Japanese onslaughts, Chiang Kaishek
organized the Central Military Committee for National
Defense, and appointed himself its chairman. This, of
course, was another paper scheme. On April 7, he called
at Loyang what was called the National Calamity Conference. Although invitations were issued to 189 prominent men throughout the country, only 70 or so responded
favorably. At the Conference there were some 140 present,
but half of them were officials under Chiang Kaishek
himself. The only tangible accomplishment of the Conference was a fervid appeal sent to the Lytton Commission.

The rupture between Chiang Kaishek and the Cantonese resulted in the reëstablishment of a separatist government at Canton, whose actual civilian and military

chiefs were, and still are, Hu Hanmin and General Chen Chi-tang, respectively. General Chen has an army of 100,000 men which he may hurl against Chiang Kaishek at some convenient time.

And as for Chiang Kaishek, he remained in the interior city of Loyang until the summer of 1932, and there again made himself the dictator of his little government, with the new title of Chairman of the Military Committee and of the Central Political Executive Committee. He had announced that his foremost task was to suppress the Communist forces which had been conducting guerrilla warfare along vast fronts in different parts of Central China. In June, he established his military headquarters in Hankow from whence he has been directing his campaign against the Communists in Hunan and Hupeh provinces. Meanwhile, he gradually got rid of Wang Ching-wei, whom he had for a while used as a puppet for purposes of domestic politics. In October, Mr. Wang went to Europe, as most Chinese politicians do when out of the good graces of their military chieftains, leaving behind him an eloquent but meaningless farewell statement.

### III

The greatest menace to Chiang Kaishek and his "national" government is the Communist army which has set up a "central" government at Juichiu in the south of Kiangsi province and has almost opened an outlet to the sea at Amoy in Fukien province. Its influence extends over large parts of Fukien, Kiangsi, Chekiang, Anhui, Hunan, Hupeh, Honan, Canton and Kwangsi provinces. Against those various fronts General Chiang has, since November, 1930, launched four drives, all of which have ended in abject failure. Since May, 1931, Chiang Kaishek has been employing 300,000 soldiers in the anti-Communist campaign, at a monthly cost of 20,000,000 dollars (silver).

In May, 1931, General Ho Ying-chin reported to his chief, Chiang Kaishek, on the appalling ravages wrought by the Communist forces in Kiangsi and Hunan provinces, and gave these figures:

> 1. In Kiangsi Province:
> Men killed ............... 186,000
> Refugees dead ............ 2,100,000
> Homes burned ........... 100,000
> Property looted ........... $650,000,000
> Crops damaged ........... $ 30,000,000
> 2. In Hunan Province:
> Men killed ............... 72,000
> Homes burned ........... 120,000
> Property loss ............. $130,000,000

In November, 1932, the government of Hupeh province gave out the following figures on Communist ravages under its jurisdiction:

> Killed ....................... 350,000
> Refugees homeless ............ 8,500,000
> Homes burned ............... 98,000
> Property looted ............... $ 60,000,000
> Crops damaged .............. $240,000,000

We may briefly describe the development of the Communist movement in China. (For the Communists in Manchuria, see Chapter XV. The Chinese Communist Party was first organized at Shanghai in September, 1920 by T. C. Chen, F. G. Chou and other radicals under the direction of Woitinsky sent from Russia by the Comintern. As China was still largely medieval in her social and industrial organizations, little affected by either capitalism or labor philosophies, there was no prospect of the Communist Party obtaining any considerable influence immediately through its own efforts alone. The Comintern, taking cognizance of this situation, adopted the policy of uniting the Communist Party with a suitable political party in China, and of converting it from within and absorb its members into the Communist ranks. The Kuomintang (Nationalist) Party of Sun Yat-sen, then out of power, was picked out under this policy. Beginning with January, 1923, Joffe, Borodin, Galen (whose real name was Bluecher, later commander of the Red army in Eastern Siberia), and others came to Canton one after another, and through their intermediary the affiliation of the Chinese Communist Party and the Kuomintang was effected in January, 1924.

Since then, the Kuomintang, assisted by the Comintern from without and supported by the Chinese Communists from within, has gained fast in strength. The Revolutionary Army, newly organized, started on its expedition northward in July, 1926.

Sweeping victoriously onward, it took the cities of Wuchang and Hankow in September, occupied Shanghai in March of the following year, thus bringing almost the entire territory south of the Yangtse River under the domination of the Kuomintang.

In the meantime, the Chinese Communist Party, which, under the direction of Borodin and other Russian advisers, had been busy organizing the workers and the peasants, and converting them to Communism, was, with the connivance of the left elements in the Kuomintang, actively engaged in a conspiracy to usurp the power of that party. But the Kuomintang leaders were not slow to realize the danger of continuing their relations indefinitely with the Communist Party. In March, 1927, as soon as the position of the Kuomintang army in South China became more or less secure, following its occupation of Shanghai, Chiang Kaishek, the Commander-in-Chief, took a decisive step and drove Communists out of Shanghai, Canton, Swatow and other localities. His action brought him into open conflict with the Hankow Government, still dominated by Communists, and led to the establishment of the Kuomintang Government at Nanking. In July of the same year, the Hankow Government following the example of Chiang Kaishek, expelled their Communist colleagues. Thus the partnership between the Kuomintang and the Communist Party, continued since January, 1924, came to an end.

After the break with the Kuomintang the Chinese Communist Party, in accordance with the order from the Comintern, cast aside its former policy of compromise and opportunism, and adopted a program of revolutionary Communism of armed uprisings and terrorism, which was responsible for the outbreak at Nanchang on August 1, 1927, and the Canton incident of December of the same year. The disturbance at Nanchang (known as the first outbreak of Nanchang) was brought about by the Communists, who had been driven out of Hankow, but who rallied quickly at Nanchang, and, by seducing the soldiers under Generals Ho Lung, Yeh Ting, and Chu Te, took possession of the city and established a Soviet régime with revolutionary committees. Although this "government" at Nanchang was broken up on August 6, 1929, by the

Nanking Government forces, three army bands under Generals Ho, Yeh, and Chu, continuing their activities in Kiangsi, Fukien, Kwangtung, Hunan and other provinces, have become the prototypes of the so-called China's "Red armies" of today. After the failure of the Nanchang outbreak the Communists scattered themselves into various localities in order to instigate the rural populace and to form "Soviet governments."

They were able to organize what they termed "the Harvest-time Insurrection of Four Provinces" (Hunan, Hupeh, Kiangsi, and Kwangtung). In December, 1927 they stormed and occupied Canton and established there a Soviet government, which, however, was destroyed by the Kuomintang army after a brief existence of three days. In this misadventure the Communist Party lost a large number of its members and peasant followers.

When the Sixth Congress of the Comintern was held in July, 1928, in Moscow, the Chinese Communist Party held its Sixth General Conference there under the guidance of the Comintern. At this conference a thorough reorganization of the party was effected and a course of future action was determined upon, which was to concentrate all efforts upon converting the city workers and upon disseminating radical doctrines among peasants and soldiers in order to achieve the revolutionary ends by the concerted action of both the urban and the rural forces. In 1929, when the "Red" armies began to show signs of expansion, the party assigned to them its representatives and political agents for the coördination and consolidation of the scattered units. Again, in May, 1930, when the military defense of the Nationalist Government in the south and central regions became inadequate, the Communist

Party called at Shanghai a conference of delegates from all Soviet districts of China, which discussed and decided upon a scheme for expanding "Red" areas in China.

Following this conference, and during the summer and autumn of that year, the "Red" armies rapidly grew in strength everywhere, especially in Kiangsi, Hunan, and Hupeh, where they had frequently defeated the local government armies and occupied principal cities and towns, including Changsha, the capital of Hunan.

The Fourth Plenary Session of the Central Committee of the Nationalist Party which was called in November, 1930, passed a resolution to the effect that the party, the army, and the Government should all unite in fighting the Red armies and exterminate them within six months. Accordingly, in December, Chiang Kaishek moved his headquarters to Lushan in Kiangsi, whither he called the heads of Hupeh, Hunan, and Kiangsi provinces for consultation on the war plan. Soon armies were mobilized from the three provinces, and the Government expedition was begun. But the Red armies, reënforced from various sources, defeated the Government forces at various points. Especially in the Soviet area in central Kiangsi, the Reds annihilated the 18th Corps under the command of General Chang Huei-tsan, killing the commander and all other staff officers, and caused the retreat of its ally, the 50th Corps led by General Tan Tao-yuan, by inflicting severe casualties upon it. Nanchang, the capital of the province, was in danger of falling into the hands of the Reds. Thus the first expedition against the Reds ended in a complete failure.

In February, 1931, Chiang Kaishek sent out General Ho Ying-chin with three army corps to fight the Reds. The

Government forces were reported to be making progress for a time but were forced to make a general retreat, in May, before a counter attack by the Red army. The second expedition was also a failure. Then Chiang Kaishek, taking personal command of a colossal army of 300,000, marched to the Nanchang front and, in mid-July, commenced a general drive on all the sectors. The Reds withdrew into the mountains for a while, but taking the offensive in August, proved themselves to be more than the equal of the Government forces. On November 7, 1931, the provisional government of the "Soviet Republic" of China was set up in Juichin in the south of Kiangsi province, and issued the following proclamation addressed to the "workers of the world":

The temporary government of the Republic of Soviet China was established formally at Kiangsi on November 7, 1931, on the occasion of memorial day of the Russian Revolution. This government is comprised of farmers, soldiers, industrial workers, and all other working classes. In cooperation with all masses of people, our aim is to fight and turn down the Kuomintang party which is composed of politicians, privileged classes, and land owners. We will have friendly relations only with proletarian Soviet Russia with a view to destroying the capitalistic and imperialistic régime, and will fight for the reversion of colonial and semi-colonial countries and for the self-determination of every race.

The Republic of Soviet China will recognize no unfair treaties, no secret treaties that have been negotiated between capitalistic and imperialistic countries and China's bourgeois government. All international bonds issued as a result of killing and suppressing the masses of people by Chinese rulers shall be void. All leased territories shall be returned without condition. All armies and navies of imperialistic countries shall be cleared out from China. No foreign interference over China's rule shall be allowed. All banks, factories, mines, and public utilities owned by imperialistic countries in China shall be taken over by us. Our last purpose is, therefore, to destroy all imperialistic and capitalistic aims of the world. With this in view, we declare that we shall endeavor to unify the world masses of people, to continue revolutionary internal war, and to continue our fight until we shall have attained permanent peace by converting the world into the Soviet ideals.

All this does not mean that Communism, as such, will engulf China, and that Communism is understood even by its Chinese protagonists, let alone the rabble who embrace it. The ringleaders of this rabble are exploiting Communism for expediency—for the help they can thus obtain from abroad—just as Chiang Kaishek, now fighting Communists, exploited it in 1926. As Mr. J. O. P. Bland says in his book, *China, the Pity of It,* "the sums of money disbursed by Moscow's agents at Canton from 1923 to 1926 would have secured followers, in large numbers, for any and every creed or campaign. When, moreover, it was instilled into the minds of peasants and other manual laborers, that the Bolshevik gospel meant more money for less work, and that refusal to accept it would involve grave personal risks, the popularity of Communism increased by leaps and bounds." The danger, then, is not a Communist revolution such as has been seen in Russia, but merely an aggravation of the chaos and disorganization which have gripped China for the past two decades.

IV

An even greater curse to China than Communism is the private armies maintained by military chieftains everywhere. These armies are estimated at 2,100,000 men. The peril of such inordinately large and undisciplined forces, not only to China's own unity but also to her immediate neighbors, particularly Japan, was so obvious even at the Washington Conference that it adopted the following resolution:

Whereas, the powers attending this Conference have been deeply impressed with the severe drain on the public revenues of China through the maintenance in various parts of the country of military forces, excessive in number, and controlled by the military forces of the provinces without coordination.

And whereas the continued maintenance of these forces appears to be mainly responsible for China's present unsettled political conditions;

And whereas it is felt that large and prompt reductions of these forces will not only advance the cause of China's political unity and economic development, but will hasten her financial rehabilitation;

Therefore, without any intention to interfere in the internal problems of China, but animated by the sincere desire to see China develop and maintain for herself an effective and stable government, alike in her own interest and in the general interest of trade; and being inspired by the spirit of this Conference, whose aim is to reduce through the limitation of armaments, the enormous disbursements, which manifestly constitute the greater part of the encumbrance upon enterprise and national prosperity:

It is resolved that this Conference express to China the earnest hope that immediate and effective steps may be taken by the Chinese Government to reduce the aforesaid military forces and expenditures.

Since the Washington Conference, the military situation in China has gone from bad to worse. No sincere efforts have been made to reduce the army. On the contrary, each and every military chieftain has been increasing his forces, getting the wherewithal by heavy levies on opium, by looting, by seizing the receipts of the railways, by blackmailing the rich, by putting a staggering load of

taxation upon the people. "A Chinese general," says Mr.
Hallett Abend, able and well-informed correspondent of
the New York *Times* in China, "who captures a city and
demands from the citizens a lump sum of money within
a given time, under threat of turning his 50,000 men
loose to loot if his demand is not met, is just as much a
bandit as is a gunman in Chicago." The only difference
is that "in China a continental area is being terrorized and
bled white by these super-gunmen, and there is no power
nor authority that can check their depredations."

The militarists, moreover, constantly interfere with the
courts of justice usually in favor of litigants who offer
them the largest sum of money. In 1926 the International
Commission, created in accordance with a resolution
passed at the Washington Conference of 1921-22 for the
investigation of the judiciary in China, made the following observations in its report:

The military interferences with the civil administration extends
to the judiciary, so that the independence of this branch of the
government is endangered. Irregularities in this respect usually
occur under the guise of the application of martial law which,
however, is declared without regard to legal provisions on the
subject. In other instances, there is simply an open assumption
of authority. Another important factor is the control by the military of the finances of the government, so that the courts are
dependent upon the military for their financial support. By virtue
of Chinese law itself, the legal position of the military renders
them immune from the jurisdiction of the ordinary courts, while
their power in fact often renders them immune from all courts.
This immunity is liable to be extended to the friends of the military and to the commercial firms and organizations in which they
are interested. Ample evidence of the foregoing is brought out
by the fact that the military are constantly committing crimes
which go unpunished, for it is generally difficult for aggrieved

civilians to obtain any redress from the military authorities, commanding their own armies, when such redress must be sought in military courts controlled by these authorities.

In 1929 the American Red Cross, that great and generous organization which had done so much for the relief of various disasters in China, sent a commission to that country to investigate into the advisability or inadvisability of continuing relief work there. The Commission consisted of Colonel E. P. Bicknell, Mr. William M. Baxter, Jr., and Mr. Ernest J. Swift. Acting upon their report, the American Red Cross issued a statement which included the following observations on militarist practices:

That the destitution which prevails in the famine areas is the cumulative result of the chronic conditions of disorder, the crushing exactions of the war lords, the depredations of bandits, the enforced payment of confiscatory taxation, and the crippling and consequent inability of the railroads to function beyond a fraction of their normal capacity—to these was added a severe drought which brought the whole to a tragic climax;

That Chinese leaders would no doubt give more thought to the removal of the causes which impoverish their people and bring on such tragedies if they realized the necessity of assuming full responsibility for resulting relief needs; any acceptance of that responsibility by foreign agencies cannot but retard this all important result.

### V

At the time of the Washington Conference, China proper was sliced up among military chieftains roughly as follows:

1. Chihli Faction, headed by General Tsaokun and General Wu Peifu, claiming as its sphere of control Chihli, Shensi, Hupeh, and Honan Provinces.

2. Anhui Faction, headed by General Tuan Chijui,

former prime minister, and including Chekiang, Fukien, and Shantung Provinces under its influence.

4. Kwangtung (Canton) Faction, headed nominally by Dr. Sun Yat-sen but really by General Chen Chien-ming, and claiming Kwangtung and Kwangsi Provinces as its sphere.

4. Kwangsi Faction, headed by General Lu Yuntien, an ex-bandit, controlling Kwangsi Province.

5. Semi-Independent Provinces of Hunan, Kweichow, Yunnan, and Szechuen Provinces.

Since then the actors have changed but the stage remains the same, except that the situation has been made much worse by Communist risings. Today China proper is divided roughly as follows:

1. Marshal Chiang Kaishek, head of the Nanking Government, controls Kiangsu province, and parts of Chekiang, Anhui, Honan, Hunan, and Hupeh provinces.

2. The Cantonese Government at Canton, dominated by General Chen Chi-tang, controls Cantung, Kwangsi, and Kweichow Provinces, though parts of these are influenced by the Communist army.

3. The Soviet Government at Jui-chin controls most of Kiangsi and Fukien Provinces, and has extended its influence into Canton, Chekiang, Hupeh, Honan, and Anhui Provinces.

4. Marshal Chang Hsueh-liang, expelled war lord of Manchuria, controls Hopei Province and a part of Honan Province. Whether he will be eliminated as a result of his defeat in Jehol remains to be seen.

5. General Yen Shi-shan controls Shansi Province.

6. General Han Fuchu controls Shantung.

7. Szechuan, Shensi, and Yunnan Provinces are semi-

independent without belonging to any particular chieftain. Szechuan is torn up with its own civil war, with carnage and pillage going on everywhere.

There is not the slightest possibility of China ever curtailing her military forces as was envisaged by the Washington resolution, unless she were compelled to do so under concerted supervision of the Powers. In Manchuria, the new independent Government, having thrown off the shackles of war-lordism, with Japanese assistance, has already drastically reduced its army and is planning to reduce it still more drastically as peace and normalcy are restored. In time, Manchoukuo will stand out before the surviving war lords of China proper as a shining example of what can be accomplished by foreign aid in the way of military reduction in compliance with the Washington resolution.

## VI

Mr. J. O. P. Bland, looking back at the Washington Conference, says in his *China, the Pity of It:*

As one crying in the wilderness, I expressed at Washington the opinion that there could be no hope of permanent improvement in the condition of China unless steps could be taken for the restoration of law and order by concerted action of the friendly Powers, and for an imposed introduction of those financial and administrative measures, which would make an effective government possible. I predicted that the Conference, by proclaiming its belief in the policy of benevolent non-interference, could only accelerate the process of disintegration and add to the grievous burden of affliction already borne by the Chinese people. Few will deny that this prediction has been amply fulfilled.

That Mr. Bland is right has been shown, at least to some extent, I hope, by the foregoing brief delineation.

And yet, not so long ago, the Chinese delegate to the
Preparatory Commission for the Disarmament Conference
at Geneva blandly declared:

China is a true democracy; it is consequently peaceful. It has
its declaration of the Rights of Man, the Three Principles of the
People. It knows how to fight against war by practising justice.
It must succour the weak and help the fallen. After many years
of internal strife, my country has quite recently achieved national
unity and political stability.

And the League no doubt took such moonshine seriously. As an antidote I recommend a careful perusal of
the following passages from a correspondence written by
the able correspondent of the London *Times* at the beginning of June, 1932:

There is little doubt that the volume of the foreign trade is
diminishing. World depression is having its effect, but few will
dispute that the biggest factor is internal insecurity and excessive
irregular taxation, which reduces the export trade and consequently affects the purchasing power of the people.

Politically, China appears to make little progress. The great
floods of last summer did not prevent Canton breaking away
from Nanking and if the menace from Japan has brought them
together again, there is little cordiality in the union, and even
now, when the Shanghai situation is not yet cleared up, and the
future of Manchuria is still an outstanding national problem, there
are signs of further differences, liable to lead to renewed conflict.
The North is full of troops, whose allegiance can be retained only
by lavish expenditure. All over China the military commanders
are looking for means to maintain their forces and any kind of
combination between them, for this purpose, is possible. Jealousy
and rivalry are outstanding, and patriotic motives are seldom
apparent. . . .

Education is being starved; the law is effective in operation
almost nowhere; Communism, after two years of military effort

on a large scale to suppress it, is rampant in four or five provinces; banditry afflicts nearly every province to an extent never
paralleled in history and there is no real State effort to better
social conditions or improve administrative methods. There are
extensive plans for reform in all branches of the administration,
and eager desire by those who prepared them to put them into
operation, but little evidence to show that anything profitable has
been done. Lack of funds is largely responsible for failure in this
respect; but behind that there is the plain indication that the
leaders, inspired by party and personal interest, have been using
the available resources much more for ephemeral political objects
than for solid national purposes. The conclusion is irresistible
that patriotism is still a weak growth, that political and administrative ability is deficient and that the leaders in general lack the
qualities necessary to the guidance of the country out of the utter
confusion into which its affairs have fallen. . . .

Such is the China of today, with which Japan has to deal in
the future at closer quarters than before. The foreign interest in
China is very great, for present and potential trade, because of
money lent and because of large investments in property and
enterprise. Foreigners therefore view with profound regret the
inefficacy of Chinese policy and the shortcomings of the statesmanship of recent times. . . .

Such has been China for the last twenty years. Another
fifty or perhaps hundred years of this condition, and
China may emerge as a united nation, not under a new-
fangled republican government totally alien to her soil
and her race psychology but under an absolute but benevolent government established by a man of iron of the type
of Ching Lung or Kwang Hsi, who will rule with a
sword in one hand and the Analect of Confucius in the
other. After all, China may, in Heaven's good time, rid
Manchuria of the Japanese and drive them to the sea.
Who knows?

# INDEX